Oregon

Judy Jewell

Photography by Greg Vaughn

Compass Am. ...IDES
An Imprint of Fodor's Travel Publications

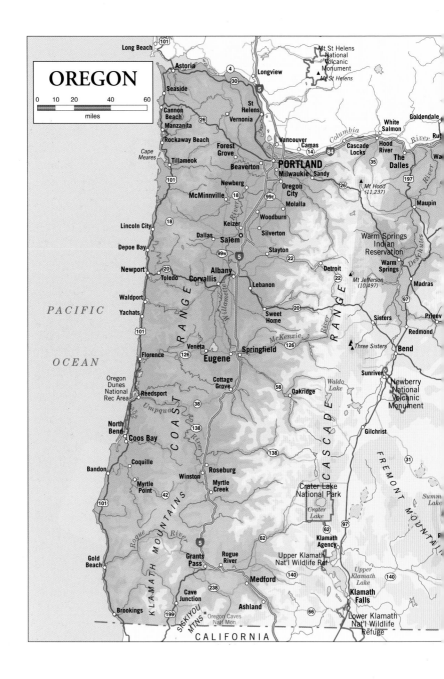

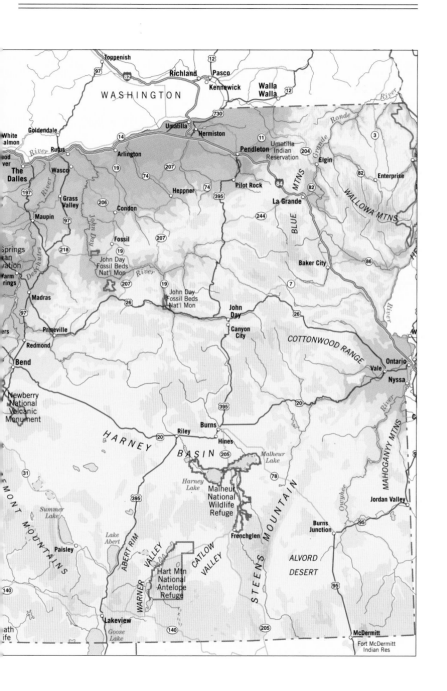

Compass American Guides: Oregon

Compass Editorial Director: Paul Eisenberg
Designer: Siobhan O'Hare
Compass Creative Director: Fabrizio La Rocca
Compass Senior Editor: Kristin Moehlmann
Editorial Production: Linda K. Schmidt
Photo Editor and Archival Researcher: Melanie Marin
Map Design: Eureka Cartography; Mark Stroud, Moon Street Cartography

Cover photo: Greg Vaughn

Fifth Edition
ISBN 1–4000–1587–1
ISSN 1543–1576

The details in this book are based on information supplied to us at press time, but changes occur all
the time, and the publisher cannot accept responsibility for facts that become outdated or for inad-
vertent errors or omissions.

Compass American Guides, 1745 Broadway, New York, NY 10019
PRINTED IN CHINA
10 9 8 7 6 5 4 3 2 1

The Publisher gratefully acknowledges these institutions and individuals for the use of their pho-
tographs and/or illustrations on the following pages: **Oregon Historical Society**, pp. 21, 34, 68-69,
84, 103, 132, 146, 150, 153, 166, 228, 248, 272, 277, 279, 283, 282; **Columbia River Maritime
Museum**, pp. 22, 27, 106, 110-111, 128; **Southern Oregon Historical Society**, pp. 41, 188, 193,
204, 206, 208, 218, 233; **Independence National Historical Park, Philadelphia**, pp. 28, 29, 43;
Underwood Photo Archives, p. 267; **City of Vancouver Archives**, p. 25; **National Archives &
Records Administration**, p. 37; **Oregon State Archives**, p. 143. We also wish to thank: Bill Wilson
for "Fly Fishing Fever;" Gary Wolf for "The Magic of Mushrooms;" John Doerper for "Willamette
Winery Tour;" Ochoco Lumber Company; Bunny Jubitz; and Dr. Eugene Hunn of the Department
of Anthropology at the University of Washington.

For my parents.

Photographer Greg Vaughn would like to thank the many wonderful people in Oregon who have let me photograph them and who have shared with me their special places. Special thanks also to Compass for continuing to showcase my work, and most all to my wife, Penelope, for her continued support, love and companionship.

C O N T E N T S

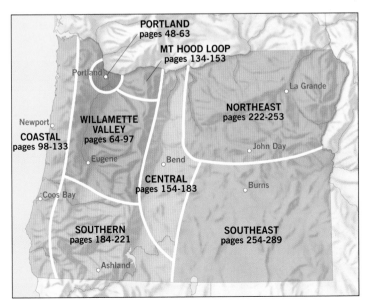

Literary Extracts

Topical Essays

Maps

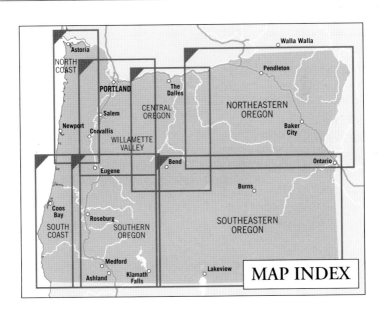

MAP INDEX

O V E R V I E W

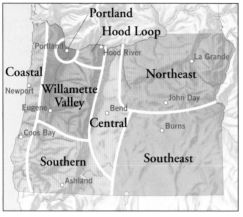

VISITORS TO OREGON usually come for the forests or the wild, rocky coast. But Oregonians know that the state's true appeal is its variety of landscapes and cultures. Head east from coastal fogs to the vineyards of the sunny Willamette Valley or Portland's casual sophistication, then to forested Cascade foothills, glacier-cut peaks, and, in eastern Oregon, high desert, big rivers, and more mountains.

PORTLAND   *pages 48-63*

One of the country's prettiest cities as well as one with a vibrant downtown and lively neighborhoods, Portland is outdoorsy and sophisticatedly urban in nearly equal measures. It only takes a few minutes to get from downtown to Forest Park's hiking and mountain biking trails.

Don't pack anything fancier than a nice rain parka: it will suit your needs on the Wildwood Trail *and* at Wildwood Restaurant. Round out a visit with a tour of the wineries in nearby Willamette Valley, or drive up the Columbia River Gorge and over the shoulder of Mount Hood.

WILLAMETTE VALLEY AND WESTERN CASCADES   *pages 64-97*

Oregon Trail pioneers settled in the Willamette Valley, where the fertile soil nourished family farms. Today, the valley's hillsides are planted with vineyards, and local wineries turn out pinot noir that seems to get better every year. East of the valley rise green hills. The western Cascades, largely National Forest land, have been heavily logged, but there are still pockets of lush old-growth forest.

OREGON COAST
pages 98-133

Oregon's wild, rocky beaches belong to the people—it's all public land, with many state parks along US 101, the coast highway. Unless you're unusually hardy, don't come to the Oregon coast expecting to sunbathe and swim in the breakers. It's best to bring a sweatshirt and be prepared for long beach walks, often punctuated with tidepool inspections, or hikes out to blustery headlands.

COLUMBIA RIVER GORGE AND MOUNT HOOD   *pages 134-153*

Misty waterfalls, hiking trails lined with wildflowers, and the great "River of the

West" itself make the Columbia Gorge a magically beautiful spot. Between Hood River and Portland, a drive along the interstate can be overwhelmingly scenic. South of Hood River (or east of Portland) Mount Hood, Oregon's highest peak and most identifiable icon, attracts skiers and mountaineers from around the world.

CENTRAL OREGON
pages 154-183

Here are soaring Cascade peaks, high desert splashed with clear, fish-filled lakes and rivers. Skiing is excellent at Mount Bachelor, and Bend is a good base, close to the mountains and full of good restaurants and friendly brewpubs.

SOUTHERN OREGON
pages 184-221

Get off the I-5 corridor and explore the wild rapids and deep pools of the North Umpqua River; check out Shakespeare or shopping in Ashland; join an eagle-watching tour south of Klamath Falls.

NORTHEAST OREGON   *pages 222-253*

The Oregon Trail traversed Northeast Oregon from the Snake River to the Columbia Plateau, and so little of the area has been developed since then that wagon ruts are still visible in several places. Some of Oregon's most rugged backcountry can be found in the Wallowa Mountains, in the far northeast corner of the state.

SOUTHEAST OREGON   *pages 254-289*

Oregon's most remote corner is little visited, even by native Oregonians. But most who have been here once will return again and again for the open spaces, the views from Steens Mountain, the birds at the Malheur Refuge, or just the hot springs.

INTRODUCTION

CONJURE UP AN IMAGE OF OREGON and it will most likely be colored with all hues of green and gray, brimming with firs and ferns, and dampened by drizzle. This would be a fairly accurate picture of western Oregon, the area between the Pacific Ocean and the Cascade Range, but that's just one face of the state.

East of the Cascades, where volcanic peaks block Pacific rain clouds, the colors turn to gold and blue, and the horizon expands for miles. Rivers dissect northeastern Oregon; the southeast's topography is marked by fault blocks and dry basins. Psychically, eastern Oregon is The West, and western Oregon is the Northwest.

Every Oregonian, and nearly every visitor to the state, pays heed to the environment. It's unavoidable. In southeastern Oregon, you're little more than a speck in space; in the Columbia Gorge or the low, wet western Cascades, you feel like a mass of carbon and oxygen, absolutely destined to nourish a fern, with only force of will and movement keeping you from becoming green and rooted.

Oregon's giant trees and abundant fish, once taken for granted, are decreasing in number, and perhaps paradoxically, the people harvesting these resources often have the deepest connections to them. Oregonians share a concern about natural resources. Not everyone agrees on what should be done, but most everybody cares. Hikers wandering through old-growth forests may pry open a nurse log with a boot toe and suddenly experience a tidal wave of feeling for nature's cycles of decay and rebirth. Campers wandering near Frenchglen during bird migration will hear coyotes howling in the night and the wing-beats of birds thundering in the dawn, and perhaps be overwhelmed by the enormity and continuity of nature's gifts.

Oregon's storytellers have long taken cues from their surroundings. Indian legends have some of the same landmarks that show up in Ursula K. LeGuin's futuristic novel, *The Lathe of Heaven.* The damp chill infusing Lewis and Clark's journal entries during their winter near the Oregon coast is so pervasive that one can only imagine the actual pages becoming water-stained and wavy from moisture. Readers enveloped by moss in Barry Lopez's *River Notes* and caught up in the rising, rushing river water in Ken Kesey's *Sometimes a Great Notion,* may decide it's time to head to the dry east side of the Cascades with a copy of C. E. S. Wood's epic, "The Poet in the Desert."

Wood, a prominent Portland lawyer in the early 1900s, also reminds readers that Oregonians, however well-bred, " . . . think that it is the right of every American to go to hell and be damned if he wants to. That is not humor—it is the truth." In contemporary Oregon culture, filmmaker Gus van Sant shows a conventions-be-damned pluck and depicts urban Portland in a light that some find a little rough-edged and unpleasant, and others find dead accurate.

No matter where an Oregonian is from, no matter what his or her livelihood, Oregonians love Oregon. Eastern Oregonians may be a little suspicious of Port-landers, and vice versa, but people are firmly rooted, with a deep sense of place and a pride in where they live. It's rare to find an Oregonian who really wants to move anywhere else. Some do it out of desperation, then immediately begin to plot their return.

While doing the research for this book, I've asked myself a number of unexpected questions, such as: Is it possible to reach perfect enlightenment while downshift-ing on hairpin turns on the McKenzie Pass Road, as empty Diet Coke cans clank back and forth on the backseat floor? I've begun to think so.

I also got a sense of being in the right place at the right time when, shortly after contracting to write this book, I took off for Steens Mountain, knowing the road would soon be closed by snow. As I dodged boulders on the final haul up Steens Summit, a battered van approached on its way down. We both slowed for the obliga-tory backroad wave, and I recognized the driver as Greg Vaughn, the photographer for this book—also racing the weather and chasing the perfect light at Kiger Gorge.

Hopefully, this book will set readers on their own path toward special moments and realizations, yet be as well a useful, practical guide to the state of Oregon.

■ ACKNOWLEDGMENTS

Friendly Oregonians statewide contributed both knowingly and unknowingly to this book, as they told me stories and revealed their favorite spots. Sarah Butler, Emily Roth, Dawn Sanders, Taylor Gehweiler, Gail Bruner, and Terry Wade all keep me informed when they travel around the state. Thanks also to Bill McRae for his tips, Michael Powell for sharing his enthusiasm for regional literature, and to Sandy and Dick in La Grande for their hospitality and advice. Kelly Duane was kind enough to track down historical photos. Special thanks to Kit Duane for her en-thusiasm, editorial guidance, and friendship.

(following pages) Mount Hood looms over the Columbia River Gorge.

H I S T O R Y

■ GEOLOGIC HISTORY

In America, power may flow from east to west, but when it comes to geology, the west is certainly the continent's leading edge. Here the oceanic plate plunged beneath the continent as island groups and miniature continental plates pulled together to create our mainland.

Before the Atlantic Ocean separated North America and Europe, parts of the Blue and Klamath Mountains were forming in the sea that buried present-day Oregon. As the North American plate edged west, offshore mountains joined the coastline.

As the continent grew, it captured a volcanic zone that would become the Coast Range. This coastal block shifted into place, tugging and stretching the continental crust. Volcanoes erupted, burying plants, animals, and rocks with lava, ash, and mud. New earthquakes ripped faults across southeastern Oregon and pushed the torn pieces into blocky mountains as volcanic eruptions left behind a lava frosting.

As the western Cascades tilted and uplifted, and the Coast Range became a north-south fold, the region caught the brunt of incoming storms that dumped intense rain and snow. Areas east of the volcanic Cascades remained relatively dry and sunny. The landscape was remade once again as glaciers swept south from Washington. During this period, roughly two million years ago, glaciers topped the Cascades, Steens, and Blue Mountains.

When the northern continental glaciers altered air flow patterns, cool, wetter weather blanketed the state. Increased rainfall turned eastern Oregon basins into huge lakes near which elephants, camels, horses, wolves, dogs, peccary, and bears lived. As glaciers retreated, the climate slowly moderated, turning hot and dry. Volcanic activity continued leaving notable landmarks like Crater Lake, created in the collapsed caldera of a mountain that blew its top.

■ FIRST OREGONIANS

During the ice ages, sea levels fell and exposed a strip of land across the Bering Sea. This became the migratory route of game animals heading south toward warmer climates. They were followed by small bands of Asian hunters who crossed the Bering land bridge and then headed south to become the first North Americans.

Small groups of hunters may have begun crossing between the continents as early as 30,000 years ago, but the largest migration occurred at the end of the last ice age about 14,000 years ago. It's impossible to say when the original wave of migrants reached present-day Oregon, or exactly how they got there. Some may have come directly, others followed waves of migration back and forth across the continent as famine, feuding, or overpopulation led to resettlement. Sandals found in Fort Rock Cave in Central Oregon date back 13,000 years. Descendants of these people may have witnessed the apocalyptic eruption of Mount Mazama (now Crater Lake) 7,700 years ago.

Anthropologists have partially reconstructed early Oregon history by tracing the migration of language groups. The experts agree that eastern Oregon and the Columbia River were settled long before people crossed the Cascades to the western part of the state. Arriving from northern Nevada were the sandal-shod cave dwellers at Fort Rock Cave. These Native Americans who lived near southeastern Oregon's big lakes spoke a Penutian language (as do Central America's Mayans).

In the hot dry spell at the end of the ice age, alluvial lakes evaporated, and the Penutian-speakers headed north to the Columbia River. Sub-groups, including some Penutian speakers, migrated to the coast between 2,000 and 4,000 years ago. About the same time, Shoshonean-speakers (the Paiute) came up through northeastern California and settled in Oregon's southeast corner. By language, the Paiute were related to the Bannock, the Shoshone, and other members of the Uto-Aztecan language family, including Arizona's Hopi Indians and Mexico's Aztecs.

The lower Columbia and portions of southwestern Oregon became home to Athabascan speakers, possibly drop-outs on a grand migration from Alaska and northwestern Canada to the southwest United States. Athabascan speakers were part of the last great migration across the Bering land bridge, about 5,000 years ago, and both the Apache and Navajo tribes speak Athabascan languages.

Coast Salish-speakers from British Columbia's Fraser River country came south to the Oregon coast around 1400. Other Salish-speaking Indians migrated east and lived across Idaho and western Montana.

Within all these language groups, there were many languages and more dialects. Under the broad Penutian heading fell Chinookan, Sahaptian, Molallan, Cayusan, Lutuamian, Kalapuyan, Takelman, Alsean, Siuslawan, and Coosan. Though it wasn't uncommon for an Oregon Indian to be multilingual, a particular language was not necessarily intelligible to someone who spoke a related language. Chinook jargon—a mishmash of Chinook, French, and English—became the common

language of people who lived and traded along the Columbia. As disparate groups were forced to live together on reservations, Chinook jargon helped these Native Americans communicate.

Were it not for the Columbia River, the Cascades could have been a formidable cultural barrier. People living northeast of the mountains led lives very different from those of their neighbors to the south. Northeastern tribes such as the Nez Perce and Cayuse were hunters and fishers. They acquired horses in the 1700s and became renowned equestrians. In the high, dry southeast, people travelled by foot in small bands and lived in willow wickiups. They often had trouble finding food. In southernmost Oregon, where the western valleys meet the Great Basin, Klamaths and Modocs took small canoes onto the large lakes and waded into marshes to harvest their most important staple food, the *woka*, or yellow water-lily seed. They wintered in well-constructed roofed-over circular pits and summered in above-ground willow-pole and tule-mat houses.

(above) Frontier artist Henry J. Warre's "Valley of the Willamette" shows the region as it looked in 1848, prior to extensive pioneer settlement. (Oregon Historical Society)

(opposite) Cecilia Bearchum keeps alive the ancient traditions of her people at the Umatilla Indian Reservation in northeastern Oregon.

Oregon's coastal people lived comfortably off the ocean and seaside rivers. Their highly stratified society included slaves. Although they were the first to trade with whites, their Willamette Valley neighbors bore the brunt of white settlement. Coastal, valley, and Columbia River tribes all travelled on Oregon's rivers in dugout canoes and sustained themselves by fishing, hunting, and gathering roots and berries. Coastal and valley tribes lived in large plank houses and wore clothing made from shredded cedar bark, tule, or grass.

East met west at Winquatt (The Dalles), where Columbia River tribes fished, traded, and lived in tule-covered longhouses. Neighbors also met in the mountains during huckleberry season, exchanging news and gossip as they picked berries. They may have also shared stories of the mythical coyote, whose roguish ways were part of western Indian mythology.

■ SHIPS ON THE HORIZON

European explorers first approached Oregon from the sea. In 1573, Portuguese explorer Juan Rodriguez Cabrillo, sailing for Spain, and his pilot, Bartolome Ferrelo, sailed up the California coast. When Cabrillo died, Ferrelo took over and came north as far as the mouth of southern Oregon's Rogue River. (Cape Ferrelo, between

An old print of "Mount Hood from the Columbia" by D. Appleton in 1874 compares favorably with a recent photograph of the same on pages 16–17. (Columbia River Maritime Museum)

Brookings and Gold Beach is named for him.)

In 1579, English adventurer Sir Francis Drake sailed around the Horn and north to the waters off southern Oregon before turning around. Perhaps he was deterred by storms, but one Drake biographer suggests that in "all his enterprises, booty seems to have been somewhere in sight." Maybe the rocky Oregon coast didn't appear to offer enough loot to merit further investigation.

For close to 200 years, maritime efforts were concentrated further south, as the Spanish sailed the South Seas, searching for the "Unknown Continent," and set up trading circuits between Mexico, the Philippines, and Japan.

Cayuse babies in papoose photographed by Lee Moorehouse in 1898.

It was 1775 before serious exploration resumed off the Oregon coast. By this time, the Russians had established fur trading posts in Alaska, hastening exploration of the Pacific Northwest coast. Any number of explorers were trying to discover a Northwest Passage linking the North Atlantic to a great river flowing into the Pacific. Time and again, ships passed right by the obvious western terminus of the mythic passage, the mouth of the Columbia River. To America's early English settlers, the undiscovered "passage" was known as the River Oregon, mentioned by Indians, sought overland by Robert Rogers, and described in an early travel book by Jonathan Carver. Yet British, American, and Spanish ships continued to sail past the rocky Oregon coast, dismissing it as difficult and harborless.

In 1775, Spanish explorer Bruno Heceta claimed he had seen the mouth of a great river, but was unable to cross its harrowing bar. For years afterward, ships' captains kept an eye out for Heceta's river but none caught sight of it.

The English, ever in competition with Spanish mariners, dispatched Capt. James Cook who had, on two earlier voyages to the south Pacific, proven there was no Unknown Continent. While he also failed to find the Northwest Passage, he did become the first European to visit the Sandwich Islands (Hawai'i). Then he sailed up the Oregon coast, naming Capes Gregory (now Foulweather), Arago, and Perpetua. Next Cook sailed past the mouth of the Columbia and landed on Vancouver Island.

In 1788, John Meares, an independent English trader known as a braggart and a liar, searched for Heceta's river, while on a fur trading expedition. This half-baked geographer thought he had discovered the mouth of a river, then decided he hadn't, and named the mouth of the Columbia "Deception Bay."

In 1792 English navigator Capt. George Vancouver, who had sailed with Captain Cook in the South Seas, commanded a British expedition to the Pacific Coast. His journey extended from the Spanish settlements of California to southeastern Alaska's Russian settlements. Vancouver paused off Deception Bay and saw the Columbia River's muddy plume, but, ". . . Not considering this opening worthy of more attention, I continued our pursuit to the N.W., being desirous to embrace the advantage of the breeze and pleasant weather, so favorable to our examination of the coast…"

Vancouver breezed on to Nootka, on present-day Vancouver Island, where he encountered Robert Gray, a vigorous Boston trader on a mission to buy furs that could be traded in China for silk. He was also bent on tracking down Heceta's river. Gray crossed paths with Vancouver in the Strait of Juan de Fuca and argued the case for a great Northwest river. Vancouver was nonplused, but the interest of his colleague William Broughton was piqued.

Several days later, Robert Gray ventured over the treacherous bar and into the "River of the West." Eventually it was named after his ship, the *Columbia Rediviva*. He only traveled a few miles upriver before turning back and resuming his fur trading mission.

William Broughton quickly followed in Gray's wake. He sailed up the newly discovered Columbia to the mouth of the Sandy River, east of present-day Portland. Naturally, he claimed the watershed for the British crown.

■ LEWIS AND CLARK

After Gray's tentative exploration, and Broughton's voyage up the Columbia, ownership of the Pacific Northwest was still up for grabs, at least as far as nation-states (as distinguished from Indian tribes) were concerned. Alexander Mackenzie, a Canadian fur trader, urged the British to claim the land drained by the Columbia. This dismayed American president Thomas Jefferson who wanted to send an American expedition across the vast, French-held Louisiana (then extending from New Orleans on the Mississippi River to the Rocky Mountains) and promptly explore the Pacific Northwest.

In 1792, Capt. George Vancouver led a British expedition to the Pacific Coast.

At the time, America was still a small, struggling country, a 26-year-old democracy in a world dominated by European superpowers. In 1802, President Jefferson started bargaining with the French and ended up taking possession of all of Louisiana Territory. If Jefferson had been interested in sending an expedition to the Northwest, he now was also interested in exploring and mapping America's newly acquired territory which lay along the way.

A transcontinental expedition was already set to go. Jefferson's personal secretary, Meriwether Lewis, was to lead the trip to the West Coast. Lewis, in turn, requested to share leadership with his longtime friend, William Clark. American acquisition of Louisiana broadened their mandate and made it all the more certain that a successful trip would land them in the history

DISCOVERY OF THE COLUMBIA RIVER

*T*he year 1792 was now come, and it was a great year in the annals of Oregon, three hundred years from Columbus, two hundred from Juan de Fuca. The struggle between England and Spain over conflicting rights at Nootka, which at one time threatened war, had been settled with a measure of amicability. As a commissioner to represent Great Britain, Captain George Vancouver was sent out, while Bodega y Quadra was empowered to act in like capacity for Spain. Spaniards and Britons alike realised that, whatever the Nootka treaty may have been, possession was nine points of the law, and both redoubled their efforts to push discovery, and especially to make the first complete exploration of the Straits of Fuca and the supposed Great River. There were great names among the Spaniards in that year, some of which still commemorate some of the most interesting geographical points, as Quimper, Malaspina, Fidalgo, Caamano, Elisa, Bustamente, Valdez, and Galiano. A list of British names now applied to many points, as Vancouver, Puget, Georgia, Baker, Hood, Rainier, St. Helens, Whidby, Vashon, Townsend, and others, attests the name-bestowing care of the British commander.

Two days later the lookout reported a sail, and as the ships drew together, the newcomer was seen to be flying the Stars and Stripes. It was the *Columbia Rediviva,* Captain Robert Gray, of Boston. In response to Vancouver's rather patronizing queries, the Yankee skipper gave a summary of his log for some months past. Among other things he states that he had passed what seemed to be a powerful river in latitude 46 degrees 10 minutes, which for nine days he had tried in vain to enter, being repelled by the strength of the current. He now proposed returning to that point and renewing his efforts. Vancouver declined to reconsider his previous decision that there could be no large river, and passed on to make his very elaborate exploration of the Straits of Fuca and their connected waters, and to discover to his great chagrin, that the Spaniards had forestalled him in point of time.

The vessels parted. Gray sailed south and on May 10, 1792, paused abreast of the same reflex of water where before for nine days he had tried vainly to enter. The morning of the 11th dawned clear and favourable, light wind, gentle sea, a broad, clear channel, plainly of sufficient depth. The time was now come. The man and the occasion met. Gray seems from the first to have been ready to take some chances for the sake of some great success. He always hugged the shore closely enough to be on intimate terms with it. And he was ready boldly to seize and use favouring circumstances. So, as laconically stated in his log-book, he ran in with all sail set, and at ten o'clock found himself in a large river of fresh water, at a point about twenty miles from the ocean.

◆   ◆   ◆

*T*he River already bore many names, but Gray added another, and it was the one that has remained, the name of his good ship *Columbia*. . . . The great exploit was completed. The long sought River of the West was found, and by an American.

—William Denison Lyman, *The Columbia River*, 1909

Capt. Robert Gray's vessel, the Columbia Rediviva, *after which the Columbia River was named. (Columbia River Maritime Museum)*

books. They were directed to follow the Missouri River to its headwaters, hop the supposedly short divide to the Columbia River, and set firm American foot in the Pacific Northwest. The pair also were charged with introducing native people west of St. Louis to the concept of American government. Jefferson sent Lewis to science tutors in Philadelphia, and asked that he keep journals and preserve specimens for the benefit of the nation.

The Corps of Discovery included 29 other men, and one woman, translator Touissant Charbonneau's 15-year-old Shoshone wife, Sacagawea (who'd been enslaved by the Hidatsas and sold to Charbonneau, or, apocryphally, won by him in a game of dice). Eventually, their baby son, Jean-Baptiste, born along the way, also made the journey, carried by his mother. Sacagawea turned out to be a better traveling companion than her unreliable husband, and she was a vital link in the translation chain. When the party met up with her long-lost Sho-shone family, Sacagawea translated the Shoshone into Hidatsa for Charbonneau, who then translated it into French. Several French-speaking expedition members provided the final translation into English.

William Clark (Independence National Historic Park, Philadelphia)

Other Corps of Discovery members were excellent hunters, and one played the fiddle. Indians were unfailingly impressed with the physical bulk, great strength, and black skin of

Clark's servant York. With the exception of one man who died early in the expedition from appendicitis, all members of the expedition successfully followed the Missouri to its Rocky Mountain headwaters, picked their way across steep, forested passes to the Columbia, and shot canoes down the wild, tumbling Columbia to the Pacific Ocean.

Anyone who's tried camping in western Oregon during a wet spell can sympathize with Lewis and Clark's journal entries from Fort Clatsop, near present-day Astoria. The words "wet, cold, and disagreeable" crop up almost daily in Clark's notes. It was an exceptionally damp winter; rain fell all but 12 days,

Meriwether Lewis (Independence National Historic Park, Philadelphia)

the sun shone for six. There's frequent mention of fleas. Acceptable food was not easy to come by and the crew subsisted for the most part on salmon and roasted dogs (obtained from the Indians). Come spring, they were eager to leave.

On the way back upstream, Chinook-speaking Shah-ha-la Indians at the mouth of the Sandy River told Lewis and Clark of a much larger river occluded by islands and bars. Clark floated back down the river and found the mouth of the Willamette River (called the Multnomah in the journals). From the size and current, Clark guessed the river's headwaters were in California.

When Lewis and Clark returned east in 1806, Americans were thrilled and eager to hear of their adventures, as the explorers had been presumed dead in the wilds.

JOURNALS OF LEWIS AND CLARK EXPEDITION
NOVEMBER 2, 1805 - MARCH 22, 1806

Expedition leader Meriwether Lewis had a knack for recording elegant, detailed observations in the journal Thomas Jefferson asked him to keep for the benefit of the nation. William Clark's passages were more earthy, and like Lewis's, rife with misspellings. Their personalities were as different as their writing styles. Lewis, scholarly and refined, was prone to depressions. During the trip, whenever he fell under a dark cloud, he stopped writing and his partner carried the journalistic load. Clark was more personable. He had good rapport with the Indians, and his knack for doctoring won him friends among the natives. When Lewis was feeling good, Clark was a slack diarist, usually just copying Lewis's meticulous notes.

[Clark]   *December 1st Sunday 1805*

The Sea which is imedeately in front roars like a repeeted roling thunder and have rored in that way ever Since our arrival in its borders which is now 24 Days Since we arrived in Sight of the Great Western Ocian, I cant Say Pasific as Since I have Seen it, it has been the reverse. Elegant Canoes…

[Clark]   *Tuesday, 24th December 1805*

hard rain at Different times last night and all this day without intermition. men all employd in finishing their huts and moveing into them.

Cuscalah the Indian who had treated me So politely when I was at the Clatsops village, come up in a Canoe with his young brother & 2 Squars he laid before Capt Lewis and my Self each a mat and a parcel of roots—Some time in the evening two files was demanded for the presents of mats and roots, as we had no files to part with, we each returned the present which we had received, which displeased Cuscalah a little. he then offered a woman to each of us which we also declined axcepting of, which displeased the whole party verry much—the female part appeared to be highly disgusted at our refuseing to axcept of their favours &c.

[Lewis]   *Friday January 3rd 1806*

At 11 A. M. we were visited by our near neighbors… they brought for sale some roots buries and three dogs also a small quantity of fresh blubber. this blubber they informed us they had obtained from their neighbours the Callamucks who inhabit the coast to the S.E. near whose vilage a whale had recently perished. this blubber the

Indians eat and esteeme it excellent food. our party from necessaty having been oblig-
ed to subsist some lenth of time on dogs have now become extreemly fond of their
flesh; it is worthy of remark that while we lived principally on the flesh of this anamal
we were much more healthy strong and more flesey than we had been since we left
the Buffaloe country. for my own part I have become so perfectly reconciled to the
dog that I think it an agreeable food and would prefer it vastly to lean Venison or
Elk…

[Clark]   *Friday the 3rd January 1806*
…as for my own part I have not become reconsiled to the taste of this animal [dog] as
yet…

[Lewis]   *Monday January 6th 1806*
Capt Clark set out after an early breakfast with the party in two canoes [to see a
beached whale] as had been concerted the last evening; Charbono and his Indian
woman [Sacagawea] were also of the party; the Indian woman was very impotunate
to be permitted to go, and was therefore indulged; she observed that she had traveled
a long way with us to see the great waters, and that now that monstrous fish was also
to be seen, she thought it very hard she could not be permitted to see either (she had
never yet been to the Ocean).

The Clatsops, Chinnooks, Killamucks &c. are very loquacious and inventive;
they possess good memories and have repeated to us the names… curiosities of the
vessels &c of many traders and others who have visited the mouth of this river; they
are generally low in stature, proportionably… reather lighter complected and much
more illy formed than the Indians of the Missouri and those of our frontier; they are
generally cheerful but never gay. with us their conversation generally turns upon the
subjects of trade, smoking, eating or their women; about the latter they speak without reserve in their presents, of their every part, and of the most formiliar connec-
tion. they do not hold the virtue of their women in high estimation, and will even
prostitute their wives and daughters for a fishinghook or a stran of beads. in common
with other savage Indains they make their women perform every species of domestic
drudgery. but in almost every species of this drudgery the men also participate.

Their women are also compelled to geather roots, and assist them in taking fish,
which articles form much the greatest part of their subsistence; notwithstanding the
survile manner in which they treat their women they pay much more rispect to their
judgment and oppinions in many rispects than most indian nations; their women are

(continued)

permitted to speak freely before them, and sometimes appear to command with a tone of authority; they generally consult them in their traffic and act in conformity to their opinions. I think it may be established as a general maxim that those nations treat their old people and women with most difference [deference] and rispect where they subsist principally on such articles that these can participate with the men in obtaining them; and that, that part of the community are treated with least attention, when the act of procuring subsistence devolves intirely on the men in the vigor of life.

After the expedition Clark married his cousin (for whom he'd named Montana's Judith River) and enjoyed good government jobs in the Midwest. Lewis drifted, eventually killing himself (though there are still those who say he was murdered) in a Tennessee hotel room.

■ FUR TRADE

The two British fur trading companies, Hudson's Bay and the North West Company, worked overland, with headquarters in Eastern Canada. American traders, including Robert Gray, typically sailed out of Boston. Although these seafaring entrepreneurs were hampered by storms, shipwrecks, scurvy, and the wrath of Indians, they built up quite a business. From 1798 to 1802, 48,500 sea otter skins were sold in Canton, China.

With numbers like these in mind, John Jacob Astor, the richest man in America, decided to base a fur business at the mouth of the Columbia River. In 1810, he sent a ship, the *Tonquin,* loaded with supplies and traders to the Oregon Coast. At the same time, an overland group departed, scouting sites for inland trading stations. Both parties were star-crossed.

By sea, the expected hardships were magnified by an unbalanced captain, Jonathon Thorne. Shortly after reaching Astoria, he took a party north to look for furs off the coast of British Columbia. His imperious treatment of the Nootka Indians led to misunderstandings and finally bloodshed. In the end virtually the entire crew of Astor's ship was murdered. In an insane act of revenge, a starving Astorian lured a band of Nootka aboard the *Tonquin.* Then he went below and lit the ship's magazine. The *Tonquin* was destroyed and everyone aboard perished. The overland party failed to follow Shoshone advice, and spent the winter in the mountains, after breaking into several small and hungry (moccasin-eating) groups.

Shortly after the Astorians arrived at their Columbia River base, Indian messengers brought word that the North West Company's David Thompson was traveling down the Columbia, staking claims for Britain along the way. Several of the newly arrived American traders set off immediately to establish upriver trading posts, ensuring American control. (Their canoes included stashes of newspapers and brochures, packed along to allay wilderness boredom). When Thompson paddled down to the mouth of the river, the Americans were trying to look well settled in at Fort Astoria.

By the time Astoria really got going, so had the War of 1812. With a war between England and the United States going on, Astor had trouble getting supply ships to the Columbia River. When an approaching British warship frightened the Americans, Fort Astoria was hastily sold to the North West Company. In 1813, Fort Astoria became British Fort George. At war's end, Astoria was returned to the Americans, but the North Westers continued to run the enterprise at Fort George.

Astoria may have been a flop, but John Jacob Astor was proud of the whole *notion* of his enterprise. He contracted one of America's most popular writers to tell the story. Washington Irving and his nephew holed up at Astor's Hudson River estate for months of research and writing. It's easy to picture Astor, straining at the library door, blurting out stories: "Did I tell you about. . . ." *Astoria* was *the* book to read in 1837, and was translated into French, Russian, and German. It has remained in print for more than 150 years.

Meanwhile, the Hudson's Bay Company, operating as a British government-sanctioned monopoly in eastern Canada, edged west. In 1821, the North West Company and the Hudson's Bay Company merged, retaining the Hudson's Bay name. In 1824, Fort Vancouver at the mouth of the Willamette River became the Company's northwestern headquarters. Although it was a hundred miles (160 km) upriver from the ocean, ships were able to reach the fort to deliver merchandise and take on furs. The new location, on a wide bench sloping back from the Columbia, was well suited for agriculture; a hog farm sprung up across the Columbia on Sauvie Island, and timber and flour mills churned away. Fish and game were plentiful, and the classy fort dining room became known as the place for a western explorer to get a really good meal.

Fort Vancouver was a place of elegance and dignity, lent largely by the chief agent, Dr. John McLoughlin, a big man topped off with a prodigious amount of

HISTORY

white hair. McLoughlin was overseen by George Simpson, a 19th-century efficiency expert and a thorn in the agent's side. Even with (or thanks to) Simpson's harping, life at Fort Vancouver was peaceful and prosperous. McLoughlin insisted on fair dealings with the Indians, and gained their respect.

Fur trading hummed all over the Oregon Country, where rivers, hills, and beaver dams were being sketched into blank spots on crude maps. One Hudson's Bay representative, Peter Skene Ogden, did his best to blanket the east side with Hudson's Bay trade. Trips to the Great Salt Lake took him across southeastern Oregon, and he made two journeys up the Deschutes River—in 1825 and 1827.

American mountain-man Jedediah Smith scouted and traded across California and Oregon. In 1828, after surviving an Indian attack in the Willamette Valley, he took a breather at Fort Vancouver. While availing himself of McLoughlin's generosity he predicted that few Americans would risk travel to such forbidding country, a prediction that pleased the company's powers-that-be to no end.

Dr. John McLoughlin (Oregon Historical Society)

To protect their lucrative fur supply the Hudson's Bay Company attempted to keep the Oregon Country unpopulated (especially by Americans). But John McLoughlin was too compassionate to refuse help to the Americans now filtering into these valleys. In 1845, McLoughlin himself moved across the river and settled alongside Willamette Falls. He took steps to become a United States citizen, but when he did, territorial authorities tried to strip him of his land, which he'd acquired under British governance.

By frontier standards, "Fort Vancouver" was a place of elegance and dignity, at least as depicted here by artist Henry J. Warre. (Oregon Historical Society)

McLoughlin was not the only Hudson's Bay employee to head up the Willamette upon quitting the company. A group of French Canadians began farming in the Willamette Valley in 1829. There were a few American mountain men there too, but it took missionaries to loosen the soil for homesteaders in western Oregon.

■ THE LORD'S WORK

European missionaries began their North American work in the 1500s, when Spanish padres began proselytizing in New Mexico. French Jesuits reached the Northeast in the 1600s, intent on saving the Hurons' souls (and ended up destroying them with disease). In the 1800s New England Protestants set out to spread The Word. Indians, suffering disease and dispossession at the hands of whites, had often been reluctant converts. So, in 1832, when four Flathead Indians appeared in St. Louis requesting the aid of the black robes, or Catholic priests, Christians everywhere were deeply moved. Among them were the Methodists, including a young graduate of Wesleyan University engaged in missionary work in Quebec. He sailed to Vancouver enthusiastically and made plans to open a mission.

By 1834, Jason Lee was building a mission in the Willamette Valley. It was not the Willamette Valley Indians who had come to St. Louis seeking to learn about Christianity, but Lee felt this was a far better place to teach the Lord's agriculture than the colder, mountain-flanked Bitterroot Valley, home of the Flatheads. His first congregation was an international one—there were French, English, American, Scotch-Irish, Indian, Hawaiian, and Japanese celebrants. (The Japanese were shipwreck survivors, washed ashore after months adrift in the Pacific.)

When missionaries could spare a moment from their own daily tasks, they tagged along with Indians, picking berries and trying to slip in holy words. In 1834, the Methodists saw Mount St. Helen's erupt and burst out singing "How awful is our God."

Of the mission's 14 original Indian students, five died and five quit school during the first year. Two more died the following year, as diphtheria and malaria spread through the valley. During the early 1830s, waves of measles, smallpox, and other epidemics crashed over the Indians of the lower Columbia and Willamette valleys. Whole villages died. As Indians fell ill and shied away from the mission, the missionaries' focus shifted to tilling the fields and educating white settlers.

Even as outreach to the natives sputtered, the missionary corps swelled. Much to the relief of the valley's French Canadians, Catholic priests arrived in 1838. Several men married by the Methodists to Indian women repeated the ceremonies in the Catholic church, igniting a theological scuffle.

East of the Cascades, Marcus and Narcissa Whitman and Henry and Eliza Spalding set up Protestant missions near today's Walla Walla, Washington, and Lewiston, Idaho (both part of Oregon territory). The Spaldings ministered to the friendly Nez Perce in Idaho; to the west, the Whitmans tried to instill the fear of God in the less tractable Cayuse and Walla Walla people. The Cayuse, in particular, weren't thrilled about Christianity, nor about the farming that seemed to be part and parcel of the church doctrine.

As white migration to the Oregon country gained steam, more and more immigrants stopped by the Whitman mission. They often arrived in ill health, but generally responded to the Whitmans' food and nursing. When the Cayuse observed that whites often recovered after being doctored by Whitman, but that Indians didn't, they suspected poisoning. It didn't help that Marcus Whitman poisoned Cayuse dogs and tainted his own garden melons to stop pilfering. The Cayuse also suspected that the growing white presence was not going to do much for the Indian way of life. The mission's work ended tragically in 1847 when the Indians killed the Whitmans and 12 other whites. The Cayuse also took hostages, who were rescued by the resourceful and diplomatic Peter Skene Ogden.

■ OREGON TRAIL PIONEERS

Well before the Whitman massacre, settlers sent word to friends and families back east that Oregon was habitable. Pamphleteer Hall Kelley was an especially vigorous Oregon booster, even before making his brief trip West. People were interested in moving to Oregon for as many reasons then as now. Some were looking for a way out of the increasingly crowded and economically depressed Midwest. Others wanted to escape the malaria and cholera rampant in the Mississippi and other valleys. Harsh winters and the specter of slavery were other contributing factors. Many were just restless, ready to try their luck in a verdant new region.

In 1843, the Organic Act allotted 640 acres of Oregon land to every adult male settler, and 160 acres per child. In this way, the federal government hoped to pack

A Conestoga wagon on the Oregon Trail, 1961.

the region full of American families, and finally tie down the United States' claims to the Pacific Northwest.

In Missouri, wagon trains gathered, ready to roll as soon as the weather permitted. Most immigrants were optimistic middle-class people. It took roughly $1,000 cash to gather the necessary trail-travel and homesteading equipment supplies. The wagon train convoys were quasi-military; captains were elected, pilots appointed, and strict rules drawn up.

The first part of the eight-month trip was mind-numbing drudgery, walking across the plains in the dust kicked up by wagons, cattle, horses, and oxen. Disease, especially cholera, often caught up with the emigrants, and almost everybody lost a friend or relative on the way west. There were plenty of marriages and births, too, neither one causing more than a few moments delay in the journey.

Oregonians are fond of remembering an apocryphal trailside marker, one arrow marked with the word "Oregon," the other with a pile of gold rocks. It is said that this sign directed readers to Oregon, and sent the greedy numbskulls south to California (where, modern interpretation has it, they belonged).

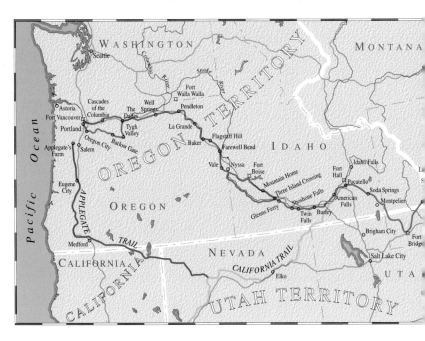

The trail crossed the Rockies at gentle South Pass, easier by far than eastern Oregon's Blue Mountains, where wagons had to be pullied up and teased down the treacherous slopes. Wagons were affixed to rafts at The Dalles and floated through the then-raging, steep-walled Columbia Gorge. Typically, this was the most hazardous part of the trip. Livestock had to swim across the river, and then cross back, at several tricky spots. In 1844, half the animals were lost in river crossings.

In 1845, rather than shooting the Columbia's rapids, Samuel Barlow led a party around the south side of Mount Hood to the Willamette Valley on an old Indian trail. A year later, Barlow built a toll road over that route. Rain, mud, steep slopes, and cold made the Barlow Road nearly as formidable as the river route.

A few wagon trains cut off the main northerly route of the Oregon Trail and crossed central Oregon. Stephen Meek's ill-fated group passed through the southeastern and central portion of this territory in 1845. Several people died from dehydration and from drinking alkaline water. However, the prospective homesteaders did find gold nuggets in the dregs of a water bucket (though nobody could say exactly *where* that pail had come from). This discovery piqued interest in

OREGON TRAIL

Modern Freeways Shown in Gray

0   100   200   300

Miles

the land east of the Cascades, even though it was Indian territory unavailable to homesteaders.

Jesse and Lindsay Applegate's route, which premiered in 1846 via northern Nevada, circled down into northern California, then up into southern Oregon. It was at least as harrowing as the northern route, and rarely used again until gold was discovered in southwestern Oregon during the 1850s.

■ GOVERNMENT TO THE RESCUE

Through the 1830s, the Oregon country was jointly occupied by the Americans and the British, and controlled by fur trader John McLoughlin and Methodist missionary Jason Lee. As the Willamette Valley's population increased, a pre-territorial, provisional government was established by fits and starts, if only to take a stand against domination by two unelected men. In 1843, a hurly-burly meeting at Champoeg took a sharp decisive note when mountain man Joe Meek shouted, "Who's for a divide?" Fifty-two settlers jumped to the American side; 50 went for the British, giving the Americans political control. Three years later, in 1846, after James Polk campaigned on a Democratic platform of "Fifty-four forty or fight," the international boundary was fixed at 49 degrees.

The provisional Oregon legislature had just assembled in Oregon City when word arrived of the Whitman massacre in distant Walla Walla. The Willamette Valley settlers threw a rag-tag militia together and headed east to mount a desultory campaign against the Cayuse; five token Indians were finally handed over and charged with the Whitman murders.

The Walla Walla violence convinced Oregonians that it was time to establish U.S. law. Ex-trapper Joe Meek went east as the legislative emissary, and arrived in Washington D.C. proclaiming himself "envoy extraordinary and minister plenipotentiary from the Republic of Oregon to the Court of the United States." On August 14, 1848, Meek's distant cousin President James Polk signed a bill creating the Oregon Territory. This "Organic Act" recognized Indian title to Oregon Territory, but two years later a new law (much lobbied for by Oregon settlers) called for Indians to cede their lands and move east of the Cascades. By 1855, western Oregon was blanketed with claims.

Oregonians had no vote in Congress, and no vote for President. The job of territorial governor was pure political patronage—a presidential appointment never given to an Oregon resident. (Zachary Taylor offered the job to Abraham Lincoln, who turned it down.) For Oregonians who'd had an active hand in the provisional government, territoriality reeked of Eastern intervention.

Fortunately, there was enough activity afoot in the West to keep the restless occupied—the 1849 California gold rush had suddenly created a market for Oregon's farm produce, as well as a new adventure for many residents. Two-thirds of the new territory's adult males headed south, heads spinning with gold fever. After gold was discovered in the Rogue Valley in the 1850s, many men migrated to southwest Oregon, where they worked relatively modest gold strikes.

In 1853, Washington Territory was split off from Oregon, and residents increasingly looked toward statehood, partly to maintain an anti-slavery position. Though Oregonians were, by and large, against slavery, they were not civil rights proponents. More than anything, Oregonians wanted self-determination. In the state constitution ratification election, slavery was voted down 7,727 to 2,645; but only 1,081 men voted to allow free blacks to settle in Oregon, and 8,640 voters chose to bar them. (Union victory in the Civil War, however, ensured the right of blacks to live in Oregon after 1865.)

President Buchanan signed the act admitting Oregon as a state on February 14, 1859. The state motto was a proud, "She flies with her own wings."

Emily Butler Blockwell of Jacksonville was one of Oregon's early black residents. (Southern Oregon Historical Society)

■ PORTLAND GROWS UP

Oregon City at Willamette Falls, and Linnton on the Willamette River near its confluence with the Columbia, were the first Willamette Valley towns. In 1845, William Overton, Asa Lovejoy, and Francis Pettygrove settled a new community between the two established communities. With grand schemes of luring settlers and building a prosperous inland port, the trio set down plats and flipped a coin, naming the city Portland rather than Boston. Portland grew quickly, and soon eclipsed neighboring towns.

Twenty years after the first stumps were pulled from Portland's streets, the Oregon Steam Navigation Company controlled Columbia River shipping. Their Portland-based fleet of sternwheelers travelled upstream as far as The Dalles. Rail links skirted river cascades that only salmon could hope to navigate. Once river traffic was theirs, so was the Pacific Northwest economy. Wheat was shipped in from east of the Cascades, and shipped out of Portland, fueling the city's growth.

In 1860, Portland was a 821-person village; ten years later, 9,565 people lived in a decidedly prosperous town whose money and cultured ways made it the envy and the scorn of the Northwest. Portland was the New England city of the West: well-to-do, with a high moral tone, and a resolute church-going populace. Despite their plump wallets, good manners, and bowed heads, most Portlanders weren't overbearing or pretentious. Historian Dorothy Johansen tells of Simeon Reed, an owner of the Oregon Steam Navigation Company: "He played cards on Sunday after church, and he did not pull the shades to hide the fact." When he attended the opera in Paris, Reed, who didn't own a dress coat, "had his wife pin back the tails of his Prince Albert to simulate the proper garb." (A similar make-do level of fashion consciousness persists on the streets of Portland today.)

In other parts of the state, Indians were herded onto reservations to free up land east of the Cascades for white settlers. Some tribes saw few options and complied easily; others fought the new limitations imposed by whites. Chronicled then as nasty little wars, these conflicts now seem like tragic epics: Chief Joseph and the Nez Perce, chased from their home in the Wallowas; Paulina, thrashing out when the Northern Paiute reservation was whittled into smaller and smaller pieces; Captain Jack and his band of 50 Modocs, who left their designated reservation and crossed into California, where they held off 1,500 troops for six months.

Scion of an old pioneer family, Capt. O.C. Applegate attends a celebration for the beginning of construction of a new rail line. (Southern Oregon Historical Society)

■ RAILROADS

Transcontinental rail lines did not come to Oregon quickly or easily, but once they arrived, life changed fast, with sleepy paddle-boat burgs becoming bustling railroad towns. The Union Pacific built west from Omaha while the Central Pacific began in Oakland, California. The two lines met in Promontory, Utah, in 1869 where a golden spike was driven to complete the transcontinental line. Various spurs were envisioned connecting Portland to the California side of this route. The rival Northern Pacific's slow pace was quickened when Henry Villard took over the company's management. He purchased the Oregon Steam Navigation Company and its Columbia Gorge railbeds, directing their transcontinental line to Portland. By September 1883, trains could travel from Portland to St. Paul, Minnesota. Other lines soon followed.

The 1880s were boom years across the Northwest. Ranchers had discovered eastern Oregon grasslands, and the big cattle outfits were in full swing. Sheep ranchers and their flocks, seen as vermin encroaching on the lovely open range, were the focus of many a cowboy's abundant outrage. On several occasions vigilantes, believing that righteousness was with the moo-ers not the baa-ers, killed thousands of sheep and their shepherds as well.

The forests were also coming into economic play—huge stacks of logs were loaded onto Union Pacific trains headed to the Midwest. Ever the hub, Portland was trying to be a real city. Rudyard Kipling visited in 1889 and commented, "All this is excellent and exactly suitable to the opening of a new country; but when a man tells you it is civilisation, you object."

When the economic bust of the 1890s set in, questionable economic and political manueverings which had gone more or less unnoticed in the excitement of discovery and growth, suddenly came to the attention of Oregon's citizens. Powerful logging companies were trespassing on public lands; certain politicians were corrupt; and there was a fuss about the railroad land grants—land that was neither taxable nor available for farming. Oregon, especially Portland, was overwhelmingly conservative and Republican, but there was a glimmer of well-bred radicalism in the Populist movement, which was, for a time, big enough to be courted by both Democrats and Republicans.

Portlander William U'Ren led a campaign intended to see true majority rule in Oregon. His vehicles were the ballot initiative and referendum, ways for voters to bring about reforms that the politically sensitive legislature would be afraid to enact. The initiative and referendum were adopted in 1902, and from the start, people were paid, a nickel a signature, to collect names on petitions qualifying a measure to appear on the ballot.

Ballot measures and developing labor unions ushered in the turn-of-the-last-century "progressive era," and an economic resurgence. Agriculture, timber, and fishing all kept up with the times. Northeastern Oregon wheat farms prospered, and young fruit trees in the Hood River Valley and in southern Oregon were soon bearing superior apples and pears. Truck farms supplied vegetables to the cities, and, on the coast, dairy farms became the foundation of a cheese industry.

Timber harvests were phenomenal, and the industry was busy trying to find new markets and standardize the lumber coming out of small-town mills.

Gill-netters fished the Columbia, and salmon canneries lined the riverbanks between Astoria and the Cascades. Chinese laborers staffed the canneries, and farther upriver, Indians used spears or dipnets to catch fish pausing before big upstream jumps. Whites engineered fishwheels and spent years pumping fish from the Columbia. In the thick of a salmon run, 20,000 to 50,000 pounds of fish a day were churned from a single wheel. Even then, it was easy to see the wheels were too efficient to sustain a fishery, and they were outlawed in 1927.

World War I boosted lumber and fisheries, and shipbuilding began. The war's end brought immediate layoffs and plant closures, but timber fueled a mid-1920s recovery that lasted until the stock market crash.

Oregon did pretty well by the Depression. Public works projects changed the landscape and put thousands of people to work. Big dams took on the Columbia River. Woody Guthrie showed up in Portland for a one-month song-writing binge—he'd been hired by the Bonneville Power Administration to popularize the new dams.

World War II brought shame along with prosperity and patriotism. Japanese-Americans were evicted from their homes (mostly in western Oregon) and sent to detention camps in Nevada. The ship building business boomed, and Oregon's black population was boosted by the influx of shipyard workers from the South and Midwest. Many war industry workers settled in the town of Vanport, on a riverside plain just north of Portland. (Vanport was destroyed by a flood in 1948, and is now West Delta Park.) Once the wartime flurry of ship building was over, Oregon returned to a resource-based economy.

Construction of The Dalles Dam on the Columbia River flooded Celilo Falls (sacred to the Indians) in 1958, obliterating the most important fishing area on the river. Two years earlier, Congress "terminated" its relationship with western Oregon tribes, including the Siletz and Grande Ronde confederations, and the southern Oregon Klamaths. Members of these tribes, which were foundering culturally, decided to divide up reservation land among members, who could then sell their property to whomever they chose. As a result, tribes lost their reservations and their government benefits, including health care, and, for some, their sense of identity. Thanks to Native American protests some tribes have been "restored" with minimal lands returned to them.

Environmental and land use laws earned Oregon a progressive reputation in the 1960s and '70s. An anti-growth climate in the 1970s was largely shouted down by local businesses, especially when the economy fell apart, first in the early '80s, then again in the early 2000s. As residents come to the wrenching conclusion that many jobs dependent on the harvest of natural resources will never return, Portland-area firms such as Nike and Intel have become the economic war-horses.

Away from the cities, people struggle on, keeping to traditional Oregonian ways, or modifying them to fit with the times. Llama ranches, sustainable forestry, and organic seed farms all thrive in modest ways, and Oregonians remain convinced that they live in the Eden that pioneers dreamed of when they followed the Oregon Trail.

From the blueberries of the Willamette Valley (above) to the vine maples and Douglas firs of the Cascades (opposite), Oregon's natural bounty and beauty continue to inspire its residents.

P O R T L A N D

Map page 51 & 54

Portland

◆ AREA OVERVIEW

It's easy to fall in love with Portland, but it's the kind of falling in love where you're friends for a long time first. Portland's not a flashy city; it's a comfortable one. It's okay to wear jeans here, even to the trendiest restaurants, and there's no purer Portland pleasure than taking a hike in Forest Park, then dropping in at a brewpub for a pint of ale.

One of downtown Portland's charms is its compact size. It's easy for most folks to tour downtown, the Pearl district, and Northwest Portland on foot. Ambitious walkers can even go from downtown to the Rose Gardens (it's not far, but it is up-hill). If walking's not your thing, then hop on a streetcar, bus, or light rail train. They're all free within the downtown core.

And one of the city's biggest assets is its proximity to beautiful and diverse outdoor areas. Many visitors will use Portland as a hub for day trips to the Columbia Gorge and Mount Hood, the northern Oregon coast, and the Willamette Valley wine country. All are wonderful, with each place offering an entirely different look at the state.

Climate: For all the talk about Portland's rain, it's not really all *that* wet here. Summer weather, which usually begins around the Fourth of July and lasts through

October, is sunny and pleasant, with daytime temperatures in the 80s. In the fall, winter, and spring, bring a raincoat and expect temperatures in the 40s or 50s.

Food & Lodging: Chain motels and hotels are abundant on the outskirts of Portland, and they're generally not bad places to stay. Lodgings in one of the city's refurbished downtown hotels lends an extra little touch of class to a visit and will position you to walk or take public transportation to many local sights.

Food can easily be one of the highlights of a Portland visit. Shop the Portland Farmers Market on Saturdays spring through fall in the Park Blocks by Portland State University; every Saturday at 10 A.M. a different local chef shows up for a culinary demonstration. Then head out to the restaurants. While the Pearl District and Northwest Portland are known for their fine restaurants, nearly every Portland neighborhood has at least one good place to eat. Good coffee, good ale, and good wine are all easy to come by. (Also see pages 62–63.)

A spectacular view of Mount Hood from Portland's Washington Park.

■ OVERVIEW

It's no surprise that a Pacific Northwest capital grew up where the Willamette River joins the mighty Columbia. The water's deep enough for a port, no falls threaten boat travel, and the setting is magnificent.

The west bank of the Willamette River was a canoe stop for Indians traveling between the Willamette Valley and the Columbia River trading markets well before Portland's first settlers took a shine to it in 1843. Mount Hood, rising up majestically in Portland's backyard, added to the fledgling city's ambiance and seemed to anchor its settlers in their lush green home. No wonder that Portland, 100 miles from the mouth of the Columbia River, quickly eclipsed early Willamette Valley settlements in population and economic vitality.

Besides its splendid location, Portland is known for its relaxed respectability. Maybe it's the rain that does it—when yet another umbrella blows out, a casual dignity may be the most appropriate response. Portlanders flock to shoe repair shops in the fall, when puddle-jumping pedestrians become acutely aware of worn soles. By December, locals show no self-consciousness about donning rubber footgear, and Nordstrom, the upright fashion conscience of the Northwest, mounts big displays of duck shoes. Pallor rules; midwinter tans are regarded with suspicion, as sort of a grave California-inspired affectation, objects of envy and scorn.

Between springtime showers, Portland sparkles. The entire city greens up in an instant, and there's a heady burst of cherry trees, dogwoods, daffodils, all damp from the last shower and pulsing with growth. The dense greenery, celebrated now, was once order's nemesis:

> The city was incorporated and the first election held in 1851… At that time the forest came down to the river's edge except that the trees were cut from Front Avenue between Jefferson and Burnside Streets. The stumps remained in the streets and were whitewashed so that pedestrians would not collide with them at night. (*WPA guide to Oregon*)

Even as the stumps were being pulled from the muddy streets, civic leaders were thinking about preserving corridors of trees and grass in the fast-growing city. In 1852, the stately **Park Blocks** were laid out through downtown, and with the exception of a seven-block stretch (which even now civic leaders are trying to reclaim) they remain intact today.

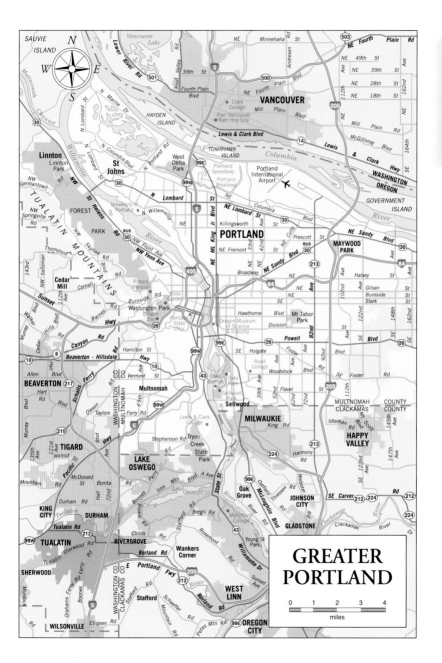

GREATER PORTLAND

0   1   2   3   4

miles

Forest Park, in the city's northwest corner—seven and a half miles long and a mile and a half wide—is one of the country's largest city parks. There are no manicured gardens or swing sets in Forest Park and even though it abuts the state's most densely populated neighborhood, it's remarkably wild. Wildlife, including deer, coyotes, and warblers use it as a corridor to the Coast Range to the west. Forest Park joggers, when they hear wet squishes under their Nikes, curse the trails for being a major slug corridor.

About two million people live in the metropolitan area now, with the population projected at four million by 2050. City planners have consulted with landscape architects hoping to establish guidelines that will ensure that the city's growth doesn't obliterate the natural setting that brought people here in the first place. Their conclusion seems obvious to Portlanders: metropolitan green spaces, access to rivers, and lively neighborhoods are important to the sense of place. The touches of old-fashioned statuary and what's now called public art, from the elk at SW Third and Main to the umbrella man on Pioneer Courthouse Square or the etched granite stairs in the Central Library at SW 10th and Yamhill, give people a chance to pause and think. Among the best-loved graceful touches are the "Benson bubblers," non-stop water fountains on downtown streets. Simon Benson, an early timber king, reputedly donated the four-pronged fountains to divert employees from the evils of whiskey.

Urban planning has not been consistently successful in preventing urban ugliness. Portland Center, the jumble of concrete south of SW Third and Market, was trumpeted in the 1960s as a beacon of urban renaissance, but it wiped out ethnic neighborhoods and replaced them with a lifeless complex of condos and office buildings, accessorized with a couple of designer waterfalls.

A more inspired project, the reclamation of the west bank of the Willamette River, gave the city the Tom McCall Waterfront Park, a three-mile swatch of green shared by tourists, transients, joggers, and bicyclists and, from late spring through the summer, a different festival nearly every weekend.

As downtown Portland spruced itself up in the 1970s, planners came up with a new idea to keep downtown traffic and parking to a minimum: within prescribed downtown borders, public transportation is free. A transit mall was built on Fifth and Sixth Avenues and is crossed at Pioneer Courthouse Square by light rail (MAX) trains. Stop by TriMet Customer Service in Pioneer Courthouse Square for bus and MAX information.

SHOOTING FRAYS APLENTY

In 1881 William Woodward, an 18-year-old farm boy from Minnesota, came alone to Portland, Oregon to look for work:

There was little activity in Portland during the winter of 1881-1882. I had no trade or profession. Boys of my age and caliber were as little wanted as today. Each day I would go forth starting on Front Street down one side and up the other; likewise on First. My search each day for work grew discouraging at times. I would sneak home mortified at the thought that every one seemed busy save myself. Finally success crowned my efforts. *For several months Charles Woodward cut cordwood for steamers that would pull up at a dock on the Columbia River. Finally, he found a* real *job at a drug store:*

Two large gambling establishments, with bar attachments, across the street furnished variety. There were shooting frays aplenty and one immediately fatal. One occasion a drunken man walked out the second story window over the way. Sidewalks in those days however, were of plank. He was quite drunk and the rebound served only to sober him. Jerry Coldwell, reporter for the *Oregonian*, came to depend on me for news items of human interest. When I told him of the drunkard's diversion, he berated me aplenty because I had neglected to take his name and address, remarking no news item was of any value if it did not carry at least these two points.

Crowing roosters in the neighborhood were a great annoyance. My employer remarked he wished to God that somebody would wring their necks. I suggested possibly a minor operation to their larynx would quiet them without loss of life and later asked a local specialist if such an operation could be performed in safety to the patients. He took the matter under advisement and informed me later the fowl's throat and vocal organs would not permit. I was incautious enough to speak of the matter to Jerry Coldwell, telling him that I was disposed to believe that such an operation was practical, however, and would go far in promoting national peace and prosperity. He printed the story and immediately arose a chorus of protests over the inhumanity of the drug clerk.

—Memoir of William F. Woodward (1863-1938),
a prominent Oregonian and state senator

PORTLAND

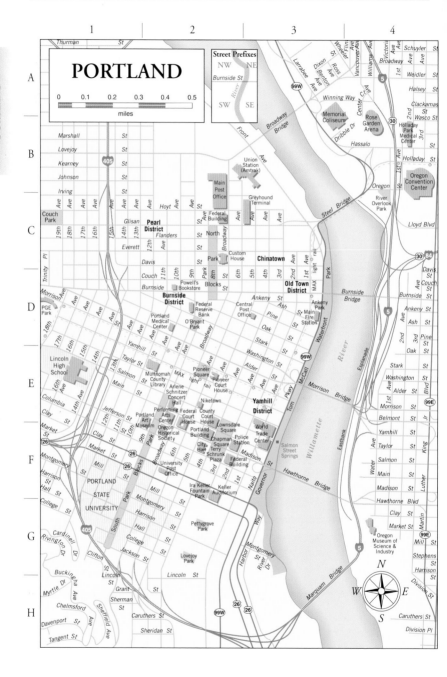

PORTLAND

0   0.1   0.2   0.3   0.4   0.5
miles

Street Prefixes
NW   NE
Burnside St
SW   SE

■ A WALK THROUGH DOWNTOWN

Pioneer Courthouse Square
map opposite, E-2

Office workers and street kids carve out their territories on Pioneer Courthouse Square, and it's a rare summer afternoon when "downtown's living room" isn't the site of a concert or rally. The square, which was built on the site of an ugly parking lot, is a good place to start a walking tour of downtown. The Visitor Information Center is here; stop in for a free copy of Powell's Downtown Walking Map. TriMet's ticket office is also here, with plenty of bus, light rail, and streetcar information.

Before its tenure as a parking lot, Pioneer Courthouse Square was the site of the Portland Hotel, an elegant building that, were it still standing, would turn heads today. The eponymous courthouse, across Sixth Avenue from the square, was Portland's earliest sign of civilization. When it was built in 1869, it was considered too distant from the city's waterfront hub. Traffic patterns changed, and for a century, the Pioneer Courthouse has marked downtown's center.

Portland Art Museum
map opposite, E/F-2

The elm-shaded South Park Blocks, a few blocks south and west of the square, are flanked by the art museum and historical museum. The art museum draws raves for its Northwest Coast Indian collection, contemporary art exhibits, and Wednesday evening "Museum After Hours" concerts. 1219 SW Park Avenue; 503-226-2811.

Umbrella Man waits for rain on a sunny day in Pioneer Square.

Oregon Historical Society

map page 54, F-2

Exhibits change seasonally at the historical society's museum, and the bookstore, facing onto Broadway, is a fine place to step in from the rain and browse. 1230 SW Park Avenue.

Performing Arts Center

map page 54, E/F-2

The elegant brick building just north of the historical society is the Performing Arts Center, the city's premier spot for live theater. Next door is the "Schnitz" (the Arlene Schnitzer Concert Hall), a grand Portland vaudeville house, host to the Oregon Symphony and the popular Portland Arts and Lecture Series.

Portland Building

map page 54, F-2

If you listen closely, you can hear the city bureaucrats complaining about the tiny office windows in architect Michael Graves's "birthday cake"—the postmodern Portland Building at SW Fifth and Main. This was Graves's first big public commission and the nation's first post-modern public building; it gets decidedly mixed reviews. Wander into the lobby, visit the balcony gallery, or sit in on a public meeting, and see whether you're pleased or appalled.

Public Art: *Portlandia* and The Elk

Portlandia, a 37-foot-tall, six-and-a-quarter-ton copper statue of a woman kneeling over the front door of the Portland Building, was barged down the Willamette before being hoisted into place, and gets as much attention as the building itself.

The elk statue in the middle of SW Main between Third and Fourth *(map page 54, E/F-2/3)* is a longtime whimsical favorite. Perhaps it was cast in dead seriousness, but when the unnaturally long neck is swathed in Christmas greenery and the statue's fountain dribbles onto the street (earning it the sobriquet "The Pissing Elk"), the elk is lovably kitschy. The plaza next to the statue was once a meadow where elk grazed. Today pigeons and courthouse workers feed here. (All manner of people use the benches here; the bathrooms are not a safe bet.)

Waterfront Park

map page 54, C-3 to G-3

The waterfront, once lined by wharfs, then overrun by a freeway, is now pleasant Waterfront Park. **Salmon Street Springs**, a fountain whose flow is timed to be highest when the city is bustling, is a great place to pause and watch it all happen. Stroll north past men dozing on park benches and teenagers honing their skateboarding skills to the **Japanese-American memorial**, just north of the Burnside Bridge. It's a quiet spot, where stone-carved words recall the lives and contributions of Portland's *Issei*, Japanese immigrants who were forced into eastern-Oregon internment camps during World War II.

Old Town

map page 54, D-3

In Old Town, near Burnside Bridge, cast-iron facades on old brick buildings hint of a grand past. The pilaster-fronted New Market Theatre (SW First Avenue and Ankeny) was the reputable place to spend an evening in

PORTLAND'S PERFORMING ARTS

Artists Repertory Theatre
1516 SW Alder St.
503-241-1278
Throughout the year, Artists Rep presents several productions, including regional premieres and classics with themes pertinent to contemporary issues.

Oregon Ballet Theatre
503-227-5538
Classical and contemporary works, performed at Keller Auditorium, 222 SW Clay St.

Oregon Symphony
503-228-1353
Over 40 classical, pop, children's, and family concerts are held each season at the Arlene Schnitzer Concert Hall, SW Broadway and Main.

Portland Center Stage
503-248-6309
Contemporary and classical works are shown in the Portland Center for the Performing Arts, SW Broadway and Main, during this group's November-April season.

Portland Opera
503-228-1353
Five operas are presented at the Keller Auditorium, 222 SW Clay St., each year.

Body Vox
1300 NW Marshall St.
503-229-0627
Freewheeling dance with great choreographic wit, performed in various locations.

---

the 1880s, though second-floor theatergoers had to put up with the din and muddle of first floor greengrocers and butchers. Outside, the four graceful bronze women of **Skidmore Fountain** hold an overflowing basin aloft. The fountain was built in 1888 for "men, horses, and dogs," and remains a lovely rendezvous for men, women, children, and dogs (well, the occasional horse, bearing a cop, still comes by).

North of Burnside, at NW Third and Everette, the **Classical Chinese Garden** is a walled sanctuary with gardens, a large pond, and a teahouse.

Burnside
map page 54, D-2
As Portland grew, the north end of First was chockablock with sailors boarding in roominghouses, drinking in bars, and sleeping with the pros. When a ship needed more crew members, drunk or drugged men sometimes woke up below deck, shanghaied to serve as a sailor.

Nightlife and comparatively wild times still thrive around Burnside. Local pundits like to say Portland has only two genuine tourist attractions: Darcelle's drag shows and Powell's Books. Even if all of Portland doesn't turn out for **Darcelle's drag shows**, it's certainly not a seedy venue, and it's a short walk from **Powell's Books**, one of the country's largest bookstores, crammed with new and used books. It is open till 11 P.M. every night at 10th and W Burnside, and it's Portland nightlife at its most typical. Drop by some evening for a reading (there's something going on at least one night out of three) or just disappear into the stacks.

Pearl District

map page 54, C-2

Powell's is on the southern edge of the Pearl District, a booming post-industrial neigh-borhood of lofts, galleries, interior-design shops, restaurants, and brewpubs. If it's the first Thursday evening of the month, check out a gallery opening or two. On a fine weekend afternoon, this is one area of town where you'll see folks wearing something other than shorts and t-shirts. Dress up to be seen sipping martinis at a sidewalk cafe, then take in dinner at Oba! or Park Kitchen. Wind up at the Bridgeport Brewpub and take a seat on the loading dock for some of Portland's best pizza and microbrew.

■ WEST OF DOWNTOWN

Though some contend that Portlanders are, by nature, a little distant from their neighbors, this modern malady may be at least partly ameliorated by the local cof-fee culture. NW 23rd Avenue, between Burnside and Thurman is perhaps the best place to dip into the caffeine scene, and stroll through trendy shops.

Northwest Portland took off in 1905, with the Lewis and Clark Exposition, an orgy of boosterism. John Olmstead, son of Frederick Law Olmstead, who de-signed New York's Central Park, came to town and designed a fairgrounds, where most of the buildings were done in Spanish Renaissance style. The building everybody talked about for years to come was decidedly different—a gigantic log "cabin" housing a forestry exhibit.

Portland must have gotten the hang of putting on a fair back then because it wasn't long before the city decided to celebrate its gardeners' penchant for roses by staging a **Rose Festival** in 1907. It's been going strong ever since, the crowning event of a quirky, old-fashioned Oregon subculture. High schools elect Rose Princesses and one becomes the city's Rose Queen—even if queens are a bit out of fashion these days. Business people aspire to become Royal Rosarians who dress up in white suits and wave straw boaters during parades. Military vessels line the

(opposite) Cafes and restaurants stand cheek-to-jowl on NW 23rd Avenue—which explains why this street seems densely populated morning, noon, and night.

The Rose Test Garden.

Willamette, and sailors flood town, taking advantage of the (for real, and officially sponsored) meet-a-sailor hotline in early June every year.

Washington Park

map page 51 center

Well-manicured Washington Park is home of the **Rose Test Garden.** Here, Portland's mania for the Rose Festival begins to make sense. From the Rose Gardens' hillside perch, (where the names of Rose Festival queens are enshrined in a cement path) downtown is framed by shiny green leaves and deep rich blooms. Even after a hundred visits to the Rose Garden, amateur photographers will find their pulses racing and hormones surging, especially on a clear day, when Mount Hood forms the photogenic backdrop for southeast Portland.

Uphill from the Rose Gardens are the peaceful **Japanese Gardens,** where water trickles through bamboo chutes. A shuttle bus or hiking trail climbs the steep grade.

Oregon Zoo, Vietnam Memorial, and **Hoyt Arboretum** are about a mile west of the gardens. The zoo, which is small but well-tended, specializes in elephant breeding. In 1962, Packy, the first elephant bred in captivity, was born, an arrival that made the whole town proud. Locals still demonstrate their curious attachment to Oregon's firstborn elephant—Packy gets a yearly peanut butter cake and a well-attended party every year. The arboretum is a lovely spot for a hike—visit the redwood grove.

Hoyt Arboretum trails join the Wildwood Trail, continuing north to Forest Park, the life blood of Portland. The 70-some miles of trails are well-used, but rarely clogged. Before the park was established in 1947, the 1,100-foot hills rising from the Willamette had been heavily logged; most of the trees are second growth, with hardy red alder eclipsing the young Doug fir and Western hemlock. Spring comes to Portland in March when the park's trilliums bloom. August means it's time to wade deep into thorny vines while dreaming of blackberry pie.

Sauvie Island

map page 51, top left corner

Determined pickers skip the trailside thickets and drive out US 30 to Sauvie Island, known for pick-it-yourself berry patches, birdwatching, and Columbia River beaches (including a nude beach). A cornucopia since well before Lewis and Clark stopped here in 1805, this was a favorite trading spot of the Chinook Indians. They swapped tuberous wapato lily, which women pulled from marshbottoms with their toes, and fished with huge cedar bark nets that they sunk to the bottom of the river with rocks.

■ EASTSIDE PORTLAND   *map 51, center right*

The Willamette River bisects Portland, with most of the wealth falling out on the hilly west side and a funky charm and rapid gentrification surrounding the shopping streets of SE Hawthorne, NE Alberta, and NE Broadway. For a breath of air, and a different view of the city, walk over one of the 10 bridges spanning the Willamette—the Hawthorne and the Broadway are good, and the Steel Bridge has a river-level pedestrian and bike span connecting to the Eastside Esplanade, a riverside trail that can lead you as far south as the Sellwood neighborhood.

Sellwood, at the city's southern edge, has had an antique row for years. Its riverside park is worth a picnic or a swim in the outdoor pool. Oaks Park, an old-fashioned, slightly down-at-the-heels amusement park, abuts Sellwood Park and is adjacent to Oaks Bottom, a wetland crisscrossed by trails ideal for birdwatching.

Portland's skyline rises above the Willamette River viewed from Sellwood Riverfront Park.

Author's Favorite Portland Food & Lodging

Lodgings

Benson Hotel.
309 SW Broadway (at Oak)
503-228-2000
City's longtime favorite fancy hotel, built by timber-king Simon Benson in 1913.

Fifth Avenue Suites Hotel.
506 SW Washington Street
503-222-0001 or 800-771-2971
A grand hotel in—believe it or not—an old department store. Rooms are luxurious and quiet. Best of all, you're right in the heart of downtown.

Governor Hotel.
611 SW 10th Avenue (at Alder)
503-224-3400 or 800-554-3456
Nicely renovated, classy hotel. Check out the robots on the outside trim.

Heathman Hotel.
1001 SW Broadway (at Salmon)
503-241-4100 or 800-551-0011
Many think this is Portland's finest hotel, though some maintain the rooms are small and noisy. You'll rarely hear the service faulted.

Hotel Vintage Plaza.
422 SW Broadway
503-228-1212 or 800-263-2305
An intimate hotel with large, comfortable rooms. Friendly and helpful staff. Wine is served in the lobby every afternoon.

Hotel Lucia
400 SW Broadway
503-225-1717 or 877-225-1717
Downtown's most stylish hotel, with fairly large rooms and great photos on the walls. Good Thai food downstairs.

Mallory Hotel.
729 SW 15th Avenue
503-223-6311 or 800-228-8657
Comfortable, like grandma's house. Close to downtown.

Restaurants

Bijou Cafe.
132 SW Third Avenue
503-222-3187
Join Portland's lawyers for snapper hash. Downtown's best breakfasts.

Bistro Montage.
301 SE Morrison
503-234-1324
Cajun spices accent everything: catfish and macaroni-and-cheese alike. Formal white table cloths contrast with the tattooed servers and capture the spirit of Portland. Dinner served 'til 2:00 A.M.; 4:00 Fri.-Sat.

Bluehour.
250 NW 13th Avenue
503-226-3394
Trendy Pearl District hangout.

Bridgeport Brewery.
1313 NW Marshall (at 13th Avenue)
503-241-7179
Portland's most atmospheric brewpub fea-

tures Blue Heron ales along with pizzas and sandwiches. Sit outside on the loading dock.

Caprial's Bistro & Wine Bar.
7015 SE Milwaukie Avenue
503-236-6457

Good-natured Caprial, known to many from her PBS show, oversees the production of Asian-influenced Northwest fare at this neighborhood cafe.

Genoa.
2832 SE Belmont Street
503-238-1464

Seven-course Italian meals, impressive wine list, and a knowledgeable staff add up to a delightful dining experience. Take a break from the formal dining room and sip your aperitif on the overstuffed furniture in the smoking lounge.

Heathman Restaurant & Bar.
1001 SW Broadway (at Salmon)
503-241-4100.

Some of the best hotel food you'll find anywhere. Fresh Northwest cuisine.

Higgins.
1239 SW Broadway
503-222-9070

One of downtown's best restaurants, where chef Greg Higgins searches out the freshest organic ingredients. There are also a couple of innovative vegetarian options on the menu here.

Oba!
555 NW 12th Ave.
503-228-6161

If the weather's nice, sit outside and watch the Pearl District passersby as you eat Nuevo Latino cuisine.

Paley's Place.
1204 NW 21st Avenue
503-243-2403

The New York Times loves this place, as does Portland's upper crust Dinner in the bistro-bar section requires less premeditation, and brings the same good food as the dining room.

Park Kitchen.
422 NW 8th Ave.
503-223-7275

Stop for a memorable afternoon snack or a full lunch or dinner along the North Park blocks.

Pearl Bakery.
102 NW Ninth Avenue
503-827-0910

One of Portland's artisan bakeries, and this one is tops; one block from Powell's Books.

Torrefazione Italia.
838 NW 23rd Avenue
503-228-2528

Where the hip and beautiful hang out and flirt over cappuccinos in ceramic bowls.

Typhoon!
2310 NW Everett Street
503-243-7557
or
410 SW Broadway
503-224-8285

Cutting-edge Thai cuisine in two locations.

Wildwood.
1221 NW 21st Avenue (at Overton)
503-248-9663

Named for Forest Park's Wildwood Trail, this northwest Portland restaurant sets trends with its food and ambience. Try Portland's best dish of mussels here.

WILLAMETTE VALLEY

◆ AREA OVERVIEW

To many Oregonians, the Willamette Valley is little more than the meadows, forests, and towns along Interstate 5 between Portland and Eugene. Even on a clear day, when the Cascades frame the eastern horizon, and the lower Coast Range appears to the west, most cars breeze through this 110 miles in as many minutes. But there are many more interesting ways to travel and places to see, so take it easy and enjoy, for it's quickly obvious why this was the destination of the pioneers who traveled the Oregon Trail. Even after 150 years of agriculture, the soil is rich enough to grow fields of tulips, iris, strawberries, marionberries, peppermint, grapes, and hazelnuts.

Take time to explore the wineries of the Willamette Valley, where some of the best wine in America is produced. Pinot noirs are outstanding, and the pinot gris is gaining acclaim.

Climate: This is a region of mild climate, with abundant rain and enough sunny summer weather for residents to psychologically withstand the gray winters. In springtime the pollen counts are astronomical, so pack your allergy medicine. Winter temperatures are are commonly in the 40s and 50s; summer days can reach the 90s. Fall is a perfect time to visit, when grape must scents the air.

Food & Lodging: It's easy to find a motel or a diner almost anyplace along I-5, but Eugene has the greatest selection in this region. McMinnville is the wine country's lodging hub and there's great food here and in Dundee (see page 80).

(opposite) Tulips are one of the Willamette Valley's many commercial crops.

■ WILLAMETTE VALLEY LONG AGO

Once bands of Kalapuya Indians lived off the fish, game, roots, and berries that flourished in the mild Willamette Valley. They traveled in canoes and migrated seasonally to fixed summer and winter camps. Once a year, they burnt the fields to keep trees and unwanted plants from encroaching on the camas meadows. Clearing away the trees also made it easier to hunt game and to spot approaching enemies. (Many Willamette Valley farmers, especially grass seed growers, still burn their fields in late summer to return nutrients to the soil and control pests.)

Trappers from the coastal fort of Astoria began traveling to the Willamette Valley in the early 1800s, more to poke around the countryside than to trap, as beaver were more plentiful elsewhere. A few French Canadians from Hudson's Bay Company turned over the sod, and pretty soon the secret was out. Missionaries rushed out to save native souls, but they were generally better at farming than at preaching. In fact, their arrival was disastrous to the Kalapuyans, who got sick with diseases from which they had little immunity.

Kalapuyans used sweat lodges to exorcise evil spirits, and since they believed that disease was caused by evil forces in their bodies, sick people would steam in a sweat lodge, then go jump into the cold river. Some died instantly from this harsh remedy, especially those suffering from pneumonia, measles, scarlet fever, influenza, malaria, and other fever-producing diseases.

Ultimately white immigration swelled. Settlers took their farming seriously. John McLoughlin, head of the Canadian Hudson's Bay Company, was supposed to discourage American settlement, but he was a compassionate and generous man, and often supplied westering Americans with seeds to start their Willamette Valley farms. Some emigrants carried seeds across the Oregon Trail, anxious to grow the same beans and sage outside their new Oregon homes as they'd cultivated in Ohio or Pennsylvania. Sometimes the attachments were fierce—one woman apparently caught the family rooster eating her prized seeds. Without a moment's hitch, she slit the rooster's throat and took out the seeds.

■ OREGON CITY   *map page 71, C-2*

Oregon City, 20 miles up the Willamette from the Columbia River and near a splendid falls, was the site of an 1829 Hudson's Bay Company settlement. Etienne Lucier was posted here, and he built three cabins and a store.

Twenty-five years later, this was Eden, end of the Oregon Trail. The trail's "official" end was at Abernethy Green, now the site of the **Oregon Trail Interpretive Center**. Look for huge covered wagons at Washington Street and Abernethy Road, which house the center's exhibits. Learn how pioneers drove their wagons over fresh graves to destroy the scent and dissuade wolves from unearthing bodies. At Oregon City, emigrants picked up land deeds from the federal office, where all the West Coast plats were held (see San Francisco's original plat at the Clackamas County Museum overlooking Willamette Falls). Call 503-657-9336 for information.

In 1845, John McLoughlin, head of the Canadian Hudson's Bay Company, became frustrated by his official mandate to discourage American settlement, and joined the Willamette Valley settlers. His house is now a **museum** at 713 Center.

Oregon City's future began to dim when Portland proved to be the more sensible shipping port. Today, the older town is practically a Portland suburb, and there's a drive-through espresso shop at the end of the Oregon Trail. At Willamette Falls, which thwarted upstream travel from Oregon City, a dam generates power, and locks ease boat travel. When the spring chinook run up the Willamette, boats line up, gunwale to gunwale, and form the "hog line" near the base of the falls, just by the Smurfit newsprint mill. Everybody has his or her own territory, there's precious little room for outsiders to squeeze in, and the chinook don't have much of a chance.

For a good view of the dam and the scene around it, ride the city's beloved pink elevator 90 feet up the basalt cliffs from the riverside business district to a roadway built on a bench above the river. The 7th and Railroad elevator, which has operated since 1913, was hydropowered until electricity took over in 1954.

■ To Aurora, Tulips, and Orchards

South of Oregon City, Hwy 99E bursts through suburban sprawl to small farms and orchards in all hues of green. Down by **Aurora,** ornamental cherry orchards and endless fields of tulips and irises lead the way to a utopian community now taken over by antique shops. In 1857, a German communist/utopian/Christian colony migrated here from Bethel, Missouri, and settled halfway between Portland and Salem. Their leader, Dr. William Keil, espoused that, "No man owns anything individually but every man owns everything as a full partner and with an equal voice in its use and its increase and the profits accruing from it." In spite of such

egalitarian ideas, Keil was rather an autocrat, and as young people began to question his dictates, the community foundered. After Keil died in 1877, the community property was divided up, and Aurora became just another well-heeled valley town, albeit one with a good utopian history museum (The Old Aurora Colony Museum, 212 Second Street NE).

■ CHAMPOEG STATE PARK   *map page 71, C-2*

Cross the freeway from Aurora and head west toward Donald, and Champoeg [SHAMPOO-EE] State Park. Roads provide easy access to scenic landmarks in the Willamette Valley, and every byway has a full complement of road signs. Bring along a decent map and you'll never be lost, even when you have only a vague sense of where you actually are. The least-traveled roads link small towns and make for splendid bike routes. Flat, grassy valley plains give way to roller-coaster hills. Thickets of willow and blackberry surround streams, patchy clearcuts dot distant hills, swaybacked barns slip by, and the rides are almost invariably pleasant.

Use Champoeg Park as a base for a bike ride. Several miles of bike paths cross the park, where families pedal past beautiful Oregon white oaks, locust, maple, and willow trees, nettles, and fields of grass (planted for seed harvest), all floating on the scent of wild roses. The Willamette River is big and fast here, much prettier than in Portland. Mount Hood marks the east. Raccoons and deer leave tracks beside streams, and harmless snakes slither away from sunny spots when they're disturbed. Blue-flowered camas dot fields; the bulbous camas roots were a staple of the Kalapuyans' diet, baked and sometimes pounded into cakes.

Champoeg marks the site where settlers jumped to Joe Meek's call in 1853 and voted, 52-50, to throw off joint occupancy with the British and establish an American provisional government.

❖

The first church within Oregon's present boundaries was a log building erected by Catholics in **St. Paul** (just south west of Champoeg). The founding Jesuits planted the state's first grapevines, presaging today's flourishing wine industry. Now St. Paul is best known for its Fourth of July rodeo, a hot, lively scene, and one of western Oregon's few big rodeos.

(previous pages) Henry J. Warre's illustration of Oregon City in 1848 was titled "The American Village." (Oregon Historical Society)

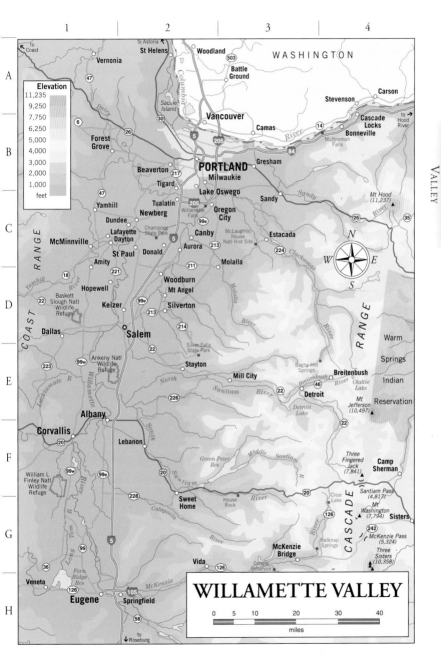

WILLAMETTE VALLEY

0 5 10   20   30   40

miles

Touring the Wineries
—by John Doerper

◆ Pioneer Vintners

While winemaking in Oregon predates Prohibition, it wasn't until Richard Sommer planted grapes in the Umpqua Valley in 1961 that wineries took off. Following Sommer's pioneering efforts, Charles Coury planted European grape varietals in the northern Willamette Valley. He was soon followed by David Adelsheim, Dick Erath, and David Lett, who established the first Yamhill County vineyards and wineries. Their first wines proved them right: this was prime wine country indeed.

Today, the valley's wineries are booming, and Yamhill County is turning into the Napa Valley of the Northwest, because the soils and microclimates are perfect for growing grapes. Vintners are just not sure yet which grapes will do best here and produce great wines. Like the Napa Valley, these vineyards are close to a major city. Portland is only half an hour's drive away, assuring a steady stream of visitors.

Pinot noir was an early favorite among locally grown grapes and makes great wines in the hands of master vintners like Ken Wright, Myron Redford, Dick Ponzi, and Dick Erath. But some vintages have proved to be disappointing; others have not aged well. Recently there's been a boom in pinot gris plantings. This pink Alsatian grape does very well here —and may make a better wine in Oregon than it does in its native Europe. It is the perfect wine for accompanying fresh salmon, crab, and other seafoods. But Oregon chardonnays and rieslings have also shown well, as has another rare European grape, muscat ottonel.

Visit a few of the vineyards listed on the following pages to get a solid introduction to Oregon's burgeoning wine industry. Memorial Day and Thanksgiving weekends are good, though busy, times to tour the wine country, as almost all of the wineries are open for tasting and tours.

◆ The Hazelnut-Filbert Connection

The orchards of low, somewhat bushy trees you see on gentle hillsides are hazelnuts. Oregon grows more than 90 percent of the U.S. harvest of these compact, flavorful nuts. They're known locally as "filberts," even though the Oregon Hazelnut Commission renamed them (and itself) a decade ago. Not more than a couple of decades before that, there were even more hazelnut orchards in Yamhill County—and no vineyards. In fact, Rex Hill Vineyards, began its working life as a nut drier.

◆ TOURING THE VINEYARDS

Ponzi Vineyards

Since its establishment in 1970, Ponzi, the winery closest to Portland, has earned international acclaim for consistently producing high quality pinot noir, pinot gris, chardonnay, vino gelato, and Arneis.

From the first four barrels produced in 1974, Dick Ponzi's name and Oregon have been synonymous with Oregon wine, and is famous today for its pinot noir and pinot gris—wines Ponzi helped pioneer.

Map Key

Adelsheim 3	Ken Wright 14
Amity 19	Knudson-Erath 9
Archery Sum. 11	Kramer 16
Argyle 7	Lange 10
Autumn Wind 4	Montinore 17
Brick House 5	OR Tasting Rm 23
Cameron 8	Panther Creek 18
Chateau Benoit 13	Ponzi 21
Chehalem 2	Rex Hill 1
Duck Pond 6	Sokol Blosser 12
Elk Cove 15	Tyee Cellars 24
Eola Hills 20	Yamhill 22

WILLAMETTE VALLEY

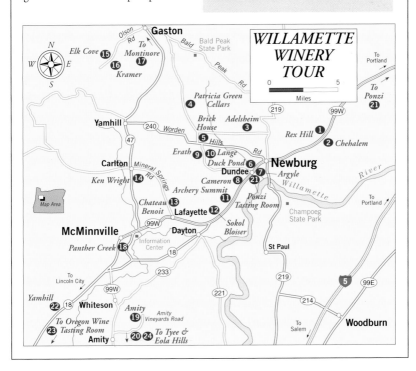

WILLAMETTE WINERY TOUR

Ponzi Vineyard: a family affair

Winery open daily at 14665 Southwest Winery Lane, Beaverton; 503-628-1227; tasting room, open daily 11-5, is on Hwy 99W and Seventh in Dundee.

Rex Hill Vineyards

The next winery you come to as you travel south on SR 99W from Portland. Shortly after you cross into Yamhill County. Where the landscape has trees and vineyards instead of subdivisions, you'll have to keep a sharp lookout for the blue sign marking the turn off. The winery rises in landscaped grounds beneath vineyards. Rose arbors and beds of flowers frame a grassy picnic area. The

The tasting room at Rex Hill Vineyards

wines to taste here are pinot noir, pinot gris, and chardonnay. 11-5 daily. 30835 N Hwy 99W, Newberg; 800-739-4455.

Chehalem

This winery is right across the highway from Rex Hill. The name translates as "valley of flowers," after the flowery valley where these grapes grow. The winery makes intense, hand-crafted pinot noirs, pinot gris, chardonnay. Tasting is by appointment. 31190 NE Veritas Lane, Newberg; 503-538-4700.

Adelsheim Vineyard

Adelsheim makes consistently good wines and is among the handful of wineries that have helped to put Oregon vineyards on the world map. Founded in 1971 by David and Ginny Adelsheim, the winery has remained small, producing a mere 20,000 cases of wine annually. There's a splendid pinot gris, a silky pinot noir, and a crisp chardonnay. The winery is only open on Memorial Day and Thanksgiving weekends. Tours by appointment. 16800 NE Calkins Lane, Newberg; 503-538-3652.

Patricia Green Cellars

Patricia Green, winemaker for Torii Mor Winery, and her cellarmaster James Anderson bought Autumn Wine Vineyards in July of 2000. Their goal is to make distinct pinot noirs that are both complex and enjoyable. Visitors welcomed by appointment only. 15225 NE N. Valley Road, Newberg; 503-554-0821.

Brick House Vineyards
All of the grapes of this beautiful vineyard are organically grown among the hazelnut orchards of Ribbon Ridge. Pinot noir, chardonnay, and Gamay noir all give excellent wine here. Production is small (fewer than a thousand cases of hand-crafted wines a year). 18200 Lewis Rogers Lane, Newberg; 503-538-5136.

Duck Pond Cellars tasting room

Duck Pond Cellars
The beautifully landscaped grounds and the well-stocked gift stock alone are reasons for visiting this winery, but the wines made by this family owned and operated winery and vineyard are also worth a special trip. Duck Pond concentrates on pinot gris and chardonnay, but also makes a superb (and reasonably priced) Columbia Valley Merlot and chardonnay. The tasting room is open daily, except on major holidays. 23145 Hwy 99W, Dundee; 503-538-3199.

Argyle Winery Inc.
The tasting room for Argyle is in a Victorian house surrounded by flowers. It's just off the highway and hard to miss.

Argyle makes very good sparkling wine and enjoyable chardonnay, pinot noir, and dry riesling. Open daily 11-5. 691 N 99W, Dundee; 503-538-8520.

Cameron Winery
Excellent pinot noir and chardonnay from three distinctive vineyards: Abbey Ridge, Brick House, and Clos Electrique. Winery open to the public only on Thanksgiving weekend. 8200 Worden Hill Road, Dundee; 503-538-0336.

From Dundee, take Worden Hill Road to Erath and Lange (turn right on Ninth in Dundee). Follow signs (the lane leading to Lange angles off to the right).

Erath Vineyards
Dick Erath is one of the true pioneers of Willamette Valley winemaking. Although the winery is best known for its complex, long-lived pinot noir, Erath also makes outstanding pinot gris, pinot blanc, chardonnay, and riesling. The winery is high in the Dundee Hills and has a picnic patio with a views. Crabtree Park next to the winery is a great place for taking a walk and clearing your head before you drive back on the winding country road. Open 11-5 daily. 9409 NE Worden Hill Road; 800-539-9463 or 503-538-3318.

Lange Winery
Take Ninth off 99W in Dundee and follow the blue signs up into the Red Hills. The pinot noir, pinot gris, and chardonnay are wines you want to take home.

Splendid views of the Chehalem and Willamette Valley from the winery's lofty ridge. Daily except Tues. 11-5. 18380 NE Buena Vista, Dundee; 503-538-6476.

The next winery is east of Erath and can be reached via Archery Summit Road, off SR 99W.

Archery Summit

Archery Summit is a surprisingly friendly place for a premium winery with snob appeal. To create distinctive pinot noir, the vineyards are planted with several clones of pinot noir on rootstocks designed to match the soils, 2,200 vines per acre. The wines are aged in the caves. Tasting 10:30-4 daily; tours by appointment. 18599 NE Archery Summit Road, Dayton; 503-864-4300.

Sokol Blosser Winery

This winery is just off SR 99W, but it sits on a hilltop with great views—on a clear day, you can look form the vineyards all the way to Mount Hood. Sokol Blosser makes first-rate pinot noir and chardonnay. The tasting room is well stocked with local foods. A shady picnic area beckons you to linger over a bottle of wine. Take the self-guided tour through the vineyard after your repast, to learn about vines and viticultural practices like trellising. 11-5 daily; tasting fee. 5000 Sokol Blosser Lane, Dundee; 800-582-6668.

Chateau Benoit Winery

Founded in 1979 by Fred & Mary Benoit, Chateau Benoit is located 1.5 miles off Highway 99W near Lafayette, high above the valley on a hilltop. Among the wines made here, you should taste the pinot noir, gewurztraminer, riesling, and the easily drinkable muller-thurgau. Taste them at Chateau Benoit's stores in the Lincoln City and Woodburn outlet malls. 6580 NE Mineral Springs Road, Carlton; 800-248-4835 or 503-864-2991.

Ken Wright Cellars

Ken Wright is a genius, a true artist of winemaking, and his wines are eagerly searched out by collectors. The winery is open to the public Thanksgiving weekend. 236 North Kutch Street, Carlton; 503-852-7070.

For the wineries north and northeast of Carlton, follow the map to the wineries, on (often narrow) roads winding in and out of the hills through a very beautiful landscape of orchards, vineyards, meadows, and oak groves. Almost all Oregon wineries are well marked by blue highway signs. Keep a sharp look-out: You might come across a new winery so young it's not yet listed in any guide.

The turnoff for both Kramer and Elk Cove is at the southern city limits, of Gaston (which is also the Yamhill County line) and can be difficult to spot.

Elk Cove Vineyards

Northwest of Newberg, near the farming hamlet of Gaston, the tasting room of Elk Cove Vineyards rises above a vine-covered "cove" actually a beautiful, saucer-shaped valley surrounded by tall trees. On the drive in, the road, winding along the slopes of the coast range foothills, offers spectacular views of the Willamette Valley farmlands. The wines are as beautiful as the setting. Elk Cove produces excellent pinot noir and pinot gris, highly enjoyable chardonnay, cabernet sauvignon, and, if the weather is right at harvest time, some beautifully balanced dessert wines. All of these are "food wines," designed to enhance Oregon's meats, seafoods, fruits, and cheeses. Open daily 11-5; picnic on the deck. 27751 NW Olson Road Gaston; 503-985-7760.

Kramer Vineyards

A short drive from Elk Cove brings you to Kramer Vineyards, a cliffhanger of a winery where winemaker Trudy Kramer handcrafts splendid pinot gris and pinot noir; also, excellent merlot and syrah. Closed January and February. 26830 NW Olson Road, Gaston; 503-662-4545.

Montinore Vineyards

The Montinore story begins with a funny twist. Folks at the winery chuckle when visitors try to show of their "sophistication" by trying to pronounce the

Montinore Vineyard

name in the French fashion. The estate, originally a ranch, was established by a tycoon who made money in the Montana mines and retired to Oregon. He decided to call his estate MONTana IN OREgon. The same stuck and was taken over by the winery established here a few years back. Highlights include crisp gewurztraminer, a lushly rich pinot noir, and a refreshing pinot gris (which happens to be a perfect wine for accompanying Northwest seafood). The tasting room staff is among the most knowledgeable and friendliest in the Oregon wine country. Open daily 11–5. 3663 SW Dilley Road, Forest Grove; 503-359-5012.

From Montinore, you can head right back down SR 47 and drive south to McMinnville (unless you want to take a detour in Yamhill, drive west into the foothills, to spend a night or two at the secluded Youngberg Hill Vineyard. McMinnville is the "capital" of the

Northern Willamette Valley Wine Country. Each July, the International Pinot Noir Celebration, a bacchanalian event stretching over a long weekend, is held at Linfield College (call 503-472-8964 for information). McMinnville has some of the Oregon wine country's best restaurants.

Panther Creek Cellars

Panther Creek Cellars, founded in 1986, occupies McMinnville's original and historical power plant. Pinot noir, melon (a little-known French white wine grape), and chardonnay are Panther Creek specialties. The winery is open to the public on the Memorial and Thanksgiving weekends, and on the second Saturday of each month. 455 N Irvine, McMinnville; 503-472-8080.

The next three wineries are south of McMinnville, along OR 99W, one of the main arteries running the length of the Willamette Valley. Except for briefly touching on towns, villages, or hamlets now and then, this is a rustic road, bordered by fields, orchards, berry patches, and the remnants of the oak grasslands which once covered much of the Willamette Valley.

Amity Vineyards

Amity Vineyards

This small family owned winery sits high on a hill, overlooking the village of Amity and the Willamette Valley. Since founding it back in 1976, founder and Winemaker Myron Redford has concentrated on pinot noir, gamay noir (a rare grape in Oregon), dry and late harvest gewurztraminer and riesling. He also makes a sulfite free pinot noir made from organic grapes, and a blush wine from pinot noir and pinot blanc. Redford is one of the true artists of Willamette Valley winemaking. His silky, full-flavored pinot noir is excellent with food as is the dry riesling. The winery's tasting room is open daily (closed in January). Open daily 12-5. 18150 Amity Vineyards Road; 503-835-2362

Yamhill Valley Vineyards

On the way to the coast, just off OR 18, these premium vineyards are tucked into the foothills where the coast range meets the Willamette Valley. A full-bodied pinot noir and an intense pinot blanc are the high points. May - November 11-5 daily 16250 SW Oldsville Road, McMinnville; 503-843-3100.

Oregon Wine Tasting Room

A great place for tasting and buying hard-to-find local wines. It's on the way to the coast at a crossroads called Bellevue. At the Lawrence Art Gallery. 11-5 daily. 19706 SW Hwy 18, McMinnville; 503-843-3787.

Eola Hills Wine Cellars

To the south of the Eola Hills, just west of Salem, Eola Hills makes great wines and also has a great reputation for its Sunday brunch at the winery; call to make reservations. 11-5 daily. 501 S. Pacific Hwy 99W, Rickreall; 503-623-2405.

As you head south on OR 99W, through Corvallis, look for a blue sign directing you to Tyee Wine Cellars. Watch for big goshawks, descending from nearby Mary's Peak to hunt on the valley floor. Long, sinuous rows of trees mark rivers and watercourses. Large, tropical looking leaves of wild cucumber vines make much of this woodland look like jungle.

Tyee Wine Cellar tasting room

Tyee Wine Cellars

Tyee Wine Cellars is among the truly great wineries of this region and well worth a special trip. The setting, too, is special. The winery is part of a "century farm" that's been run by the same family for more than a hundred years. The place is as rustic as ever: the tasting room is in an old dairy house. Highlights include the pinot noir, pinot gris, chardonnay, and a gewurztraminer that ranks among the very best of its kind in the Northwest. A picnic area in the pristine meadow is shaded by ancient Oregon oaks. This portion of the farm has never felt the bite of a plow. Look for beavers in the marsh below (they make paths in the shoreside reed and leave toothmarks on riparian trees). Open June–Aug., Thurs.–Tues. 12–5; Apr., May, and Sept.–Dec., weekends 12–5. 26335 Greenberry Road, Corvallis; 541-753-8754.

WILLAMETTE VALLEY

◆ WINE COUNTRY FOOD & LODGING

Downtown **McMinnville** is not particularly scenic or charming, but what the town itself lacks, the **Hotel Oregon** has in abundance. Portland's McMenamin brothers have refurbished this old downtown hotel into a place full of hidden corners decorated with whimsical art and topped with a great rooftop bar. 310 NE Evans Street; 888-472-8427. Just down the street, the storefront **Nick's Italian Cafe** offers top-notch five-course meals and a fine selection of local wines.

Dundee has two fine restaurants, both highlighting the local wines. **Tina's,** 760 SW Hwy 99W, 503-538-8880, is almost like a rural French auberge, only with Willamette Valley wines. Every wine-country town should have a comfortable restaurant like **The Red Hills Provincial Dining and Fine Wines.** 276 Hwy 99 W; 503-538-8224. In this old house by the side of the road, local wines enhance excellent food.

Over in **Dayton,** the **Joel Palmer House** is known for its way with wild mushrooms. Sure, there are other things on the menu, which changes seasonally, but why pass on the chance to order roast elk with chanterelles? 600 Ferry Street, Dayton; 503-864-2995.

(above) Chardonnay grapes. (opposite) A premium Oregon pinot noir from the WillaKenzie Estate Winery.

WILLAMETTE VALLEY

■ SALEM AND VICINITY   *map page 71, D-2*

Most people who visit Salem, the capital city, go there on official business. For the more casual traveler, there's not much here but two nice parks (Bush and Minto), and the capitol building. Built in 1938 after the original burned, the statehouse is a dome-topped Orwellian-looking marble building with a golden pioneer perched like a wedding cake ornament on top. The best part of the capitol is its interior. Striking WPA murals are inside the front door; fans of 1930s art should definitely stop and take a look at the gargantuan, muscled logger and fisherman. Other murals and friezes play out the state's history, and an odd modern painting of Tom McCall pays tribute to one of the state's best-loved governors.

Salem may be damned by bureaucracy and strip malls, but it does host the state fair around Labor Day, and there's lovely country surrounding town.

To stay nearby try **A Creekside Garden Inn,** a colonial house surrounded by trees, overlooking quiet Mill Creek—you'd be hard pressed to find a more serene lodging within walking distance of Capitol Mall. The rooms are very comfortable and the breakfast is sumptuous; 333 Wyatt Court NE; 503-391-0837. For food try **McMenamin's Boon's Treasury.** This is where Salem's equivalent of the counterculture hangs out, drinking microbrews in the old brick treasury building; 888 Liberty NE. Near the capitol, the Sassy Onion Grill is a favorite for breakfast or lunch; 1244 State Street.

◆ SILVERTON AND SILVER FALLS STATE PARK   *map page 71, D&E-2*

On your way to Silver Falls, you'll pass through **Silverton.** Be sure to arrive hungry for there's good food (and good wine) at **Silver Grille**, a tiny Main Street cafe with a sophisticated menu; 206 Main Street.

Also in Silverton, the **Oregon Garden** is a large display garden that's still setting its roots. It showcases Oregon's nursery industry, one of the less well-known workhorses of the state's economy. The garden is also home to Oregon's only house designed by Frank Lloyd Wright, which was moved there after the owner of the house attempted to tear it down. 879 W Main Street; 503-874-8100.

At **Silver Falls State Park,** about 25 miles east of Salem, a seven-mile trail passes 10 waterfalls. Silver Falls is often overlooked by travelers intent on mountain peaks or ocean spray, but the falls here are as thick as in the Columbia Gorge, and the air is refreshingly cool when hot spells still the cities.

◆ MOUNT ANGEL   *map page 71, D-2*

Mount Angel, north of Silverton on Hwy 214, is one of the Willamette Valley's most interesting towns. A hilltop Benedictine abbey dominates Mount Angel, and the museum there is a fascinating mishmash, even for heathens. (Where else can you find a Coke bottle collection, or a giant hairball under glass?) Used to be, a nun would just give the odd visitor a skeleton key to the museum, but the place has been spruced up a bit recently, and there's a less haphazard feel to it now. The state-of-the-art library, designed by Finnish architect Alvar Aalto, houses a surprisingly good collection of ancient manuscripts. Mount Angel celebrates Oktoberfest every September (try that timing on for size), and tries to maintain a Bavarian theme year round. If "Bavariana" begins to get a little trying, stop in at Tiny's Tavern, and you'll quickly re-enter the ambiance of western Oregon.

■ WESTERN CASCADES   *map page 71, A to H-4*

East of the Valley's broad agricultural floor are the western, or old, Cascades. Their volcanic peaks are 10 million years older, more weathered, and lower than the high Cascade peaks cresting to their east. These tree-covered mountains are home to the spotted owl and site of the old-growth forest controversy that has brought logging on federal property, and local economies, to a near standstill.

For a tour of timber towns, begin in **Albany,** which gains most of its reputation from the big pulp mill right on Interstate 5. In spite of new technology designed to mitigate toxic emissions, passersby are still greeted by wafts of sulfur from the chimneys of paper mills, combined with the memorable scents of a nearby chemical plant. For those who take the trouble to scoot into town, Albany is a treasure trove of historic homes. These Victorian and Craftsman houses are reminders of Albany's turn-of-the-last-century prosperity, when produce and flour were shipped out, and the town was a commercial center. (Pick up a map of historic homes from the kiosk in the Market Place, 300 SW Second Avenue.)

West of Albany on Hwy 20, the town of **Corvallis** is the home of **Oregon State University** (founded in 1868) and the Linus Pauling Institute of Science and Medicine. The two-time Nobel Prize winner graduated from OSU in 1922. On Refuge Road off Hwy 99W lies the **Finley National Wildlife Refuge**, a bird sanctuary with scenic trails.

WILLAMETTE VALLEY

◆ EAST OF ALBANY ON US 20   *map page 71, F&G, 2&3*

As you drive east, blue-hued mountains can be seen across the broad valley on clear days. Closer, patches of dense green stand out against paler areas where the big trees are gone, and replanted strips are still no more than brushy fields with saplings. On US 20, which traces the South Santiam River east from Albany, the economy is still timber-based, and foothill towns like **Lebanon** and **Sweet Home** are surviving, but not prospering. Log trucks still barrel down the road towards the mills. (Be sure to give these trucks plenty of room.) You'll pass big corporate mills, some quiet, others still chugging along. Nearly every household keeps a chainsaw out in the shed, and even if the forests can't be depended upon to put food on the table, wood still heats many homes.

After Sweet Home, the road hits the riverbank and follows its bends past herb farms and hiking trails into stands of big Douglas firs and western hemlocks. The Santiam Wagon Road once crossed the Cascades, and traces of it remain near the **House Rock** Campground, 24 miles east of Sweet Home, where a huge trailside boulder sheltered early travelers. Old-growth trees now form a broad canopy, and the short trail leads to a waterfall on the South Santiam River.

◆ NORTH SANTIAM   *map page 71, F/G-3/4*

At Santiam Junction, continue the westside forest drive by swinging north on Hwy 22 to Detroit, where the North Santiam is dammed to form Detroit Lake. (Or continue east into central Oregon's ponderosa pine.) Some of the state's finest stands of old growth western hemlock and Douglas fir are here, north of Detroit, near Hwy 46 and the Breitenbush River. Viewed from a small plane, it becomes obvious how extensive the clearcutting has been.

◆ BREITENBUSH HOT SPRINGS   *map page 71, E-4*

Off Forest Road 46 northeast of Detroit can be found a western Cascades landmark of New Age spiritual environmentalism. You needn't be part of an organized group to rent a cabin or soak in the hot pools. Ex-hippies and New Agers will feel at home. Others will want to hide in their rustic cabins. Call 503-854-3314 for more information.

(opposite) "Steam Donkeys" were used to haul timber up and down steep mountain slopes in the early days of logging. (Oregon Historical Society)

Just north of the Breitenbush campground (run by the Forest Service), turn east to the South Breitenbush Gorge trail. The trailhead is not far from the main road. This is a splendid example of westside old-growth forest. Leggy rhododendrons and Oregon grape break through the moss floor; cedars and Douglas firs top out to the sky or lie wrecked on the ground, decaying and nourishing younger trees. Whole slopes of trees were uprooted in a violent 1990 windstorm are slowly decaying and becoming "nurse logs," supporting the growth of saplings. The forest is home to an amazing variety of wildlife, and you don't need to be a biologist to recognize much of it. Keep an eye out for black bears scrambling up and down tree trunks. Consider it a special treat to come across a bear, but do keep your distance.

◆ OLALLIE LAKE   *map page 71, E-4*

Turn off Hwy 46 about 27 miles north of Detroit for an 18-mile trip into Olallie Lake. It's worth the long, slow drive. In the Chinook jargon (19th-century trader's pidgin) "olallie" means huckleberry, and huckleberry bushes dominate the understory beneath the lodgepole pine and mountain hemlocks. (These days olallie berries are something quite different—a cross between a blackberry and a loganberry.) Olallie Lake, with its no-frills resort and campground, is the largest of the many lakes in the area (for resort and campground information call 541-504-1010), most of which are small shallow basins scooped out by glacial ice. Climb four miles to Olallie Butte for a great view of the lakes and, if the weather cooperates, Mount Jefferson will seem as close as the trailhead parking lot.

Past the Olallie turnoff, Hwy 46 takes up with the Clackamas River. Pullouts and trailheads dot the road, and steam plumes rise from hot spots in the river.

The mile-long hike from Hwy 46 to **Bagby Hot Springs** is a great old-growth tour. Bagby is popular with Portlanders, who reach it via Estacada and Hwy 224; midweek visits are the most relaxing, and there's less of a wait for a soaking tub. Bagby is maintained by regular users—it's not a commercial resort, but it's nice to leave a contribution in the donation jar. The live-in caretakers keep this clothing-optional place peaceful, but occasionally a rough and rowdy crowd shows up.

(opposite) The Roaring River is typical of the many beautiful streams coarsing through the Willamette National Forest in the Western Cascades.

WILLAMETTE VALLEY

■ EUGENE

Eugene revolves around the University of Oregon, but it's a loose, elliptical orbit. Eugene may be the one town in America where tie-dyed T-shirts have been in fashion for 30 solid years. It's certainly one of the few places in the state where the corner grocery stocks soy milk. In spite of the preponderance of soy products, a culinary tour of Eugene won't disappoint those with more sophisticated and carnivorous tastes—the local restaurants are quite good. *(See page 91 for ideas.)* Humble Bagels, Nancy's Yogurt, Grizzly's Granola, Emerald Valley Kitchen Salsa, and Prince Puckler ice cream are all worth sampling.

There's as much partying here as in any college town—*Animal House* was filmed in Eugene—and there's the expected fraternity-type beer guzzling, but at least half the student body at the University yawns at the idea of joining up with the Greeks. What sets the town of Eugene apart from the pack is the hippie atmosphere at its fairs and markets. Enjoy the weekly **Saturday Market** downtown; the **Oregon Country Fair** in Veneta in early July; and the **Eugene Celebration** in late September. The Saturday Market offers the expected mix of beads and dried

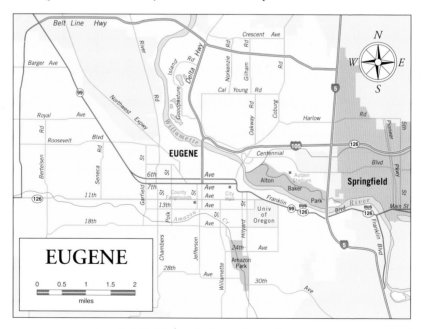

(opposite) Musicians at the Oregon County Fair—a premier counter-cultural event held just outside Eugene.

herbs, and the **Eugene Celebration** is lively, but not too giddily foreign for the un-prepared visitor.

The **University of Oregon Museum of Natural History,** at 1680 E 15th Av-enue, offers tourists proof of the town's more serious side. Here you'll find the 13,000-year-old Fort Rock sagebrush sandals, as well as Thomas Condon's fine fossil collection. Call 541-346-3024 for more information.

Oregon Country Fair (late July) requires a certain fearlessness—a willingness to *feel* stoned, even though the fair now has a strict drug-free policy. Hordes of crafts-people set up elaborate booths along a meandering creekside. If the sun shines, dust rises, and tanker trucks come in to dampen the ground and spray the sweat from fair-goers, who seldom hesitate to strip down for a cool shower. There are *se-rious* hippies here—people who live in the hills and aren't in the habit of making concessions to "straight" society. For anyone who's in the mood to cut loose, dance to marimba bands, pretend they're shaking a headful of dreadlocks (and there are probably more dreadlocked white people here than anywhere else in North Amer-ica), watch the guy in the loincloth chipping Early Man tools from flint, and remi-nisce about the times the Dead showed up; it's a blast.

Alternative thinking shows up even on Eugene's city streets. Bike paths line many streets, and routes run out to the hinterlands. Any direction out from town, in car or on bike, it doesn't take long before you feel like you're out of Eugene, and back into the real Oregon. Drive or cycle south to **Spencer Butte,** bounded by Willamette Boulevard and Fox Hollow, for good views of the old Cascades and the Three Sisters. Mountain bike and hiking trails run along and across the butte.

■ MCKENZIE RIVER ROAD   *map page 71, H-2 to 4*

Or, head east from Eugene, past Springfield (as conservative as Eugene is liberal), and up the McKenzie River, whose valley is broad and, once agricultural, now prey to creeping subdivisions. Highway 126 is studded with pull-outs and state parks with river access. Both powerboats and classic McKenzie River drift boats are pulled up in front of houses, occasionally tagged with a "for sale" sign. Loaded log trucks zoom down from the hills around McKenzie Pass. Stop by the covered **Goodpasture Bridge** for a photo shoot or a picnic, then continue upriver through hazelnut orchards. Vida, along with Dundee, produces most of the world's supply.

Author's Favorite Eugene Lodgings & Restaurants

Lodgings

Excelsior Inn and Restaurant.
754 E 13th, near the University
541-485-1206
Small inn whose Northwest sophistication will make you feel more elegant than you really are. Fine restaurant; see below.

Valley River Inn.
1000 Valley River Way
541-687-0123.
A beautiful, modern resort.

Restaurants

Ambrosia
174 E. Broadway (at Pearl)
541-342-4141
Italian, with new-wave pizza.

Cafe Zenon.
898 Pearl Street
541-343-3005.
There's always something tempting on the ever-changing eclectic menu in this bustling bistro.

Savouré.
201 W. Broadway
541-242-1010
Stop in for tea and scones in the elegant salon.

Chanterelle.
Fifth and Pearl
541-484-4065.
A small, charming restaurant with accomplished dishes made from the freshest local ingredients. Don't skip dessert.

Excelsior Inn and Restaurant.
754 E 13th, near the University
541-485-1206
The Excelsior was one of Eugene's first fine restaurants. See Lodgings above for more.

Glenwood Cafe.
1340 Alder Street
541-687-0355
University students walk over to enjoy the big breakfasts.

High Street Cafe.
1243 High Street, near 13th
541-345-4905
Pub fare, microbrewery.

Marché.
296 E Fifth Avenue
541-342-3612
Eugene's hottest spot for French-inflected Pacific Northwest cuisine.

Poppi's Anatolia.
992 Willamette Street (in the mall)
541-343-9661
Greek and Indian cuisine. They serve both lunch and dinner, specializing in different curries, spanakopita, kotta psiti, and salads.

Steelhead Brewery and Cafe.
199 E. Fifth Avenue
541-686-2739
The faux-British pub decor doesn't detract from the good pizza and microbrews.

Above **Vida,** the valley's shoulders hunch in, and it's just the road and the river, a few trees, and sometimes a flat space cleared out just enough for a mobile home or a cabin, quite a change from the proper little ranchettes downstream. In places the valley widens out enough to accommodate a small community and views open up enough to expose hillsides painfully scraped clean of trees due to clearcutting.

Dense forests, including some old growth surround **Cougar Reservoir**, where the lovely natural **Terwilliger Hot Springs** are helped along by volunteers who move rocks to form soaking pools. Fifty miles east of Eugene on Hwy 126, take Road 19 halfway down Cougar Reservoir road.

Tokatee Golf Course, near Cougar Reservoir and McKenzie Bridge, is one of Oregon's loveliest and most celebrated. (Modern Oregon folklore has it that renegade foursomes golf naked here once a year.) Don't resist the temptation to linger along the McKenzie. The nearer you get to the headwaters (at Clear Lake, on Hwy 126), the more mysterious the river becomes. **Clear Lake**, formed by a lava dam, flooded a forest that is still visible underwater. In the fall, when the lakeside vine maples turn, the bare-branched underwater forest seems to grab for the brilliant red and yellow leaves floating on the lake's surface.

*The Goodpasture Covered Bridge where it crosses over the
McKenzie River is a good place for a picnic.*

Scott Lake reflects a full moon with the Three Sisters as a backdrop.

The **McKenzie Pass Highway,** Hwy 242, is a forever-winding road. Take a break and spend the night at the **Log Cabin Inn** at 56483 McKenzie Hwy (126), a classic resort with the restaurant in the 1906 lodge; 541-822-3432.

Ferns and trees, thick near the town of **McKenzie Bridge,** become sparse at higher elevations—then, shockingly, plant life gives up altogether to crusty, brown-black lava fields. The McKenzie Pass Highway terminates at Sisters. It isn't plowed in the winter, and travelers then should cut north at Belknap Springs on Hwy 126 and cross into central Oregon on Santiam Pass. A place to stop in the area is **Belknap Hot Springs,** six miles east of McKenzie Bridge, a well-tended resort with a pool.

FLY FISHING FEVER

For me, as a small boy growing up in northwestern Oregon, the allure of fly fishing was not instantaneous. Whatever skills I may now have in fly casting came gradually, as little emphasis was given to fly fishing as a particular way of angling in the 1930s. Fiberglass and nylon were unheard of, and graphite was a lubricant.

When I was six, my father took me on a fishing trip. We camped on the bank of the Deschutes River in central Oregon, a major expedition in the old Dodge with running boards and isinglass side curtains. Unlike the Presbyterian minister in Maclean's *A River Runs Through It,* my father was neither a dedicated nor an accomplished fly fisherman— but on this trip he fished exclusively with a dry fly. I remember his old bamboo rod. It seemed 20 feet long at the time, and the scarlet windings were about an inch apart over each of its three sections. Mine was a telescoping steel job and I fished with a single egg weighted with one split shot. After my father landed his first large "redside," I persuaded him to remove my split shot and tie on a fly. My first attempts were awkward flailings which nearly emptied his fly "book" in the brush and tree limbs, and I soon learned to sneak up on likely water where I could dabble the fly at rod's length and lure a few smaller fish to the surface. It was the spawning of my desire to fly fish—a desire yet to mature.

Our family had a Mount Hood cabin on the upper Sandy River, near Zigzag, Oregon, and it was here that my brother and I made our first independent efforts at fly fishing. Across from our cabin was a uniquely beautiful and small tributary— Clear Creek. In the warmer months, the upper Sandy was always turbid from the glacial melt near its source on lower Mount Hood. The sand stung our legs as we waded out to swim in the current; but Clear Creek was gin clear and very cold— and it was a visual and biotic paradise from its source to its confluence with the Sandy. It was also boy-sized and accessible to a couple of kids in their slippery Keds and rolled-up overalls. Lastly, it was heavily populated with small rainbow and cutthroat which, because of the stream size, had to be stalked.

Each summer, my younger brother and I would return to familiar rocks, riffles, and pockets where we knew the fish were waiting. At particularly good holes, we would flip a coin to see who fished first; and each year we would start higher upstream to discover new water. We still used telescoping steel poles. We hadn't learned the term "rod." They were inexpensive at Monkey Wards—important during Depression years—and well suited to single egg fishing on a on a small, brushy creek.

We bought our jars of single eggs at the Zigzag store, and always asked Gladys Rypzinsky—owner and postmistress—how the fishing was. Our good friend always said, "I hear it's pretty good, boys, if you know where to find them." On one such occasion, I looked longingly at the few flies displayed in the small case—blue uprights, professors, royal coachmen—all snelled with a six-inch length of looped leader. I bought two of them for a quarter, along with a length of silk gut leader which had to be soaked between moistened felt pads. Nylon was yet to be invented.

My brother and I discovered that even with those heavy buggy whips and a badly cracked level line of coated silk, we could make small roll casts to reach good water. And we did a lot of "dabbling"—sneaking quietly behind a rock or tree to drop the fly into a likely pocket. We discovered the thrill of seeing a fish come to the surface in a rush and a swirl. We were also learning to "read" the water—to know where fish were most apt to be waiting for a floating morsel. And we bought more of those lovely flies and fewer jars of eggs. By preference, we found ourselves making the transition to fly fishing.

As we grew older, we became more adventuresome—seeking the larger streams nearby, such as the Zigzag and the Salmon. We saved our money to buy bamboo rods, for even the cheapest ones at Monkey Wards improved our casting—even with those old level lines. It was to be several years before I had my first double taper line —an oiled silk Newton which was instant magic.

♦ WHERE TO LEARN

Fishing is different things to different people and there's no need to rush into any one aspect of it, but opportunities abound for learning. There are fly fishing clubs, rod manufacturers, and local fly angling shops—all offering instruction in casting and fly tying. In Eugene, The Caddis Fly is superbly stocked and is staffed by knowledgeable and courteous people who will offer suggestions and sound advice on where and how to fish.

The McKenzie River near Eugene is a relatively large and still very beautiful river for fly fishing. Wading is difficult and bank fishing is limited to short and infrequent stretches. The preferred way of fly fishing this river, for both the novice and the experienced, is from a McKenzie drift boat with a competent guide at the oars. It is heavily fished but also regularly stocked with legal-size rainbow. Larger "native" fish must be released unharmed in the hope that we may thus increase the population of "wild" fish.

The North Umpqua River, east of Roseburg, is best known for its summer-run steelhead fly fishing. These rainbow are anadromous—meaning they have the ability to live in both fresh and salt water. When they return to Oregon's rivers they average around seven to eight pounds, beginning their ascent from the Pacific in July and remaining in the river and its tributaries until spring spawning. The best fishing may occur in the late summer and early fall, depending upon the vagaries of the run and the weather. I would urge the uninitiated to contact Steamboat Inn for reservations, information on the fishing, and the names of knowledgeable guides. The North Umpqua is worth seeing if only for its pristine beauty, but it is a post-graduate course in casting and wading—not a fishing river for children. Several miles of this beautiful river are closed to all angling other than fly fishing. Anglers are encouraged to release wild steelhead for the same reason that this practice is required on the McKenzie for native resident rainbow.

◆ How to Know a Wild Fish

To make sure you've caught a planted fish, check to see that one of the two pelvic fins on the lower belly is clipped off. (If neither has been you should return the fish to the river.) Another sign of a fish reared in hatchery tanks is a damaged tail (caudal fin) and a disfigured dorsal fin, the result of their constant contact with concrete tank walls. Additionally, planted rainbows do not have the darker red sides characteristic of "wild" fish. They are pretty plain and silvery colored. If they survive more than their first season in the river, they usually take on the "redside" coloring.

Steelhead "smolt" are usually about six to ten inches long when planted. Those that make it downstream to the ocean will feed in that smorgasbord for one to three years before returning to their river, and they will run from one to fifteen pounds in weight, and be 14 to 30 inches long. When they first arrive back in the river, they are all bright silver except for their steely gray backs—planters and wild fish alike.

—Bill Wilson

(above) From his McKenzie driftboat, architect and river guide Bill Wilson casts a long line into the McKenzie River, while another angler (opposite) casts his into the Metolius River in Cascades Deschutes National Forest.

O R E G O N   C O A S T

◆ **AREA OVERVIEW**

On the Oregon coast cold green waves thunder toward evergreen headlands and craggy shorelines. Seafoam cold as shaved ice rolls up onto beachcombers' bare feet and curls around the fantastic forms of gray driftwood. Offshore are fog-shrouded rocky islands filled with nesting seabirds. In winter, storms thunder in off the Pacific; during the summer, fog hovers over the coast. On clear days the sky overhead is steel blue. The ocean spray is so refreshing that even sedentary people seem game for long walks, but the surf is so cold it's easy to resist a swim.

Cliffside houses range from the palatial to weathered shacks, and the generally uncrowded beaches belong to the people. Unlike many states, where oceanfront property owners control beach access, Oregon's beaches are public. This goes back a long way. In 1913, before roads connected coastal towns, Gov. Oswald West told the legislature that the beaches' tidal spans should be designated a public highway. The legislature agreed, thwarting the state's early attempts to sell tide lands. (Of course, it wasn't much of a highway, and until US 101 was completed in 1932, coastal towns were very isolated and grew up with distinctive personalities.) In 1967, a Beach Bill was enacted to provide public access to the dry sand areas above the high-tide mark. This law did a lot to confirm the protective way Oregonians think about their coast and gave the state a national reputation for environmental preservation.

State parks, many with campsites, stipple the Oregon coast. Even on summer weekends, when Portlanders flock to Lincoln City and Cannon Beach, the long, broad beaches don't seem crowded. For real solitude, head to the south coast, pick a remote wayside, walk a hundred yards from the parking lot, and it'll be you and the sandpipers, investigating wave-tossed logs and huge hanks of kelp.

Alluring as the beach may be, a look east toward the coastal mountains completes the picture. It's obvious that these hills haven't been protected as the beach zone has—in places, entire mountainsides have been deforested, and the streams clogged with silt. The coastal forests that remain are as integral as the tidepools and the basalt cliffs.

Climate: Better bring a sweater. And a windbreaker. And warm socks. In July? You bet! Summer fogs can keep the coast cool and damp while the rest of the state broils. But it's just as likely that the clouds will burn off early in the day and by mid-morning you'll be strolling the beach in shorts. Winters are generally mild and wet on the coast, though the roads over the Coast Range frequently become ice-glazed.

Food & Lodging: Every town on the coast has at least a handful of motels. One of the state's largest resorts is Salishan, south of Lincoln City, and one of the most elegant hotels is Cannon Beach's Stephanie Inn. But many coastal visitors never set foot in a motel. State park campgrounds line the coast, and almost all of them have a few wonderfully dry, heated yurts or cabins for rent; 800-551-6949.

There are surprisingly few good seafood restaurants on the coast, but we've mentioned those which do exist with the town they are in. Don't be afraid to stop at the roadside crab and oyster vendors in dilapidated shacks near fishing ports—you'll get great picnic fare and, almost undoubtedly, a few pearls of local wisdom.

Harris Beach State Park.

COAST

COAST

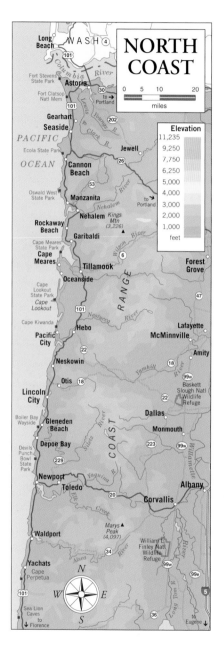

NORTH COAST

0   5   10   20

miles

Elevation	
11,235	
9,250	
7,750	
6,250	
5,000	
4,000	
3,000	
2,000	
1,000	
feet	

■ BICYCLING THE COAST

A bike route, essentially along the wide shoulder of US 101, with a few detours, runs the entire length of the coast. A week long ride is one of the best ways to really get into the scenery. After you pump up the steep hills you'll feel entitled to stop at beaches, bakeries, and ice cream shops.

Coastal bike trips are best from north to south, because they take advantage of the prevailing winds and ocean views. Fifty miles a day is a reasonable goal. State park campgrounds have hiker/biker areas with hot showers and, if the weather is good, it's a great and inexpensive way to go. There are plenty of motels if that suits you better. Anyone who is not used to this will want to think twice before starting off on a loaded bicycle. Coastal hills are steep, and can be long—don't expect momentum to do all the work. For the inexperienced cyclist, an organized tour with a sag wagon or a credit card ride (every night in a motel) may be a more enjoyable way to go.

Cyclists who make the 367-mile trip from Astoria to Brookings can leave their cars at the Visitors Center in Astoria and cobble together a return trip via Curry Public Transit bus from Brookings to Coos Bay (800-921-2871), Amtrak Thruway bus from

Coos Bay to Eugene, Amtrak train from Eugene to Portland, and Greyhound from Portland to Astoria. Or, ride the public bus to Coos Bay and rent a car there (541-266-7100) for the drive back to Astoria.

■ COASTAL INDIANS

Up and down the coast, indigenous people shared certain customs, though rarely the language of their neighbors. Over thousands of years, migrations down the coast from Alaska and across from the state's interior left a patchwork of languages, encouraging many people to become multilingual.

It would be a stretch to say life was easy for coastal Indians, but the ocean, the estuaries, and the coastal forests supplied abundant food. Wealth was important, and poor people often ended up slaves of the rich. The well-born members of northern coastal tribes secured a board to a new baby's skull, gently molding it to a flat slope that was the signature head shape of the upper class. Southern tribes rarely flattened their heads, but women were often tattooed with three vertical lines on the chin.

Winter villages, usually located on a coastal river estuary, were the main bases. People harvested shellfish from the beaches and trapped salmon and

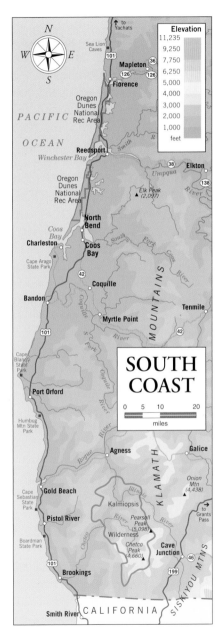

other fish in elaborate weirs. Though they traveled by canoe, they weren't really seafarers; trips from headland to headland were the extent of ocean travel. Indian women along the coast wove spruce roots into baskets, which were used as hats, baby cradles, and storage containers.

In the 1850s, white settlers and the territorial government wanted all Indians removed from western Oregon. The Indians were unwilling to leave and in 1855 two reservations were established for coastal tribes: the long narrow Coast Reservation on the central coast and the Grande Ronde Reservation in the Willamette Valley. The Coast Reservation was whittled away at the middle when whites took over the area around Yaquina Bay (the site of present day Newport), creating the Siletz Reservation to the north and the Alsea Reservation to the south. Tensions between tribes on the Alsea Reservation led some Coos, Umpqua, and Siuslaw people to purchase a six-acre reservation in Coos Bay. The tribes on these reservations had their relationships with the U.S. government severed in 1956 by an act that essentially dissolved all tribal entities in western Oregon. In 1977, the Confederated Tribes of the Siletz regained federal recognition and, eventually, a small, forested reservation northeast of Newport. The Confederated Tribes of the Coos, Lower Umpqua, and Siuslaw, federally reinstated in 1984, have a tribal hall in Coos Bay.

■ ASTORIA AND VICINITY   *map page 100*

History buffs obsessed with the adventures of Oregon's first explorers, Lewis and Clark, may want to drive to the coast on US 30, the Columbia River road. With copies of the Journals cradled in their laps, they'll recite entries describing "wet, cold and miserable" weather, and perhaps smile slightly when the windshield wipers are switched to "high."

Other US 30 travelers will wait for a sunny day and stop to ride the Cathlamet ferry from Westport, Oregon, through the braided Columbia River channels to Cathlamet, Washington, then back again. Or perhaps they'll detour south past thick Coast Range forests and massive clearcuts, many replanted with Douglas fir seedlings, to Jewell Meadows on Hwy 202. Elk come down from forested hills to feed in the meadows in the early morning and evenings.

The Columbia River ushers travelers into Astoria and becomes a more important directional aid than compass points. This first coastal town is set away from the surf on the broad mouth of the Columbia. Here, the river's treacherous bar is a force to contend with and has been since mariners first passed this way looking for the fabled "great river." At first the bar obscured the river from them entirely, and ships passed it by time and time again. Finally, in 1792, Boston sea captain Robert Gray, having been told by English navigator George Vancouver that there was no great river in the vicinity, took a chance and sailed toward the bar and into what turned out to be the Columbia River.

Lewis and Clark spent a wet winter at Fort Clatsop near here in 1805, and half a dozen years later, John Jacob Astor set up a fur trading company. It foundered and was tossed around like a hot potato amongst American and British players. It takes some looking to find the site of Fort Astoria now, but it's there—a little street-corner park at 15th and Exchange, with a replica trading post that could just as easily be a child's playhouse.

As the "soft gold" of the fur trade became scarcer and less fashionable, Astoria's prosperity increasingly came from the export of timber and fish. Limitless (or

Fort Astoria's name was changed to Fort George at the time Henry J. Warre drew this illustration in 1848. Later the name of the village that grew here was restored to Astoria. (Oregon Historical Society)

(following pages) The view towards Cannon Beach from Ecola point. Haystack Rock is visible in the distance.

renewable) as big trees and husky salmon once seemed, their numbers are now decimated, and every year they provide less and less of an income to the area. Now Astoria hangs on with a gritty grandeur.

From a hillside vantage point, or from a seat on a wharf, it's easy to imagine days long gone by, when Scandinavian fishermen ran gill-net boats and Chinese laborers skinned fish in the riverside salmon canneries. Mammoth logs from the coastal mountains were, and still are, hoisted onto ships and sent to Asia. (Since this shipping of raw, unmilled logs takes jobs away from American millworkers, the practice is almost universally abhorred, and logs cut from public land may not be exported "raw.")

To get a sense of local topography, follow the signs uphill to the **Astoria Column**, a 125-foot tower adorned with a historical mural. From the top of the tower, the geography of rivers, bays, and estuaries becomes clear, and the urge to

View of Astoria and harbor circa 1880s. (Columbia River Maritime Museum)

climb down and explore the countryside comes on strong.

You might want to set aside an hour or two for a visit to the first-rate **Maritime Museum** on the river. It's on the south side of US 30 as you drive into town from the east, at 1792 Marine Drive; 503-325-2323. You can't miss it—there is a lightship moored outside.

Stop at **Fort Clatsop,** southwest of Astoria on the west bank of the Lewis and Clark River. Here, at Lewis and Clark's winter camp, the reconstructed quarters seem quite cramped for 33 people and Lewis's Newfoundland dog. In the summer, park staff goes all out with historical reenactments, but a damp, chilly winter visit on a day when the sun never really shines, and then sets at 4 P.M., will etch the experience deeper than any staged deer hunt can.

Before striking out southbound on US 101, drive west to **Fort Stevens State Park,** near the town of Hammond, where a road leads to the end of Clatsop Spit. It's here that the Columbia flows into the Pacific. Neon orange pilot boats guide freighters over the bar, which smaller fishing boats take on their own, sometimes with a few knocks.

■ SEASIDE AND CANNON BEACH   *map page 100*

Back on US 101, in Seaside, Oregon's northernmost full-fledged beach town, be prepared for unrestrained ticky-tacky high-camp tourism. Ben Holladay, a Portland transportation mogul, built a resort here in the 1870s, and it became a Victorian-era hotspot. It's the coast's only town with a boardwalk (called "The Prom"). There's also a cruising street—Broadway, with a beachside loop ("The Turnaround"). The coast's cheesiest aquarium is here—it once exhibited a large lobster acquired from the seafood department at the Safeway across the street.

Cannon Beach, nine miles down US 101 from Seaside, has long been labeled "artsy." Low-life partiers went to the Seaside arcades; book-reading types stayed in Cannon Beach cottages. A surge in development has brought more people to the area, and the streets are jammed on summer weekends. Stop here on a blustery spring day, linger at the Cannon Beach Book Company, browse the White Bird Gallery, and then, when there's a break in the weather, walk down the broad, sandy beach, where thousands of seabirds crowd onto big-shouldered Haystack Rock and tidepools cradle anemones that look like peppermint candies.

(following pages) Heceta Head lighthouse, just north of Sea Lion Caves.

There's a summer theater in Cannon Beach, but the social event of the year is the Sandcastle Contest, held in late May or early June, when thousands of spectators come out to watch teams build elaborate shell- and seaweed-trimmed fantasies. Prospective sculptors should call 503-436-2623, then hope for a gray day that will keep the sand damp and sculptable.

An erstwhile loggers' boarding house is now a cozy hotel—the **Cannon Beach Hotel** at 1116 S Hemlock Street; 503-436-1392. **Stephanie Inn** is an elegant accommodation with all the extras at 2740 S Pacific; 503-436-2221 or 800-633-3466. For refreshment try the **Bistro**, a long-time Cannon Beach hangout; 263 N Hemlock; or the nearby **Lazy Susan Cafe** at 126 N Hemlock.

(below) In 1894, a second sprit-sail was added to gill-net fishing boats racing in the Astoria Regatta. The practice, which continued thereafter, earned these boats the sobriquet "The Butterfly Fleet." (Columbia River Maritime Museum)

■ OSWALD WEST STATE PARK   *map page 100*

Oswald West State Park grows up around Short Sands Beach, a sheltered cove at the foot of Neahkanie Mountain 10 miles south of Cannon Beach with waves big enough to amuse wet-suited surfers and kayakers. The coast's best campground is here in an old-growth grove nestling 36 hike-in campsites. Hike from the campground through big trees and a thick understory out to the tip of Cape Falcon, with views south to Manzanita. Or, cross the highway from the campground and hike up Neahkanie Mountain, where, at the top, you'll feel like an early-day cartographer, ready to draw the lay of the land for miles around.

■ MANZANITA   *map page 100*

Some of the north coast's best views are from US 101 between Oz West Park and the town of Manzanita. Manzanita is still small and unhurried, "what Cannon Beach used to be," people lament. For local political sagas or surfing tips, stop by Manzanita News and Espresso, and read the latest issue of "Upper Left Edge."

The beach is long and wide at Manzanita, perfect for a spin on a beach cycle. See the bike guy on the beach about rentals, and don't get discouraged if recumbent cycling doesn't come easily at first. (Here's a tip: slouch down in the seat.)

Spring and fall storms come in hard from the west and bring good beachcombing. Oregon's most intriguing and unlikely shipwreck treasure—ancient, mysteriously inscribed chunks of beeswax—have been washing up near Manzanita for as long as people can remember. The wax is reckoned to have come from a Spanish ship in the 1700s, and it was probably intended for liturgical use. In recent years, the supply has dwindled. According to one local, "Every few years you hear of somebody finding a chunk, but you wouldn't want to stand around on the beach waiting for it to wash up."

Other bonanzas happen all the time. A ship from Asia lost a container a few years back, and Nike sneakers began washing up on the northern Oregon coast. A shoe exchange was set up and people swapped shoes to make complete pairs.

For a small inn with well-appointed rooms a block from the beach, try **Inn at Manzanita** at 67 Laneda Avenue; 503-368-6754. **Blue Sky Cafe** at 154 Laneda Avenue is a comfortable cafe where locals mingle with visitors. The innovative food is worth the wait. **Manzanita News & Espresso** at 500 Laneda Avenue serves good coffee and is great place to hang out.

◆ NEHALEM   *map page 100*

Nehalem, just southeast of Manzanita, on the eastern edge of tiny Nehalem Bay, is even smaller and less rushed than its neighbor. It's an easygoing place to learn about Oregon coast nightlife. Blackjack devotees come in off the bay and beaches, and spend their evenings sizing up the three regular dealers and their deals at Bay Way Tavern.

■ TILLAMOOK BAY AND VICINITY   *map page 100*

The first black person to reach Oregon, Marcus Lopez, was killed by Indians at the mouth of the Tillamook Bay. Lopez, who joined Robert Gray's 1788 trip to the northwest as a cabin boy in his native Cape Verde Islands, was exploring near present-day Barview, on the northern edge of Tillamook Bay, when he realized an Indian had stolen his knife. When the young sailor tried to recover his property, he was murdered.

◆ GARIBALDI   *map page 100*

Today, Tillamook Bay's main fishing port is Garibaldi, near the Bay's northern edge. Fish merchants line US 101, which runs around the large bay. For the best seafood prices and a fresh haul, turn in at the Texaco station, go down past the docks, and find Garibaldi Charters. Travelers can make an easy picnic of Dungeness crab, which come cleaned, cooked, and ready to eat.

Wander around Garibaldi's docks, where charter and commercial fishermen moor. It doesn't take too long to want a piece of the action. Join an ocean-going charter for salmon or bottomfish at **Garibaldi Charters; 503-322-0007.** Or, rent a skiff and crab pots from the Garibaldi Marina, and venture into the bay. Out on Tillamook Bay, thoughts may wander to the lives of Tillamook Indians. Tillamook men used the bay not only as a fishery, but as a duck-hunting ground. A duck hunter would cover a basket with feathers, making as lifelike a decoy as possible, and wade into the water. With the feathered basket on his head, he'd crouch low, and slowly approach a flock of ducks. Then he'd dip underwater, grab a duck by its feet, and pull it beneath the surface.

Today stalking ducks with binoculars is great fun. Some of the coast's best bird watching is found at the cluster of roadside rocks just east of Garibaldi (it's east rather than south because the highway bends around the bay here). Cormorants, oystercatchers, grebes, Harlequin ducks, and an assortment of gulls are often spotted here.

❖

The wet, green area around Tillamook is known for its pasture land. Local dairy farmers co-operatively own the Tillamook County Creamery Association, which supplies the **Tillamook Cheese Factory.** More people stop at the cheese factory, on the northern edge of Tillamook, than any other single spot on the coast. And it's

not just the RV crowd—every so often you'll spot a motorcycle gang licking ice cream cones in the corner of the parking lot. Most people just run in for ice cream and a restroom, but there's also a self-guided tour of the factory and an exhibit extolling the virtues of butterfat.

■ A SPIT, THREE CAPES, AND A HEAD *map page 100*

South of Tillamook, US 101 makes an inland run down to Lincoln City, bypassing three coastal capes, any one of them more interesting than the inland route.

Leave Tillamook on the Three Capes Loop and drive northwest along the edge of **Tillamook Bay.** The long spit coming up from the south end of the bay used to hold the resort town of Bayocean, but jetty construction at the bay's mouth changed the pattern of the waves and washed away Bayocean. Now the seven-mile-long spit beckons birdwatchers. In late summer, thousands of sandpipers run across the mudflats. Walk or bike out the spit, with Tillamook Bay to the east, the Pacific to the west, and look for ghost town rubble.

At **Cape Meares State Park,** up a steep hill from both Tillamook Bay and the Pacific Ocean, pull out binoculars and scan the ocean rocks for sea lions, harbor seals, puffins, and murres. (The Portland Audubon Society regularly gets calls from people reporting dead penguins on the coast; they're actually dead murres, whose body shape and markings resemble penguins.) Puffins nest in the cliffs—a careful search may be rewarded with a bright bill sticking out from beneath a rock overhang.

Cape Lookout, the next cape south, sticks out into the Pacific like a finger pointed to Japan. A hike through big old spruce, hemlock, and cedar trees to Cape Lookout is a yearly ritual for coast-lovers who appreciate the long views north to Cape Meares and south to Cascade Head. Such ocean panoramas make for great whale-watching.

Whales migrate southbound December to February; then they go into reverse and head north from March to May. April is the peak of whale migration, and if Cape Lookout or any headland makes a good land base, **Depoe Bay,** south of here between Lincoln City and Newport, is the best place to join a whale-watching charter boat. For good storm- and whale-watching from very comfortable rooms perched right on the edge of Depoe Bay, try the **Channel House Inn** at 35 Ellingston Street; 541-765-2140.

(opposite) Tillamook Bay's main fishing port is Garibaldi.

Cape Kiwanda, the southernmost cape on the Three Cape Loop, is a fine place to pit your legs muscles against sand. Trudge up the mountainous sandy cape to its windy head, find a sheltered spot, and watch the waves crash far below. This is a place to feel big as king of the hill, small as a speck of blowing sand. On the way back down the sandy slope to the beach, become a bounding, soaring wingless Icarus. Hang gliders go a step further, and take off from Kiwanda for a slower, more circuitous trip to sea level.

In the mid-1960s, plans to develop **Cascade Head,** between Neskowin and Lincoln City, were thwarted when, through a patchwork of donations, the Nature Conservancy acquired the land. Preserved are the sitka spruce, hemlock, and alder forests and the often-foggy native prairie on the headland. The world's largest land salamander, the Pacific giant salamander, lives here. It grows up to a foot long and eats mice. Reach the two-mile trail to the head from Three Rocks Road; the parking area is just beyond the Sitka Center for Arts and Ecology.

Five small towns between Cascade Head and the Siletz River grew together at their heads and tails and in 1965 legally became **Lincoln City,** a name found on

(above) Weathered buildings such as this one at Depoe Bay are a familiar sight along the coast. (opposite) Female and undersize Dungeness crabs are returned to the sea at Weber's Pier, Bandon.

no pre-1965 map. From the north end of town, Hwy 18 takes off toward McMinnville and Portland; minutes from the coast, in the hamlet of **Otis**, is the **Otis Cafe** which serves some of the state's best pie. (People say they're going to take a hike, but they really spend the day here eating strawberry-rhubarb pie); 1259 Salmon River Hwy (Hwy 18). Fuel yourself, then prepare for a long slow drive through an unrelenting strip of fast-food vendors and beach curio shops, culminating in an outlet mall. The mall and two big casinos are the focus of many a Lincoln City vacation. In Lincoln City, the Siletz Tribe runs the Chinook Winds Casino. Some 20 miles inland on Hwy 18 is Spirit Mountain casino, run by the Confederated Tribes of the Grand Ronde.

To experience high-1950s Oregon on the beach, stay at the **Ester Lee Motel**, 3803 SW Hwy 101; 541-996-3606. Nearby **Salishan Lodge** is a sheltered, exclusive resort that has everything you'd want except the beach—it's a long walk through mud flats to the ocean. Come for golf, tennis, or walks through wonderfully landscaped wooded grounds. The restaurant is said to be one of Oregon's best. 7760 Old Hwy 101 N between Lincoln City and Depoe Bay; 541-764-3600. **Blackfish Cafe** has some of the best-prepared fresh seafood on the coast—it's one of the few coastal restaurants offering true Northwest cuisine; 2733 NW Hwy 101. **Chez Jeanette** is an intimate and unpretentious restaurant with good French food on 7150 Old Hwy 101 N, just south of Salishan in Gleneden Beach.

■ NEWPORT AND VICINITY   *map page 100*

Newport's sprawl is somehow more purposeful than Lincoln City's. Perhaps the active bayfront fishing port redeems it. It's certainly given a boost by the renovated bustle at **Nye Beach,** an old-time beach resort gone derelict until the Sylvia Beach Hotel launched a neighborhood renaissance in the mid-1980s. The Sylvia Beach, a "hotel for book lovers," is as good as they come.

Newport's big draw is the **Oregon Aquarium**, 2820 E Ferry Slip Road, 541-867-3474, where jellyfish swim through a room-sized cylindrical aquarium that glows like a beautiful lava lamp, and a giant octopus lives outside in a rock crevice surrounded by an aviary, where puffins and other seabirds fly. Walk through a clear acrylic tunnel, passing sharks, rays, and other deep-sea denizens. (Keiko, the killer whale from the "Free Willy" movies, lived here before being moved to Iceland. He eventually swam 1,000 miles to Norway, where he died in 2003.

After a morning at the aquarium, head to the old town bayfront fishing village. A windowside seat at Mo's Annex is a good place to enjoy a bowl of their much-vaunted clam chowder and to watch boats sail in and out of the harbor. Gum-booted fishermen unload their catches, and sea lions bob in the waves.

A Newport hotel with class and personality, **Nye Beach Hotel** has a good cafe open for three meals a day to all. 219 NW Cliff Street; 541-265-3334. **Sylvia Beach Hotel,** the "hotel for booklovers,"offers theme rooms devoted to favorite authors, and the library is the place to hang out. Good management and interesting guests keep it from feeling contrived. Dinners here are family style, with lots of good conversation between diners. 267 NW Cliff; 541-265-5428.

For clam chowder try **Mo's.** Admittedly the restaurant is kind of a zoo, and you may feel like you're on an assembly line, but it's an Oregon classic; 622 SW Bay Boulevard. You'll pay just a bit more for a bayfront meal at Saffron Salmon, but the food is better and the ambiance less frantic; 859 SW Bay Blvd. Across the street, **Shark's Seafood Bar** has delicious steamed and poached seafood; 852 SW Bay Blvd.

■ YACHATS AND CAPE PERPETUA *map page 100*

South of Newport, the coast range presses closer to the sea, and commercial hustle gives way to tidepools, sea lions, and whales. For such reflectiveness, Yachats [Yah-hots] may be the perfect coast town. It's down close to the water, nearly buried in salal and huckleberry. From April till October, sea-run smelt hurl themselves up the Yachats River, aiming straight toward locals with clever triangular smelt nets and oily diets.

Cape Perpetua, the epitome of the rocky wild Oregon coast, is just a few miles south of Yachats. The picture window at the Cape Perpetua visitor center is a good place to watch for whales in nasty weather. Even if it's raining, take the short walk to the **Devil's Churn,** where the ocean cleaves a thick basalt flow into a narrow chasm. People raise their voices over the thunder of waves crashing against rocks, and see and feel the high-flying spray. Starfish keep a stubborn suction-grip on the sides of the wave-battered basalt cliffs. Chartreuse rock-top slime grows a stone's throw from a damp, dark green forest. An oceanside trail continues south from Devil's Churn, and it's easy to spend a full morning staring at the waves and poking around tidepools.

People may have lived here for the past 8,000 years. Alsea Indians used the beach regularly, and left middens, or piles of clam, oyster, crab, and mussel shells. Middens formed when, after a seafood feast, diners threw sand over the shells to lessen the odor. After many shellfish meals, the middens resembled small dunes.

The area around Yachats and Cape Perpetua comprises the largest intact coastal temperate rainforest in the continental United States. Two small wilderness areas, **Cummins Creek** and **Rock Creek,** are enveloped in a canopy of sitka spruce, Douglas fir, western hemlock, and western red-cedar. A trail up Cummins Creek leads to a rainforest with nine-foot-diameter spruce trees growing among downed and decomposing nurse logs. Almost everything is covered by a dense green mat of salal and ferns. The delicate yellow salmonberries are safe to eat, and some berry connoisseurs rate them above all others. (Make sure an expert identifies them for you!) Birders look for marbled murrelets in these groves. For years, nobody knew where this seabird nested. It turns out that old-growth coastal forests are its nesting habitat, and this intact stretch of old growth is considered crucial to the murrelet's

COAST

A hike along the coast reveals colorful marine flora (opposite) as well as abundant marine fauna, among them these harbor seals at Strawberry Hill State Wayside (above).

survival. Though the slopes are steep and the soil unstable, much of the area is currently managed by the Forest Service for timber production. The Ten Mile Creek Association, based in Yachats, is working to establish a coastal rainforest reserve.

To stay in Yachats, try the **Shamrock Lodgettes** on US 101 S, just south of the bridge; 541-547-3312. These well-kept cabins and motel rooms are in a wonderful location. Eat at the Drift Inn Pub, a family-friendly informal spot with surfing videos on the bar TV, occasional live music, and good food; 124 Hwy. 101 S.

■ FLORENCE AND VICINITY *map page 101*

If you have more money and more time than you think you're going to need, take the elevator 208 feet down to **Sea Lion Caves,** tucked under the cliffs between Cape Perpetua and Florence. It may be a commercial roadside attraction, but at the bottom of the elevator, there are great close-up views of the 800-pound behemoths lounging and playing in the cave.

Sea lions are usually visible in the ocean near the cave's entrance from the clifftop parking lot. With a good pair of binoculars, this is a reasonable, and free, alternative to a descent into the cave (where finicky noses may be offended by the smell of sea lion droppings).

It's usually pretty easy to tell Oregon coast pinnipeds apart. Sea lions tend to be larger than seals, and unlike their smaller brethren, they have ears and can get up onto all fours. Most seal and sea lion populations have rebounded since 1972, when marine mammals became officially protected. Anglers still have the right to shoot marine mammals (typically harbor seals) that tangle with their nets. Some commercial fishermen claim the pinnipeds' salmon diet is partially responsible for declining salmon populations. (Research doesn't bear this out, but it is true that harbor seals can make a real feast out of fish caught in an underwater net.)

Turn from fauna to flora at the **Darlingtonia Garden,** four miles north of Florence. Big cedars, Oregon grape, salal, kinnikinnick, and delicate ferns surround a sphagnum bog chock full of the coast's most fascinating plant, *Darlingtonia californica,* also known as cobra lily or pitcher plant. Sweet nectar and flashes of color on this plant's calla lily–like calyx lure insects into a hooded mouth-like leaf opening. There bugs get lost in a maze of slippery transparent tubes. Sharp, downward-pointing hairs direct them deeper into the plant, where they finally fall into a liquid and are digested. In the bog, a damp, raindrop-flecked spiderweb hangs precariously close to darlingtonia, setting the stage for a carnivorous drama.

All the original bridges on US 101 are distinctive, but the **bridge spanning the Siuslaw River at Florence** is particularly charming—the posts look like giant concrete bishop's hats. It beckons one to leave the car and walk across, inspecting the dark green river and the old town beneath the bridge. Even more so in Florence than in other coast towns, the old town is the place to linger.

After a good glance at the river and some remarkably good clam chowder in old town's **Bridgewater Restaurant,** 1297 Bay Street (at Laurel), go a step further upriver and rent a motorboat. The marina's a casual place—they can spot an honest face here, and that's more security than a driver's license or deposit. Cruise upstream past drippy moss-draped trees and a few searing clearcuts. Pass waterlogged islands where lush wild gardens surround abandoned houses and where herons fly up and down the river.

Explore another facet of upstream life at **Alpha-Bits Cafe** at 10780 Hwy 126, 10 miles east of Florence. It has great veggie food and hippie atmosphere.

■ OREGON DUNES   *map page 101*

The dense forests and seaside basalt cliffs stop short at the mouth of the Siuslaw, where they're replaced by giant sand dunes all the way south to Coos Bay. Volcanic basalt cliffs never formed a barrier here, and the ocean bottom sand was free to blow inland, forming huge shifting hills. The dunes are vast; in some places, they reach a couple of miles inland.

To get a sense of their scale, just walk toward the ocean. There's an observation wayside halfway between Florence and Reedsport (10 miles from either town) where blue-topped posts guide hikers and ease anxieties about getting lost in the sandhills. On a sunny day, even in the early spring, you can find warm spots tucked between dunes. Pause to spend an hour or two reading and napping in the sand. Or, if the giant dunes make you feel more fiesty than contemplative, stop at one of the many dune buggy rental shops on US 101 between Reedsport and Florence.

European beach grass, introduced around 1900 to hold sand down and prevent it from blocking river channels, is forming a mat over the sand, and the dunes no longer blow and shift as they once did. Once the dunes are held firmly in place, other vegetation can take hold, and the unpredictable blowsy wild cards of the landscape will be replaced by more permanent features.

■ COOS BAY *map page 101*

Coos Bay, with its Siamese twin North Bend, is the coast's largest city, a small-scale megalopolis. It's the only place where buildings rise to five or six stories, and where the feeling is unreconstructedly working class. (Of course, you'll still find crowded espresso bars here. It's still the Pacific Northwest, after all.) The shipping port here exports more timber than any other port in the world, much of it now wood chips headed to Japanese paper mills, and it's the best natural harbor between San Francisco and Puget Sound. The lower Coos River is lined with smokestacks, big mounds of wood chips, and warehouses. **Blue Heron Bistro** is a comfortable spot with good seafood and salads at Commercial Avenue and S Broadway (US 101 S); 541-267-3933.

■ CHARLESTON AND SOUTH SLOUGH *map page 101*

Coos Bay is a place to stop for lunch, to service a car, or re-up in the longshoreman's union. If you'd rather just kick back, head eight miles southwest to Charleston. It's a fishing town, and much smaller and easier to negotiate than its big city neighbor.

If you head due south on Seven Devils Road you'll reach **South Slough**. The broad estuary empties into the ocean at Charleston, and the tidal brew of salt and fresh water extends half a dozen miles south. Experienced canoeists can, with a little planning, use the slough's tides to travel north (towards Charleston and the ocean) with the outgoing tide and return to the launch site as the tide comes back in. When the tide's out, the waterway turns to mud flats sprinkled with golden brown diatoms. At high tide, perch, salmon, and crabs feed on the clams, shrimp, and worms that live buried in the mud. Farther up the slough's tributaries, narrow channels of water reach into agricultural flats and yield broad, low views of fields and fringes of forests.

Explore the slough on foot if you don't have a canoe. Several hiking trails visit different habitats; the best trail takes two hours to hike. It passes through coastal forest and 19th-century logging sites down to a boardwalk, which traverses a swamp—a wetland with trees—and a salt marsh—where no trees grow, but sharp-edged grasses brush bare legs, and the humidity is broken by wisps of ocean breeze. Coos County was once strewn with such marshes (the city of Coos Bay

(opposite) Oregon Dunes National Recreation Area, just north of Coos Bay.

was originally named Marshfield), but they've largely been diked and turned into "productive" land.

West of Charleston is a cliff-edged stretch of coastline with three state parks. Shore Acres, with its lush gardens, is the real surprise here.

■ BANDON *map page 101*

Between Coos Bay and Bandon, the soggy ground is planted in cranberries. The closer you get to Bandon, the greater your craving for a tart berry—something far removed from the gelatinous stuff that slides from a can at Thanksgiving. Autumn travelers may catch glimpses of a cranberry harvest. It starts when the fields are flooded. Then a sternwheeler-in-reverse floats through the flooded bog, the bow-mounted rotary blades clipping berries free like a waterborne push mower. The loose berries float, and the foliage begins to sink. Harvesters in chest waders shove log booms around the flooded bogs, corralling the berries to the side of the bog, where a conveyer belt shuttles the berries into trucks.

It's not necessary to base a culinary pilgrimage solely on cranberries. Bandon is also known for its cheddar cheese. The factory's small, and the sharp full-fat cheese surpasses Tillamook's in flavor.

Any town with such deep roots in food is off to the right start. Add in the artists and craftspeople who've been trickling into Bandon's old-town since the 1970s, and you've got a cultural boomtown on the coast. A couple of high quality craft galleries, good restaurants, and a youth hostel with an adjacent guest house give the town just enough artsy gentility to counter both the typical coastal shell-shack-and-myrtlewood syndrome and the soulless resortification that could have resulted from the fancy new Bandon Dunes golf course. Across the mouth of the Coquille River from Bandon, a restored stucco lighthouse marks the bar. Though fishing boats tie up in downtown Bandon, summer winds make the bar crossing hazardous. That danger combined with an ever-shortening commercial salmon season means that anglers generally choose to sail out of Coos Bay or Port Orford, or stay put for much of the summer.

To stay here try **Sea Star Hostel and Guest House** at 375 Second Street; 541-347-9632. Budget travelers should stay in the hostel; for a little more privacy and breakfast at the bistro, go for a guest room.

■ PORT ORFORD *map page 101*

Some of the coast's most spectacular views are from the bluff at Port Orford where Humbug Mountain, south of town, is often shrouded in misty clouds. The overlook may be lovely, but to get a real feel for the town head down to the port. Since there are no boat slips or rampway, a hoist plucks boats out of the water and lifts them onto the dock. Some boats stay at anchor, and boaters use dinghies to shuttle to and from shore. On the dock, divers hang around the fish cleaning table, wetsuits pulled down to the waist, long knives strapped to their legs. These aren't the commercial fishers; they're sport fishers going after rockfish, ling cod, and other bottomfish. Stacks of crab traps and mesh net traps suspended inside chickenwire cubes crowd one end of the dock—the latter are used to catch sablefish, or black cod.

Port Orford's name has long been identified with a tree—the Port Orford cedar. Its wood resembles that of a valuable, and now quite rare, Japanese tree, the hinoki cypress. Much of Oregon's Port Orford cedar harvest goes to Japan, where one tree will fetch up to $10,000. A virulent root fungus has destroyed entire drainages of cedars, but you can still see and smell these exquisitely fragrant trees at the **Grassy Knob Wilderness Area,** seven miles east of the Cape Blanco turnoff.

■ ROGUE RIVER AND GOLD BEACH

If it weren't for the Rogue River, Gold Beach would have disappeared as quickly as the gold found in its sands in the 1850s. (Floodwaters swept the beach clean of gold in 1861, though upstream mining continued for years.) Mail boats started making the upstream trip to Agness in 1895, when it took several days of rowing to travel the 32 miles upstream from Gold Beach; now, jet boats shoot upriver in two hours. Even with the river traffic and a narrow winding road linking it to Galice and Grants Pass, Agness is remote. Not far from the old wooden mercantile, a mowed airstrip crosses the road. Pick up the **Lower Rogue River Trail** near Lucas Lodge (just down from the airstrip) for a hike or mountain bike ride along remnants of a 19th-century road. Pass ospreys tending their nests along the green Rogue and giant banana slugs inching across the trail.

■ BOARDMAN STATE PARK   *map page 101*

Boardman State Park, north of Brookings, is a long strip with many waysides. Steep cliffs impede access to the beach, but many trails lead down to sheltered coves. These beaches are rarely crowded; venture a hundred yards past the parking lot and your companions will be birds, waves, and rocks. Scuff through the sand, numbing your ankles in the water, poke around the mussel-laden rocks. It's okay to gather up to 72 mussels a day (but check to make sure no signs warn of red tide or other contaminants); steam them up with butter, white wine, and garlic.

If, after a quiet beach walk, US 101 traffic seems too harrowing, turn east at Pistol River and drive the old highway (Carpenterville Road) past small ranches and abandoned gyppo logging operations. Pistol River got its name in 1853, when a guy dropped his gun into the water, and it's still the sort of place where, if something of that magnitude happens, you'll hear about it. (The big buzz about Pistol River now is that it has great wind and has begun to attract windsurfers.)

(above) The Glennesslin *was one of many ships to be lost along the rocky Oregon coast. (Columbia River Maritime Museum) Still in operation, the lighthouse at Heceta Head (opposite) was built in 1894 to warn mariners of the treacherous shores.*

■ BROOKINGS   *map page 101*

Brookings has fallen prey to the long strip sprawl of coastal towns, but off US 101 it's one of the coast's most spectacular areas. All winter long, it's the warmest spot in the state. (Of course, during the summer, coastal fogs settle in and make for spectacular botany and lousy tans.) The fishing port on the south side of the Chetco River (technically, this is the town of Harbor) is a good place to hang out and chat with the locals.

As logging and fishing jobs fall off, some people look for work in the lily fields south of town. (Brookings grows most of the world's Easter lilies.) Others go into the woods and pick brush, which they sell to florists' brokers for bouquet "greenery."

Gravel companies have been dredging the broad, shallow Chetco River for years, but it remains a pleasant waterway. Myrtlewood trees grow along its banks; their bay-like leaves can be used as a flavoring in stews. Up the coast in Coos Bay, the wood is fashioned into highly polished clocks, coffee tables, and salad bowls.

Follow North Bank Road up the Chetco to **Loeb Park,** flush with salmonberries and myrtlewood trees, then on to **Quail Prairie** on the edge of the Kalmiopsis Wilderness Area. It's a short hike in to a glacier-scratched red peridotite basin nesting Vulcan Lake. By the time you get here, you're far from the fringe of coastal fog and into the hot, dry summer zone characteristic of the Kalmiopsis. **Vulcan Lake** is a favorite swimming hole for Brookings residents, who also use it as a trailhead hub for day hikes deeper into the Kalmiopsis.

The huge 2002 Biscuit Fire burned throughout the Kalmiopsis, but the land is quickly recovering while debates rage about the logging of burned acreage within the forest's roadless areas.

A Japanese bomb was dropped on Mount Emily in 1942, and the bomb site is now a place of some local pride. The bomber pilot was a guest of honor at the azalea festival in the early 1960s, and the trail to the bomb site is the closest thing to a historical site/shrine you'll find on the south coast. To reach it, drive up South Bank Road and follow signs to the "bomb trail."

Powerful surf and rocky shores conspire to make the Oregon coastline a wild and dramatic place. At Shore Acres State Park near Coos Bay (opposite), vigorous waves pound the headlands.

LOGGERS

*A*s the trees fell and the hours passed, the three men grew accustomed to one another's abilities and drawbacks. Few words actually passed between them; they communicated with the unspoken language of labor toward a shared end, becoming more and more an efficient, skilled team as they worked their way across the steep slopes; becoming almost one man, one worker who knew his body and his skill and know how to use them without waste or overlap.

Henry chose the trees, picked the troughs where they would fall, placed the jacks where they would do the most good. And stepped back out of the way. . . . Hank did the falling and trimming, wielding the cumbersome chain saw tirelessly in his long, cable-strong arms, as relentless as a machine; working not fast but steadily, mechanically, and certainly far past the point where other fallers would have rested...

...Joe Ben handled most of the screwjack work, rushing back and forth from jack to jack, a little twist here, a little shove there, and whup! she's turning', tippin', heading out downhill! Okay—get down there an' set the jacks again, crank and un-crank right back an' over again. Oh yeah, that's the one'll do it. *Shooooom,* all the way, an' here comes another one, Andy old buddy, big as the ark... feeling a moun-tain of joyous power collecting in his back muscles, an exhilaration of faith rising with the crash of each log into the river.

—Ken Kesey, *Sometimes a Great Notion,* 1963

Giant Douglas firs such as this are rare sights nowadays. (Oregon Historical Society)

Mike Brownson, logger and co-owner of the Brownson Logging Company near Dillard.

COLUMBIA GORGE
MOUNT HOOD LOOP

COLUMBIA GORGE
MOUNT HOOD

◆ HIGHLIGHTS   *page*

◆ AREA OVERVIEW

The day-trip most deeply ingrained into the Portland psyche is that up the Columbia River, past steep basalt cliffs overflowing with waterfalls and verdant with ferns. At Hood River, turn south and head for Mount Hood. Glimpsed time and again from a distance, Hood can come to represent all things Oregonian. When you're actually on the mountain, the details—the cold streams, the wildflowers, the summer snowfields—are as intriguing as the big snowy triangle pointing up into the sky. Take in a sunset at Mount Hood's Timberline Lodge and return to Portland in the dark. There's plenty of reason to stretch this trip into a two-day excursion, with a night in the town of Hood River, at Timberline, or in a campground on Mount Hood's northern flank.

Climate: At the western end of the gorge, skies are frequently gray. Around Hood River the sun often breaks through the clouds and spring days can quickly warm to 80 degrees. With elevation things get colder. Up at Timberline Lodge snow can fall almost any time of year, although July and August are usually sunny and warm, with temperatures in the 70s.

Food & Lodging: Hood River has a wide selection of restaurants and accommodations, with the Columbia Gorge Hotel leading the pack in elegance and price. Other good places in which to spend the night or eat a meal are Edgefield, in Troutdale, and Timberline Lodge, high on Mount Hood.

■ OVERVIEW OF THE COLUMBIA RIVER GORGE

Mist may envelop the river, but rainbows are over almost every shoulder along the Columbia Gorge. As you travel the gorge, you'll notice it's fairly level. Lewis and Clark kept to this route, and so did a number of pioneers, although it was by no means an easy one.

Ancient lava flows laid down the dark layers of Columbia River basalt. Then, 10,000 years ago, an ice dam in northern Idaho backed up a huge lake over most of western Montana. Periodically, the dam would bob up, like an ice cube in a drink, releasing torrents of water across eastern Washington and through the Columbia River channel. The floodwaters scraped the basalt clean, leaving steep walls.

When Lewis and Clark floated down the Columbia in 1805, cedar plank long-houses up to 200 feet in length dotted the riverbanks. Cedars were also crafted into long canoes, and Chinook Indians (including Cascades, Wascos, and, on the Washington side, Wishrams) took the rapids in canoes.

Oregon Trail migrants preferred to portage their belongings past the river's roughest section after an 1842 wagon road was built around the five-mile-long Cascade rapids. Francis Chenoweth filed a claim and built a mule-drawn tramway along the north bank of the river. Soon the south shore also featured a portage rail-road. Portage railroads around rapids were spliced together, often using the wagon road as a railbed, and in 1883, formed part of a transcontinental line.

The Columbia River just barely squeezes through basalt cliffs at several points along the gorge, leaving little room for a roadway. In 1872, the Oregon legislature called for a wagon road between Troutdale and The Dalles, and a few stretches of the narrow road are still visible at Shellrock Mountain near milepost 52. But the road was no match for its setting; rock and mudslides crumbled it early on.

Sternwheelers could "float on mist," and they made it through some dodgy rapids and shoals, but railroad portages around the Cascades were essential until 1896, when the Cascade Locks, a 3,000-foot-long canal, cleared a path for boats. Sternwheelers could finally make it upstream to the Snake River. It's still possible to ride a sternwheeler along the Columbia River, but it's strictly a party boat now. Barges and tugs took over most of the river work in the 1940s, when being a tug captain was as glamorous a job as any Oregonian could hope for.

COLUMBIA GORGE
MOUNT HOOD

(following pages) The view of the Columbia River Gorge from Women's Forum Park looking towards Crown Point at sunset.

Sam Hill, son-in-law of the Great Northern Railway's James J. Hill, began scheming to build a road through the Columbia Gorge in the early 1900s. Hill was something of a dreamer, and his Maryhill, Washington home is now the **Maryhill Museum,** a funny half-cultured jumble of Rodins, Ukrainian Easter eggs, and chess sets in a huge, poured concrete Italianate mansion on the dry hills opposite Biggs Junction on Hwy 14, 360-773-3733. A few miles east of Maryhill, Hill built a cement-slab replica of Stonehenge and dedicated it to locals who died in World War I.

Hill hired Samuel Lancaster to build a riverside highway, and together they went on a European tour. They traveled through the Alps and drove Roman roads and thought of the rustic natural designs of the American Craftsman movement. When construction started, Lancaster worked with Italian–American stonemasons, whose arched guard rails still seem more graceful than bulky. The road was finished in 1916, and its remaining stretches are nearly as popular now as they were then.

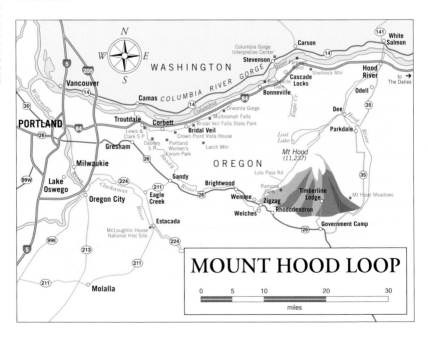

MOUNT HOOD LOOP

■ LOOP ROUTE

◆ SANDY RIVER

The Sandy River smelt runs, like many fish runs, are not what they used to be. But when the oily, pint-sized fish are running strong, they're scooped up with nets and dumped into garbage pails. Unfortunately, most families cannot eat an entire garbage pail full of smelt. In fact, both the memory and the aroma of one small meal of fried smelt seems to linger until the next run.

Fortunately, there's sustenance beyond smelt on the Sandy—Tad's Chicken and Dumplings, less than a mile from the Troutdale bridge, is a Sunday-dinner favorite. Or, forego a meal and stop at **Dabney State Park,** with riverside trails, fishing, and boat launches. When the water warms up, the Sandy's swimming holes fill up with local kids, and its modest rapids host floaters in inner tubes.

◆ CORBETT

Past Dabney, the scenic highway cuts away from the Sandy and heads through upland orchards to Corbett. The Columbia is finally visible at the Portland Women's Forum Park, a great vantage point for photographers, where round, blended green hills give way to blocky, dark basalt upstream.

The **Crown Point Vista House** is on the next bluff upstream from the park. The Vista House was dubbed the "$100,000 outhouse" when it was built in 1918, but nobody's ever disputed its great views up the gorge. The stocky stone octagon is an architectural oddity that works—picture windows are topped by streaky stained glass and a copper-green dome. A few historical displays share the space with vases of wildflowers.

◆ CROWN POINT TO MULTNOMAH FALLS

This section is the old highway at its best. The arched stone guard rails are softened by moss, and ferns grow in every interstitial niche. When the maples are newly leafed out and sun shines through the thin leaves, there's a splendid arboreal feeling. The trees are just as captivating in the fall, when they turn red and gold above the silver moneyplants lighting up the ground.

◆ MULTNOMAH FALLS   *map page 138*

Everybody stops here. The falls drop 620 feet, and they are unfailingly impressive. It takes an hour to hike to the top of the falls, and the trail continues on to Larch Mountain (another five miles uphill). Little exertion is required to see naturalist John Muir's favorite bird here—even in the iciest weather, American dippers plunge their faces into the stream at the base of the falls.

If you don't have time for more than a two-hour hike, try the **Horsetail Falls/ Oneonta Trail loop,** which has a nice mix of waterfalls and river views. From the tall spray-spitting plume at the scenic highway, it's half a mile uphill to the step-behind Upper Horsetail Falls. Giant wet slugs glide across a trail lined by spring-time trilliums and lavender bleeding heart. False Solomon's seal reaches long lily-leaved, flower-tipped arms toward shafts of light. The trail then follows a sun-struck ridge above the Columbia, where pikas, or rock rabbits, squeak from their rockslide homes. The short descent into the next drainage offers a look down

COLUMBIA GORGE
MOUNT HOOD

Multnomah Falls with a 620-foot drop is one of the highest waterfalls in the U.S.

*Part of the botanical preserve in Oneonta Gorge in the
Columbia River Gorge National Scenic Area.*

COLUMBIA GORGE
MOUNT HOOD

through the narrow Oneonta Gorge and a return to the highway. On the roadside walk back to the car, it's tempting to wander back into the **Oneonta Gorge.** If it's warm enough for wet feet, go with the urge; there's no place quite like this dark chasm, home to rare shade-loving plants.

The historic highway merges with Hwy 84 at Ainsworth State Park, but bicyclists and pedestrians can travel sections of the old highway between Tanner Creek (Exit 40) and Eagle Creek and between Hood River and Mosier.

◆ BONNEVILLE DAM   *map page 138*

The Bonneville Dam was one of the great Depression-era public works projects and a source of pride for decades. The Bonneville Power Authority hired Woody Guthrie for a month in 1941 to popularize the dam-building project. It turned into a song-a-day marathon. To feel the spirit of the times, pick up a copy of Guthrie's Columbia River songs (Portland's Music Millennium stores keep it in stock), and listen to it on the way up the Gorge. Bonneville and the other Columbia River dams generated huge amounts of electricity and spawned an aluminum industry, a notoriously power-thirsty business.

The dam's engineering is no doubt interesting to an occasional visitor, but the fish ladders and the navigation locks draw the masses to Bonneville. Barges and their tugs, sport fishers and Indians in outboard motorboats, and an occasional kayaker all lock up together, waiting for a flood of water to buoy them to the upriver side of the dam, or for the lock's plug to be pulled, lowering them downriver. If there's no action at the locks, head to the sub-basement fish-viewing window in the dam's visitor center. Official fish-counters sit in their own darkened cubicle, chronicling the salmon's decline. When salmon do swim past the windows, they're treated like champs. Everybody in the viewing room roots for them to make it back to spawning grounds.

Above the dam, anglers go for northern pikeminnow, officially declared an enemy of young salmon. The Bonneville Power Administration offers a bounty for every Columbia River pikeminnow turned in to damside monitors, hoping that in de-

In the 1930s, when the Bonneville Dam was built, Woody Guthrie was hired to sing its praises.

creasing the number of predators on the juvenile salmon, the impact of the dams will be blunted—an unlikely result, at best.

◆ EAGLE CREEK TRAIL

This trailhead is about a mile east of Bonneville, and is, after Multnomah Falls, the Gorge's most popular stop. In the spring, water streams down in dozens of makeshift falls, turning portions of the trail into a refreshing shower. Hikers mark the spring's wetness by the number of falls and the intensity of the wildflower display. Equisetum (horsetail fern), sword ferns, maidenhair ferns, and salmonberry bushes grow beneath maples and towering Douglas firs. When the sun hits right, flocks of little lavender butterflies mix up in hikers' legs. It's no place to bring an acrophobe—the trail's nearly

A Native American angler displays his Celilo Falls salmon.

always edged by a cliff, and it's downright dangerous to venture off the path.

◆ CASCADE LOCKS   *map page 138*

At Cascade Locks Marine Park, a grassy, relaxing riverside spot, the focus shifts back to the Columbia River. Slow down here and watch the river traffic—since Bonneville Dam has quieted this stretch of the river, boats pass around the lock. A footbridge spans the now obsolete 1896 lock. Below it, Indian dipnet platforms hang from guy wires like a window-washer's rigging above rushing water.

The sternwheeler *Columbia Gorge* departs from the Marine Park several times daily from June through October (during winter, it runs less frequently).

◆ BRIDGE OF THE GODS   *map page 138*

The Bridge of the Gods spans the Columbia at Cascade Locks. Actually, it's reckoned to be the second Bridge of the Gods—the first was a natural span over the Columbia. As the legend goes, two sons of the Great Spirit were in charge of the Columbia Gorge. Pahto ruled north of the river; his brother, Wy'East, controlled the southern bank. Both brothers were enchanted with the lovely Loo'wit, and they began to fight over her, hurling fiery rocks across the river. Their battle collapsed the existing rock bridge and provoked their father into turning his sons into basalt guardians of the Columbia. Pahto became Mount Adams, Wy'East became Mount Hood, and Loo'wit was turned into Mount St. Helens.

◆ HOOD RIVER   *map page 138*

Even when the west end of the gorge is clouded over, the sun often breaks through at Hood River. The climate here is nearly perfect for fruit trees, and the steep gorge walls funnel winds into a fury near Hood River, making it the windsurfing capital of the Northwest, if not the nation. The sport really does permeate the local culture. Wind reports are regular features on every radio station, and it's a great place to shop for a sailboard or wetsuit. An uncommon number of boardheads have settled here, and make good livings peddling windsurfing gear.

Windsurfing and its newly popular cousin, kiteboarding, are late-risers' sports; winds rarely pick up before noon. By late afternoon, the narrow beach at the Hood River Marina is thick with windsurfers and gawkers. Gawking is, incidentally, a perfectly respectable pursuit. If you feel tempted to windsurf, take a lesson before venturing into the water. The Columbia River is too big and too busy to risk being stranded in the channel, trying to figure how to return to shore.

After timber-king Simon Benson built Portland's Benson Hotel, he turned his sights upriver and built **Columbia Gorge Hotel** in 1921. For a really expensive (albeit good) breakfast or dinner, stop here. Lunches are only medium-expensive and the views are lovely. 4000 Westcliff Drive; 541-386-5566 or 800-345-1921.

To watch windsurfing on the river, try the comfortable, modern Best Western **Hood River Inn;** 1108 E. Marina; 541-386-2200. **Hood River Hotel** is a nicely restored old downtown hotel at 102 Oak Avenue (at First Street); 541-386-1900.

(left) The Columbia River near the town of Hood River is known as one of the windsurfing capitals of America.

COLUMBIA GORGE
MOUNT HOOD

FISHING CELILO FALLS

*R*ed Shirt had taken Danny to Celilo Village before The Dalles Dam flooded the falls. More than five thousand Indians came that year for the salmon fishing and the feast. They took turns dipnetting from the flimsy wooden platforms that extended over the churning whitewater. Most wore raingear to keep the mists from soaking their clothing, and they smoked their pipes upside down to keep the tobacco dry.

Danny and Red Shirt were Sammy Salwish's guests at the celebration. Danny was surprised to see Sammy feed his dog raw salmon because he thought salmon poisoning would kill her. Sammy grinned, explaining that Celilo dogs had developed an immunity over the years.

Red Shirt tried fishing from Sammy's platform, but he had been drinking and was too unsteady. Danny had no raingear and was soon shivering from fright and cold. The platform shuddered with the water's force, and the treacherous wind nearly blew him from the scaffold. When his father forced him to eat a salmon eye, Danny vomited and left the platform.

As the sun was setting, fishermen came off the platforms carrying their dipnets and gunnysacks filled with salmon. They cast dark shadows against the fiery mists, and it seemed to Danny they were walking out of campfires.

After supper, his belly stretched with salmon, roots, and strawberry pop, Danny listened to his father tease Sammy about going elk hunting in the Wallowa Mountains after the fishing sites had been destroyed.

—Craig Lesley, *River Song*, 1989

COLUMBIA GORGE
MOUNT HOOD

Indians platform fishing in the 1930s at Celilo Falls—since inundated by the lake behind The Dalles Dam. (Oregon Historical Society)

Bette's Place at 416 Oak Avenue is where the windsurfers chow down. **Big City Chicks** at 303 13th Street offers healthy, tasty food from around the world. At **Full Sail Brewing Company Tasting Room and Pub,** 506 Columbia, you can sit on the deck, look down on Interstate 84 and the Columbia River, and sip a Full Sail Ale (it's some of Oregon's best beer).

◆ SWIMMING THE COLUMBIA

People fret about the river's cleanliness because the Hanford Nuclear Reservation is a couple of hundred miles upstream, and has a history of leaking radioactivity. But hundreds of swimmers can't be dissuaded from crossing the river every Labor Day. Early in the morning, before boat traffic gets going, swimmers ride the stern-wheeler *Columbia Gorge* to the Washington side of the river, where they jump off the bow and swim one and a quarter miles back to Oregon. It's a ritual, not a race; call the Hood River Chamber of Commerce to register; 800-366-3530.

After a brisk swim across the Columbia, a tubful of hot sulfurous water may sound appealing. Over on the Washington side of the river, **Carson Hot Springs** is a classic way to warm up either from a swim or from the chill of a rainy-weather getaway. Attendants usher clients from claw-foot bathtub to cot (where a mummy-wrap in wool blankets encourages a good, cleansing sweat) to masseuse. It's a little scary the first time out, but the post-wrap euphoria keeps the bone-chilled and world-weary coming back for more; 509-427-8292.

◆ EAST OF HOOD RIVER   *map page 138*

From Hood River, Hwy 35 heads south up Mount Hood, and the freeway, Interstate 84, continues east. A surviving stretch of the old highway splits off the freeway at Mosier (17 miles east of Hood River) and climbs past cherry orchards, through scattered oak and pine trees, to the Rowena Plateau, where the transition from a wet west-slope habitat to a drier east-side environment is manifest. From the wildflower-fringed high plateau, it's all mounds and swales down to the river. Yellow daisy-like balsamroot and deep blue-violet broadleaf lupine, exclusive to the Gorge, grow on meadows spread out on top of basalt flows. The dry open views from the often-blustery Rowena trails are different from the typical dense, green gorge hike.

COLUMBIA GORGE
MOUNT HOOD

◆ SOUTH TO MOUNT HOOD

Hwy 35 heads south and uphill from Hood River's laid-back trendiness, toward orchard country. Before windsurfing arrived on the scene, Hood River meant apples and pears, and they still grow in force. The **Mount Hood Railroad** runs from Hood River south to Parkdale; it's a popular springtime trip, when snowy Mount Hood is the backdrop for pink and white blossoms. Call 541-386-3556 or 800-872-4661 for reservations.

The road wastes no time before beginning the long pull up Mount Hood. Stop at a fruit stand for a trunkload of apples and pears. **Rasmussen Farms** has a good farm store at 3020 Thomsen Road, 800-548-2243. Turn off at Parkdale toward a perfect canoeist's view of the mountain from the middle of Lost Lake. Little **Lost Lake Resort** is a fine place to take in the beauty of the mountain and has lakeside cabins, a restaurant, and canoe rentals; Forest Road 1340; 503-386-6366. For a daytrip from the resort, drive to Lolo Pass Road past flaming rhododendrons, hiking trails, and Mount Hood views.

■ MOUNT HOOD   *map page 138*

The erstwhile Wy'east has, in recent years, proved calmer than lovely Loo'wit. Mount Hood erupted sporadically through the 1800s but never with the devastating force of Mount St. Helens' 1980 blast. An 1859 *Oregonian* article reported:

> *I*t became hot about midday . . . in the evening occasional flashes of fire were seen. On Thursday night fire was plainly visible . . . A large mass on the northwest side (of Mount Hood) had disappeared, and an immense quantity of snow on the south side was gone.

Oregon Trail emigrants who chose the Barlow Road route from The Dalles to Oregon City enjoyed a close-up of the mountain, and learned, on the steep slopes, how to hold back a wagon to prevent it from nipping the heels of the animals.

Perhaps it's the ancestral memory of the Barlow Road, perhaps it's that wonderful vision off on the eastern skyline, but Portlanders have long looked to Mount Hood when they needed to feel intrepid.

Four Portlanders climbed 11,237-foot Mount Hood in 1857, and it caught on. Two hundred people climbed through sleet and thunder in 1894, the inaugural

Mount Hood seems to float above the Hood River Valley its summit rising to 11,237 feet.

climb of the Mazama Club. This mountain club is restricted to those who have climbed a glaciated Cascade peak. The Portland-based Mazamas still sponsor mountaineering classes and climbs; 503-227-2345.

Developers have long eyed Mount Hood; in the 1920s, the Mazamas fought against a tramline up to the peak. By 1937, there was nothing but applause for **Timberline Lodge**, built as a WPA project. Unemployed artisans were put to work fashioning beams from giant trees, carving newelposts into owls and bears, and weaving rugs and chair covers. (Workers lived below timberline, at Government Camp, and many of their bunkhouse cabins still stand, as charming as the lodge is grand.) There's now a separate, 1980s, concrete-bunker-style day lodge filled with contemporary crafts, ski rental shops, and snack bars. But Mount Hood savants know the second-floor bar in the old lodge has comfortable sofas, great sunset views down the Cascades, and a happy blend of rusticity and comfort for weary hikers and skiers. Off Hwy 26; 503-622-7979.

Built on the slopes of Mount Hood under the auspices of the Works Projects Administration, Timberline Lodge remains one of the nation's most elegant country resorts. (The lodge's "role" in Stanley Kubrick's film The Shining—*that of a terrifying Grand Hotel of the Damned—was not exactly "in character.") (Oregon Historical Society)*

Sunday climbs up Mount Hood's south face were popular into the 1940s, when hikers would wake up early, eat a big breakfast and pack sandwiches, drive to Timberline Lodge, lace on hobnail boots, shove a pair of sunglasses and some lampblack into a pocket, and set off uphill. At the final steep slope they were aided by a dangling rope and snow-carved steps.

People have become more cautious, and a Mount Hood ascent is no longer a Sunday afternoon outing. The safest time to climb the mountain is from May through early July. Climbers start from Timberline Lodge around 2 A.M., aiming to reach the summit by mid-morning, and be off the mountain when the afternoon sun increases the chance of an avalanche.

For those who prefer to see the horizon a little bit at a time, a 40-mile trail circles the mountain at timberline; pick up the trail at Timberline Lodge and walk the loop (allow a few days). Or, light out west to Paradise Park, a lavish alpine meadow five miles from the lodge. Continue another five and a half miles past a deep V of a chasm holding the cascading headwaters of the Sandy River to **Ramona Falls**, where basalt terraces split the creek into a multitude of thin falls, then funnel them back together at the bottom of the 100-foot drop. From Ramona Falls, it's a short hike out to the Zigzag Road (off US 26, and an easy hitch back to Timberline), or a 10-mile return to Timberline Lodge, or another few days around the mountain.

◆ Mount Hood Skiing

Downhill skiing and snowboarding runs through the summer at Timberline's above-timberline Palmer glacier snowfield. During the winter, **Mount Hood Meadows** overtakes Timberline in popularity—it's just east of the pass (on Hwy 35), which frequently means good weather in Oregon's westside/eastside precipitation sweepstakes.

Cross-country skiers will enjoy the groomed Teacup Lake trails, just across Hwy 35 from Mount Hood Meadows. The Trillium Lake trail, about a mile east of Government Camp, is, after an initial slope, a flat and easy loop. More advanced cross-country skiers head for Bennett Pass and the great views from the "Terrible Traverse." Rent cross-country ski gear in Government Camp. For ski reports call Timberline at 503-222-2211, or Mount Hood Meadows at 503-227-SNOW.

OREGON TRAIL, 1853

Wednesday, June 1st It has been raining all day long and we have been traveling in it so as to be able to keep ahead of the large droves. The men and boys are all soaking wet and look sad and comfortless. (The little ones and myself are shut up in the wagons from the rain. Still it will find its way in and many things are wet; and take us all together we are a poor looking set, and all this for Oregon. I am thinking while I write, "Oh, Oregon, you must be a wonderful country." Came 18 miles today.)

Wednesday, June 15th . . . passed Independence Rock this afternoon, and crossed Sweetwater River on a bridge. Paid 3 dollars a wagon and swam the stock across. The river is very high and swift.

Wednesday, July 27th Another fine cow died this afternoon. Came 15 miles today, and have camped at the boiling springs, a great curiosity. They bubble up out of the earth boiling hot. I have only to pour water on to my tea and it is made.

Monday, August 1st . . . This evening another of our best milk cows died. Cattle are dying off very fast all along this road. We are hardly ever out of sight of dead cattle, on this side of the Snake River. This cow was well and fat an hour before she died. Cut the second cheese today.

Monday, August 8th We have to make a drive of 22 miles, without water today. Have our cans filled to drink. Here we left unknowingly our Lucy behind, not a soul had missed her until we had gone some miles, when we stopped a while to rest the cattle; just then another train drove up behind us with Lucy. She was terribly frightened and so were some more of us when we found out what a narrow escape she had run . . . . The little ones have curled down and gone to sleep without supper. Wind high, and it is cold enough for a great coat and mittens.

Friday, August 19th Quite cold this morning, water frozen in the buckets. Traveled 13 miles over very bad roads without water. After looking in vain for water, we were about to give up as it was near night, when husband came across a company of friendly Cayuse Indians about to camp, who showed him where to find water. The men and boys have driven the cattle down to water and I am waiting for water to get supper. This forenoon we bought a few potatoes from an Indian, which will be a treat for our supper.

Thursday, September 1st . . . we have encamped not far from the Columbia River. Made a nice dinner of fried salmon. Quite a number of Indians were camped around us, for the purpose of selling salmon to the emigrants.

Thursday, September 8th . . . There is very little chance to turn out of this road, on account of timber and fallen trees, for these mountains are a dense forest of pines, fir, white cedar or redwood (the handsomest timber in the world must be here in these Cascade Mountains). Many of the trees are 300 feet high and so dense to almost exclude the light of heaven. . . . We have camped on a little stream called Sandy.

Tuesday, September 13th . . . here we are in Oregon making our camp in an ugly bottom, with no home, except our wagons and tent. It is drizzling and the weather looks dark and gloomy . . .

Friday, September 17th In camp yet. Still raining. Noon—It has cleared off and we are all ready for a start again, for some place we don't know where . . .

A few days later my eighth child was born. After this we picked up and ferried across the Columbia River, utilizing skiff, canoes and flatboat to get across, taking three days to complete. Here husband traded two hoke of oxen for half section of land with one-half acre planted to potatoes and a small log cabin and lean-to with no windows. This is the journey's end.

—Diary of Amelia Knight, 1853

COLUMBIA GORGE
MOUNT HOOD

Frontier camping. (Oregon Historical Society)

CENTRAL OREGON

◆ HIGHLIGHTS

◆ AREA OVERVIEW

Central Oregon is a volcanic tapestry, edged with towering peaks and basalt cliffs, and textured with geometrically perfect cinder cones. Forests, mountain lakes, and rivers embroider glints of blue and piney green; skiers, floaters, and anglers skid and cast across this rugged quilt.

Reminders of a volcanic past are everywhere. Volcanic peaks dominate clear skies, and the lava underfoot may not even have a dusting of soil covering it. Most of central Oregon's lava topping was laid down 14 to 16 million years ago during a burst of volcanism so intense that lava covered all but the tips of the Blue and Wallowa mountains. All this foreshadowed the birth of the Cascade volcanoes.

The high spine of the Cascades defining central Oregon's western boundary began when the oceanic plate took a dive beneath the North American continental plate. The friction generated heat; lava got cooking, and eventually poured from a chain of volcanoes. Mount Hood, Mount Jefferson, Three Fingered Jack, Mount Washington, the Three Sisters, Broken Top, Mount Bachelor, Mount Thielson, Mount Mazama (now, in a truncated form, Crater Lake), and Mount McLoughlin are the high Cascade peaks. These high peaks are ages younger than the low western Cascades, worn-down piles of ash and lava, just off their western shoulders.

For a headlong pitch into big-time scenery, central Oregon's Cascade peaks can't be beat. Yet in some of the region's more level spots, the air is so charged that the mountains drop to the background and a traveler stops short at the prospect of such pristine space. On the right days, when the strong sun is foiled by a few clouds, and the light becomes dramatic, the Metolius headwaters or the Crooked River canyon at Smith Rock are as mesmerizing as anyplace on Earth.

Climate: Summers are hot, winters are cold, and flash floods can follow drought on the east side of the Cascades. Tourist bureaus say the sun shines 310 days a year, but plenty of snow falls from these supposedly cloudless skies, especially at higher elevations. Winter daytime temperatures are typically in the high 30s, summer afternoons in the 80s. Some spots, notably Smith Rock State Park, can easily hit 90 on a summer afternoon.

Food & Lodging: There are more out-and-out resorts here than in any other part of the state, and they run the gamut, from funky little log cabin resorts on a mountain lake to upscale Sunriver condos.

Paulina Lake at sunset in Newberry Crater National Volcanic Monument.

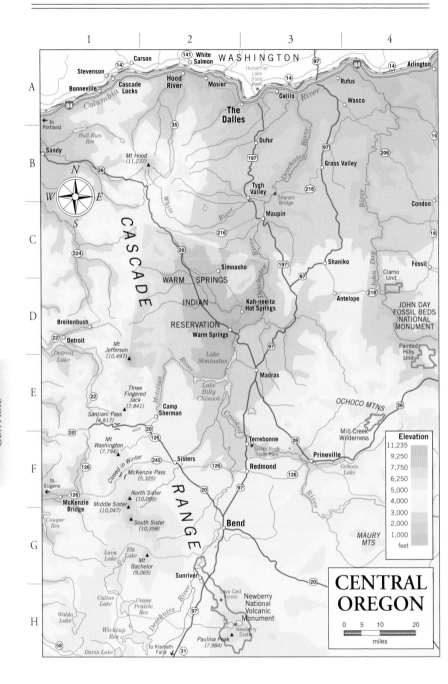

CENTRAL OREGON

■ THE DALLES *map opposite, A/B-2/3*

At central Oregon's northern edge, the Columbia River divides Oregon from Washington and hacks a level path through the Cascade mountains as it travels west to the Pacific. Back before French-Canadians named the Columbia's basalt-walled narrows after giant Gaulic flagstone gutters ("les dalles"), The Dalles was called Winquatt, a "place encircled by rock cliffs."

For Indians, this was a prized fishing area. Salmon resting in eddies and pools were easy dipnet or spear targets, and once caught, valuable currency in a big trade mart. Traders were drawn to Winquatt from all over Oregon, bringing items from across the West: Minnesota pipestone, Southwestern turquoise, Vancouver Island dentalium, Alaskan copper, and Puget Sound clams, mussels, and whale products.

Two main groups of Indians lived on the Columbia's south shore: Sahaptin-speakers and Chinook-speakers. (The Chinookian language is not the same as Chinook jargon, a pidgin language that developed because so many languages were spoken in such a small area. Chinook jargon is based on a pared-down Chinookian vocabulary and has words borrowed from English, French, and other Indian languages.) Several Sahaptin-speaking tribes wintered in wind-sheltered spots just south of the Columbia. During the warmer months, they fished the river or went farther south to hunt and gather roots and berries on the Columbia plateau. Among the Sahaptin speakers were the Tenino, who lived just east of Winquatt, and Wyams around the mouth of the Deschutes, just above Celilo Falls. A tribe later called the John Day lived near the mouth of that river; and the Tygh lived up the Deschutes and in Tygh Valley. All the mid-Columbia tribes were traders (especially the Chinook-speaking Wascos, who lived west of The Dalles), had cultural ties to downriver Chinook people, and were considered particularly worldly, status-conscious business people.

Explorers Lewis and Clark were the first whites to travel along this stretch of the Columbia, and their visit went well. The Indians were used to traders stopping by, and the Corps of Discovery brought intriguing people with good stories (told through sign language and a long chain of translators) and out-of-the-ordinary trade items.

The tribes of north central Oregon stayed on good terms with early white settlers and Indians did a brisk business ferrying Oregon Trail pioneers through the Columbia River rapids. But as settlers from the east wanted more land, they set up a territorial government and legal structure that allowed them to push the Indians onto a reservation. Oregon's Superintendent of Indian Affairs, Joel Palmer, was charged with forging treaties with the Indians. Between 1853 and 1855 he signed 11 treaties that took most of the tribal land in western Oregon and the Columbia Plateau away from the Indians. In 1855 the Warm Springs Reservation was created, throwing land around the Columbia and Deschutes rivers open to white settlement and forcing tribes away from the big rivers.

During the late 1800s, when steamboats plied the Columbia, The Dalles was a bustling stop on the trip up from Portland. Wheat from eastern Oregon was transported here, where it was transferred onto Portland-bound boats, and the town appeared prosperous and respectably staid. Rudyard Kipling rode a steamer up the Columbia to The Dalles in 1898 and reported that "all the inhabitants seemed to own a little villa and one church apiece." Later that evening, he went to the hotel bar and raised an eyebrow at the drinking, swearing, and "prurient servant-girl-slush yarns" that The Dalles residents indulged in after sundown.

Now, there's a certain sadness to The Dalles, a sense that it was at its most exciting in its Winquatt incarnation, when the river raged, tens of thousands of salmon jumped, and people came from all over looking for a fair trade. Now, standing beside the backwaters of **The Dalles Dam**, there's a tugging sense that the power of that lost world can never be equaled by all the dam's kilowatt hours.

◆ THE DALLES DAM   *map page 156, A/B-2/3*

To make the most of your visit, stop in at the **The Dalles Visitor Information Center** at 404 W Second Street; 541-296-2231 or 800-255-3385. Also, the Dalles Dams Visitor Center (north and east of Interstate 84, exit 87) offers a look at the dam's history, as well as rock carvings that were removed before the dam was built.

Cherry canneries, quiet most of the year, come up to the riverbank edge of downtown. Early in the summer, they whir into action, and The Dalles hums with business from migrant pickers who come to town. The Dalles has escaped the gentrification that's crept up the gorge—it's a no-nonsense place, stuck tight to the basalt, with half an eye cast across Interstate 84, Oregon's big east-west highway, to the Columbia.

A fine side trip from The Dalles lies across the river. At **Horsethief Lake State Park**, a trail leads to more riverbank petroglyphs that escaped the floodwaters of the dam. Vandalism has forced the closure of the trail, but the park ranger still leads tours on Fridays and Saturdays; for reservations call 509-767-1159. Here, the petroglyph called Tsagigla'lal, or She Who Watches, forever watches over the river. The Wishram Indians, a Chinook tribe that lived here on the Columbia's north bank, told this story about her:

> *A* woman had a house where the village of Nixlu'idix was later built [present-day Wishram, or Spedis]. She was chief of all who lived in this region. That was long ago, before Coyote came up the river and changed things, and people were not yet real people.
>
> After a time Coyote in his travels came to this place and asked the inhabitants if they were living well or ill. They sent him to their chief, who lived up in the rocks, where she could look down on the village and know all that was going on.
>
> Coyote climbed up to her home and asked: "What kind of living do you give these people? Do you treat them well, or are you one of those evil women?"—"I am teaching them how to live well and build good houses," she said. "Soon the world is going to change," he told her, "and women will no longer be chiefs. You will be stopped from being a chief."
>
> Then he changed her into a rock, with the command, "You shall stay here and watch over the people who live at this place, which shall be called Nixlu'idix."
>
> All the people know that Tsagigla'lal sees all things, for whenever they are looking up at her those large eyes are watching them.

■ COLUMBIA PLATEAU *map page 156, B-2/3*

From The Dalles, US 197 climbs away from the river south to the Columbia plateau, where the light bounces off wheat fields with a high bright glow, and the spaces get big in a hurry. This road leads from the ancestral riverside home of the mid-Columbia tribes to their current Warm Springs Reservation.

Drive south as far as the crossroads town of Tygh Valley, overlooked by rimrock and home of the mid-May all-Indian rodeo, then turn east, and stop at the **White River Falls State Park.** A triple-tiered waterfall splashes down to the stony bones of a hydroelectric power plant—it's lovely in an eerie, ruined way, as though a river finally won a round in its match with technology. The road continues, descending through dry canyons to the Deschutes River to Sherar's Bridge.

Sherar's crosses a frothing river at the bottom of high canyon walls, topped off by a wedge of sky that promises to grow huge and blue at the gorge's top edge. What gives this spot spirit as well as beauty is the work that happens here—it's one of the few remaining Indian dipnet fishing spots.

Rickety-looking platforms, many accessorized with a kitchen chair or two, reach out over rapids; tribal fishers snare salmon with long-handled nets. Warm Springs members have struggled to keep this tribal tradition going. Dams have shut down many dipnet sites and destroyed much of the habitat of the salmon themselves.

◆ MAUPIN   *map page 156, C-3*

From the east bank of Sherar's Crossing, the road south to Maupin is a nearly continuous fishing riffle and campground. Maupin, built on a mesa-like bench above the river, is a close-to-perfect place to fish, float, or sit and watch the play of light on the Deschutes. It's illegal to fish the Lower Deschutes from a boat, but anglers are free to engage in plenty of thigh-strengthening wading as they cast into the fast Deschutes water. Steelhead, wild trout, and salmon keep anglers busy year-round. In the summer, Maupin's river outfitters run whitewater trips down the Deschutes (see page 293); come fall, the town overflows with hunters. To stay in lodgings with a great riverside location next to city park, try **Imperial River Company** at 304 Bakeoven Road; 541-395-2404.

■ WARM SPRINGS AND VICINITY   *map page 156, D-2*

In 1855, the **Warm Springs Reservation** was allotted to the Tenino, Tygh, John Day, and Wyam people, who lost land along the Columbia and lower Deschutes rivers. These tribes are now, together, called "Warm Springs." They were soon joined by the Wascos, and later, by some Northern Paiutes from the northern Great Basin. Though the Warm Springs and Wasco people were used to being neighbors on the Columbia, there was long-standing enmity between the Columbia River tribes and the Paiutes. In the 20th century, the reservation's three tribes banded together legally—the Confederation of Warm Springs Indians includes the Warm Springs, Wasco, and Paiute tribes.

As part of the 1855 treaty, the river tribes retained fishing rights on the Columbia and Deschutes rivers. When The Dalles Dam flooded sacred Celilo Falls

Indian dancer at Pi-Ume-Sha Treaty Days Celebration on the Warm Springs Indian Reservation.

fishing sites in 1957, the federal government paid the confederated tribes $4 million in restitution. The tribes commissioned an economic study, then began investing the restitution money in land and businesses. A plywood mill and sawmill, a hydroelectric dam on the Deschutes, clothing companies, and a construction company have been the result. The tribes bought out all the private holdings within the reservation, including the hot springs that now form the core of the Kah-Nee-Ta resort.

Kah-Nee-Ta (root-digger) was named after a woman who once lived in the Warm Springs Valley. Now, it's an upscale resort, with 168-degree water diverted into an enormous swimming pool. The dry country has been greened up enough for a golf course, but there's no hiding the raw, essential beauty, awash with punchy scents of pine and juniper, and complemented by views of Mount Hood and Mount Jefferson.

At **Kah-Nee-Ta,** you can stay in a tepee or a regular room, and enjoy the hot-springs swimming pool, golf, tennis, fishing, salmon bakes, and a casino. 541-553-1112 or 800-831-0100.

More traditional activities, both spiritual and economic, still go on. Fishing platforms at The Dalles and Sherar's Bridge are used, though they yield fewer salmon than they used to. For tribal fishers, it's a balance between a traditional economy and preserving the runs. Too often now, it's necessary to let the fishing platforms sit empty over the river so that the remaining salmon have a chance to spawn. The season's first salmon are feted, blessed, then eaten at a ritual dinner, but as far as ritual celebrations go, since the establishment of the Warm Springs Reservation, the First Salmon Feast has been supplanted by the Root Festival.

In the spring, the Root Festival draws celebrants from across the Northwest. Honored tribal members dig the tuberous *piyaxi* (bitterroot). Then, after several days' preparation, the roots are cooked, as dances are performed. When the meal is presented, initial sips of water and bites of food are taken as the name of each food is called out. Once the first ritual bites have been taken, everybody chows down. In June, Pi-Ume-Sha celebrates the 1855 treaty and pride in the reservation with a pow-wow and rodeo. Non-tribal members are welcome at these events, but it's important to remember that they're not "shows" put on for entertainment.

Warm Springs Museum started buying cultural artifacts from tribal members in the late 1960s. By the time the museum opened in 1993, an unparalleled collection of beadwork and basketry had been amassed. The museum presents the reservation's cultural context in a way that's more immediate and manageable than just endless displays of artifacts. The building, on US 26 in the town of Warm Springs, is handsome and well designed. Its value goes beyond that for tribal members, who recognize the symbolism of the reservation's three tribes in every feather-bustle doorhandle and basketweave wall panel and see the high-tech video and audio displays as a way of keeping their culture vital and accessible. For a non-tribal visitor, this is a great introduction. Call 541-553-3331 for information.

The Kah-Nee-Ta Resort features campground teepees as well as a comfortable lodge.

■ PRINEVILLE AND THE OCHOCO MOUNTAINS *map page 156, E/F-3*

The rolling, juniper-studded road from Redmond to Prineville looks over chaparral to the Ochoco Mountains, pale hills patched with dense purple-green forests. When the road drops off steep rimrock and plunges into the Crooked River Valley, the sky suddenly seems very far away. **Prineville,** at the base of the flat-topped hills, is dominated by a complex of aqua metal prefabs—the world headquarters of Les Schwab Tires. Downtown are some reminders of the past—a grand, old, dark stone courthouse and an old house that's now home to the Bowman Historical Museum.

In Oregon the lumber business runs in the family. When Ed Wilson (left) retired, his son Ron (right) took over as sales manager at Ochoco Lumber Co. in Prineville. Their cousin John Shelk is president. All of them, including a visitor (center), are related to the founders of the old Clarke Wilson Lumber Company in Linnton.

CENTRAL

Prineville grew up in the 1870s around Barney Prine's ranch house store and was the first real town in central Oregon. Even though there weren't any other towns to choose from, some visitors reported that Prineville lacked a certain *je ne sais quoi*. One early observer of Barney Prine's empire sneered that Prine was "all of one day building it" and that "his liquor consisted of a case of Hostetter's Bitters."

Between the 1870s, when the first ranchers came, and 1885, when laws were proclaimed and courts established, vigilantes ruled. They killed seven men (who deserved it, no doubt), sparing them the agony of a courtroom trial.

Even after sheriffs, lawyers, and judges moved in, the do-it-yourself spirit lingered. A hundred years ago cattlemen were proud to announce they'd slaughtered 10,000 sheep (called "woolly monsters," "hooved locusts," and "range maggots," they were, indeed, shot down by the hundreds, often along with their herders).

Today's backroad traveler should head nine miles east of town on US 26, and take Mill Creek Road (Road 33) from the east end of the Ochoco Reservoir toward the Ochocos' rounded hills. Follow signs to **Stein's Pillar,** where a three-and-a-half mile round-trip hike to the landmark phallic tower of volcanic ash and tuff yields plenty of views onto the Cascade peaks. Wildcat Campground, a couple of miles past the Stein's Pillar turnoff on Road 33, is the jumping-off spot for the quiet **Mill Creek Wilderness Area,** where big ponderosa pines reign— though "ochoco" is the Paiute word for willow. During the winter, when snow covers Forest Service roads, the Ochocos become a gentle, cross-country skiing paradise. Particularly hardy souls can ice fish on Ochoco Reservoir.

■ SMITH ROCK *map page 156, F-2/3*

As it heads west from Prineville, the Crooked River cuts through **Smith Rock State Park.** (US 97 travelers will reach it by turning east at Terrebone—there are plenty of signs for the park.) Half the fun at Smith Rock is the people-watching. From a distance, red-orange rock faces and pinnacles are traced against deep blue sky; closer in, the cliffs are speckled with rock climbers, inching upward through prisms of pure color. Somehow their sunburned legs and muscular shoulders don't detract from the luminosity.

A meander down the Crooked River's south bank follows a low rimrock ledge; on the north bank, a trail and some climbers squeeze in between the river and the cliffs. For most visitors, Monkey Face and Morning Glory Wall are best seen from the bottom up. There's a good network of trails and some easy rock scrambles for non-climbers. Hike the riverbank trail to the base of Monkey Face and scramble up just until the Cascade peaks come into view. If this isn't enough, call First Ascent or Timberline Mountain Guides *(see page 293)*.

Several groups offers services to climbers at Smith Rock *(see page 294 for a list of services)*.

One of the pleasures of a visit to Smith Rock is climber-watching.

(previous pages) The Crooked River meanders through Smith Rock State Park.

A railroad bridge over the 320-foot-deep Crooked River gorge near Terrebone was a tough bit of engineering and construction when it was built in 1911, brokered by equally tough politicking. Crews from both the Great Northern and the Union Pacific railroads worked from opposite sides of the river to determine which rail line would control the way to central Oregon markets. Sabotage became commonplace; workers would swim the river at night and explode their rivals' supply of dynamite. Occasional gunshots were fired across the canyon, though no one was ever hit. An 11th-hour truce called for the Great Northern crew to finish the span but for the two lines to share the use of the completed bridge.

True crime buffs and

A precarious rope ladder is used by workers building a rail bridge over the Crooked River in 1911. (Oregon Historical Society)

CENTRAL

legal scholars know the neighboring highway bridge as the place where a distraught woman threw her children into the river in 1960. Then-governor Mark Hatfield couldn't abide putting a woman to death and pardoned her. (The voters soon abolished capital punishment, but restored the death penalty in the 1980s.) The rest stop here offers a spectacular view—peer over the dizzying gorge and imagine railroad builders scaling rope ladders up and down the canyon walls.

■ SISTERS AND VICINITY *map page 156, F-2*

Sisters is a sprightly place. It *feels* high and Western, with its namesake trio of snow-capped peaks, once called Faith, Hope, and Charity, now North, Middle, and South Sister, in the town's backyard.

Sisters is written up in travel magazines as a "Western theme town," but it's more than that. Real ranchers and cowboys stick out pretty easily from the tourists flocking the false-front shops. For fashion and culture purists, Leavitt's Western Wear is a reliable place to buy duds for the mid-June Sisters' rodeo.

Leavitt's customers include llama wranglers from the 30-some (and counting) llama ranches in the Sisters-Prineville-Bend area. These fleecy ruminants have a status never granted to their sheep kin. Llama ranchers are an easygoing lot, ready to scout the big llama exhibits at the Crook County Fair (third weekend of August in Prineville) for the latest breeding and marketing trends. The animals are raised to pack gear on wilderness trips, though all over rural Oregon they do double duty as lawn ornaments. The Hinterland Ranch, east of Sisters on Hwy 20, is the biggest llama outfit, and their herd is usually visible from the road. On the same stretch of road, you may also see an emu ranch.

From Sisters, two very different roads cut west across the Cascades, one through lava fields and the other through a pine forest. Southwest-bound Hwy 242 climbs to **McKenzie Pass,** closed for about half the year, when cross-country skiers and snowmobilers gain access. For the rest of the year, McKenzie Pass offers a view of windswept lava fields that look like plowed soil crusted over. Parts of the flow are only 400 years old. Just 30 years ago, these lava fields stood in for the moon, when astronauts practiced landing and walking on the lunar-like surface here. (Apollo astronauts left a central Oregon lava rock on the moon, in exchange for the moon rocks they ferried back to Earth.)

The Pacific Crest Trail crosses the road at the pass. During the summer, hike it southbound along a ridge running the west slopes of the lava-strewn, wildflower-lit, and glaciated **Three Sisters** peaks. North Sister is the oldest. The Middle and South Sisters are younger and less sculpted. South Sister, at 10,358 feet, is the highest of the three; there's a crater with a small lake at the top. (The best trail to the peak starts from the Cascade Lakes Highway.)

The forested road, US 20, the Santiam Pass road, leaves Sisters and heads northwest through pine forests. A few miles from town, just west and north of Black Butte, is the casual paradise of the **Metolius River.** Unlike most rivers, which have uncertain starts in trickles of mountain snowmelt, the Metolius flows in a big rush from some rocks at the base of Black Butte. With clear, piney air, Mount Jefferson in the background, and, during the fall, kokanee spawning at the headwaters, this area is searingly beautiful. The Metolius runs 30 miles through a volcano-laid, glacier-scoured basin before it's swallowed up by Lake Billy Chinook. Float or fish the river (campgrounds provide the best access), but stay to the south bank—much of the northern side is on restricted Warm Springs Reservation land.

To eat in Sisters try **Bronco Billy's Ranch Grill** at 190 E Cascade (at First); 541-549-7427. **Papandrea's Pizza** at 442 E Cascade serves tasty thick-crust pizza popular with the locals. To lay back and enjoy the outdoors in a luxury setting, try **Black Butte Ranch.** It offers hotel rooms, condominiums, and houses; horseback riding, golf, and tennis, and its lodge restaurant is the area's most elegant, with views that are at least as good as the food. 13653 Hawksbeard; 541-595-6211 or 800-452-7455.

♦ CAMP SHERMAN AND THE METOLIUS RIVER   *map page 156, E/F-2*

Camp Sherman, just downstream from the Metolius headwaters, is a minor mecca for fly anglers. Fish thrive in the clear, 46-degree water. Wild bull (Dolly Varden) and rainbow trout share the stream with brown and brook trout, whitefish, and kokanee salmon. The Metolius was once full of chinook salmon, but Round Butte Dam blocked their runs to and from the sea and effectively killed the entire anadromous population in 1966. (Anadromous fish are born in fresh water, spend much of their adult life at sea, and return to their home river to spawn.) The remaining salmon are kokanees, landlocked sockeyes. Stop for a snack at the Camp Sherman store and linger at the riverside deck, or venture downstream to the Wizard Fish Hatchery, renowned for its spectacular setting and tank of oddball fish.

Good places to stay are **Metolius River Lodges,** which have a beautiful riverside site with well-kept but rustic cabins; 541-595-6290. **Metolius River Resort** is a fancier place to stay in Camp Sherman; call 541-595-6281.

(following pages) Canoeing on Sparks Lake with South Sister Peak beyond.

CENTRAL

■ BEND AND VICINITY *map page 156, G-2/3*

Bend is the hub of central Oregon and a good place to pause before exploring the eastern flanks of central Oregon's Cascade peaks and the high lava plateaus.

Since the turn of the last century, people have moved to Bend to be near the mountains and out of the rain. Rails were laid to Bend in 1911, and within five years, trains were shuttling ponderosa pines into and out of two big new mills on the Deschutes. Tracks went out to the logging sites, where loggers and their families lived in cabins trundled from site to site by rail. Scandinavian timber workers started skiing around town in the early 1920s, and the sport caught on. Outdoorsy Californians and western Oregonians began moving here in the 1970s and the boom continues.

From the moment you arrive in Bend, people will ask if you've been to the **High Desert Museum** (six miles south of Bend on US 97, 541-382-4754). Don't skip it—it's a good introduction to central and eastern Oregon history and ecology. The natural history exhibits are as good as everyone claims, but the real surprise is the sophisticated diorama exhibit. No grade school shoe-box displays here; birdsongs and the scent of sage envelop a marshside Paiute wickiup, and the trapper's tent smells like dirt. More than anything, it'll make you want to get out and do some exploring. Outdoor exhibits of river otters and porcupines get you out walking, and agreeing with Donald Culross Peattie who once said: "It is an aroma rosinous and timbern, that pervades much of the life of the west, and many towns, like, Bend, Oregon are perpetually steeped in its wholesome zestful odor."

If you've come to fish or raft, try **Ouzel Outfitters** in Bend, 800-788-7238, for trips on the Deschutes and other Oregon rivers. Stop by the **Fly Box** at 1293 NE Third St, 541-388-3330, to stock up on gear.

Deschutes Brewery and Public House at 1044 NW Bond offers good pasta, seafood, and burgers served with excellent Black Butte Porter or Mirror Pond Pale Ale. The locals' favorite "fancy restaurant" (remember, this is Oregon, so you don't have to dress up) is **Pine Tavern Restaurant** at 967 NW Brooks. Its great woodhewn building is at the foot of Oregon Avenue. Make reservations. 541-382-5581. **Cafe Rosemary** a tiny, spare cafe which has every detail just so, especially the food; 1110 NW Newport Ave., 541-317-0276.

If you can afford to stay at one of the country inns nearby, the tranquility and scenery will be worth it. **Rock Springs Guest Ranch** is a lovely, well-run spot just outside Bend, with horseback riding, fishing, tennis, swimming pool. Price includes full board; 64201 Tyler Road; 541-382-1957.

Inn of the Seventh Mountain is a full-scale resort offering any activity you could want, and is as close as you can stay to Mount Bachelor. Century Drive, five miles west of Bend; 541-382-8711 or 800-452-6810.

■ MOUNT BACHELOR *map page 156, G-2*

Mount Bachelor (first called "The Bachelor," then "Bachelor Butte," until the Chamber of Commerce decided to elevate its status) is 20 minutes from town on Century Drive (aka the Cascade Lakes Highway), 9,065 feet high, and has alpine slopes and cross-country ski trails. Separate lodges for downhill and cross-country skiers offer food and warmth, but no overnight accommodations are available. (Most skiers stay in Bend; the Inn of the Seventh Mountain, a condo-cum-motel, is closest to Bachelor's slopes.) The ski season is long and powdery: skiers know Bachelor as the ultimate intermediate mountain, with not-too-scary blue runs right from the top of the mountain. Expert skiers and snowboarders should ride the Northwest Express lift for access to challenging terrain. Bachelor usually opens around Thanksgiving and has snow well through the spring. Come winter, casual hikers become devoted, obsessive skiers, spending winter weekdays fixated on weather reports, and weekends on the trails or slopes. Call Mount Bachelor at 800-829-2442 for general information; 541-382-7888 for a ski report.

Sunriver Resort, on Hwy 97, 15 miles south of Bend, 541-593-1221 or 800-547-3922, was planned to blend in with the natural surroundings, and it does a credible job. You'll find three golf courses, 28 tennis courts, and 26 miles of paved bikeways. Sunriver maintains its own nature center with displays and classes.

The mid-May **Pole Pedal Paddle race** is one of Bend's defining cultural institutions. Several thousand contestants start out on Mount Bachelor's downhill ski slopes, swoosh down to a cross-country ski circuit, then hop on bikes for a 22-mile ride to the Deschutes, where it's a five-mile riverside run to kayaks and canoes, which racers paddle to a final sprint through Bend's Drake Park. For most participants, it's a relay race, though individuals are welcome to race the entire course. For information call 541-388-0002.

CENTRAL

Mount Bachelor ski area.

■ CASCADE LAKES *map page 156, H-1/2*

A road to the Cascade Lakes area southwest of Bend was started in 1912. Originally built to facilitate firefighting and forest ranger business rather than recreational pursuits, it's now part of the Cascade Lakes scenic byway and a great long-cut alternative to busy US 97 (or it can be linked with 97 to make a full daytrip from Bend). The paved-road tour starts in downtown Bend near Drake Park, passes a thicket of condos and resorts, and begins climbing. Look for the Swampy Lakes area to the right, a maze of mountain bike and cross-country ski trails. (The Nordeen Loop has the best views and, like most of the trails, a warming hut.)

During the winter, the road is plowed only as far as Mount Bachelor. After Bachelor, the mountain lakes, many formed by lava dams, really start in, and a new Cascade peak springs into view at every break in the lodgepole pines and bend in the road. Visit early in the summer, and you'll find this lava-flecked land glistening with snow-melt trickles and lupine meadows. Trails into the **Three Sisters Wilderness Area** sprout from the road; virtually every lake has a few campsites on its shores, and resorts at Elk Lake, Cultus Lake, and South Twin Lake have lakeside cabins.

One of the first lakes on the drive, Todd, is just off the main road. From late spring through the summer, it's surrounded by violet lupine, pink penstemons, red Indian paintbrush, and red-and-yellow columbine, all crowned by the rugged beauty of Broken Top. For even closer views of Broken Top's caved-in crater and craggy peak, continue past Todd Lake on Forest Service Road 370, turn left onto Road 380, and pick up the Ditch Trail. It follows a ridge around Broken Top to Green Lakes.

Strong hikers can climb 10,358-foot **South Sister.** It's a steep five and a half mile hike to the top. Take off from Devil's Lake where the highway takes a sharp turn to the south, and follow the trail 'til it quits. Make sure to hike under sunny skies, and at the top you'll have all the central Oregon peaks as neighbors.

After you've enjoyed the mountaintop panorama, return to the Cascade Lakes Highway and head south toward more lakes. Pull off at Little Lava Lake and ponder the beginning of the **Deschutes River.** The Deschutes headwaters spurt up

The Twin Lakes Resort features lakeside cabins.

from springs beneath the lake. Dribbles of water at the lake's outlet pick up force quickly and become a real river in no time.

The **Crane Prairie Reservoir,** which impounds the fledgling Deschutes, is home to a fascinating osprey colony. They nest on snags in the reservoir and dive for rainbows, brookies, kokanee, and largemouth bass. Ospreys are often mistaken for bald eagles, but the osprey's dive for fish is far more graceful than an eagle's feet-first snatch. (If an eagle topples into the drink, it swims to shore with a woebegone butterfly stroke; ospreys fly right out of the water.)

Road 42 joins the Cascade Lakes Highway just south of Crane Prairie and shoots east to Sunriver, passing Twin Lakes and Wickiup Reservoir before joining US 97 at the base of Newberry Volcano.

■ LAVA LANDSCAPES   *map page 156, H-2/3*

Bulky, more felt than seen, **Newberry Volcano,** 23 miles south of Bend, may be central Oregon's most unprepossessing peak. The slopes of the massive volcano are riven with fissures. Vents and over 400 cinder cones, including Lava Butte and the Lava Cast Forest, have lined up along the fissures, where the weaker surface gave easy outlet to lava. Most of the effluent from Newberry came out these side vents. As the volcano's guts oozed out, its top collapsed, leaving a five-mile-wide (8-km) caldera, **Newberry Crater.** Once the caldera was formed, it too became a snorting, pustulant mess. The glassy, obsidian flow in the caldera is from Newberry's most recent eruption, some 1,300 years ago.

Newberry's really staggering view is from **Paulina Peak,** the high point on the volcano's rim. Look into the forested caldera, with its two perfect lakes (one, East Lake, comes complete with a stinky, milk-of magnesia-textured, dig-it-yourself hot springs). Non-native trout and kokanee, the Big Obsidian Flow, down home re-sorts, and a handful of campgrounds are there too. The mountain is big enough to create its own weather; expect it to be colder up here than in Bend, and it's likely to be wetter as well.

Pint-sized bears, no paleontologist's find but the living, breathing things, were spotted and trapped on the lava fields south of Newberry Volcano in the 1920s. The 30-pound black bears aren't around anymore (curious trappers hastened their demise), but the lava bears live on in the names of the sports teams at Bend High School.

A view over Paulina and East Lakes in Newberry National Volcanic Monument. Note the massive obsidian flow overrunning the forest in the lower right of photo.

Walk from the **Lava Lands Visitor Center** (16 miles north of the Newberry Volcano turnoff on US 97) to the base of Lava Butte over jagged ʻaʻa lava. A narrow, spiraled road leads careful, non-acrophobic drivers to a butte-top viewpoint. Stop by the visitor center before a scramble through the nearby **Lava River Cave,** where hot lava continued to move beneath the crusted-over surface, leaving caves and tubes. It's a rough ride to the stony tree-trunk molds in the Lava Cast Forest (nine miles east of US 97), where basalt flowed in, then out of, a forest, leaving tree trunks coated with molten rock. The trees slowly burned from the hot lava, but the hollow black lava casts remain.

(following pages) South Sister, Broken Top, and Mount Bachelor rise above the far shore of Lava Lake.

Hoo-Hoo Golf Tournament

*E*d was cooking up pancakes and elk, making an especially nice breakfast for his brother, an architect who'd driven over from Eugene. Now they stood together in the kitchen swapping stories about rattlesnakes: rattlesnakes that jumped out of hay bales, and rattlesnakes that sunned themselves at a fishing spot by Boxcar Rapids.

Ed's brother reached over and picked up a red felt hat that was sitting on the dining table. About five years before he'd given it to Ed for his birthday, and now he saw it was shot full of bullet holes and held together with scotch tape. "Someone try to shoot you in the head?"

Ed set plates piled up with pancakes and backstrap down on the table by the hat. "That hat got drilled at a Hoo-Hoo golf tournament." Hoo-Hoo was a lumbermen's fraternal organization. Men from all walks of the industry could join, and there were chapters all over the world, including Australia and Japan. Ed himself was manager of sales for a mill in Prineville that had been privately held by his cousin's family since the late 1880s.

After passing his brother the syrup and melted butter, Ed started to explain about the hat. He said that the night before one of the Hoo-Hoo golf tournaments he'd been up on the highway near the dam playing poker with some guys who'd come over from Bend, when he'd gotten the idea they should go down to the Pioneer Club.

"The place was jammed full of people. We'd already had quite a little bit up there on the dam and we were pretty well tanked. It was full of locals, and we hooked up with a guy we knew, a Hoo-Hoo in a ruffled shirt, but he can get away with it because of his size. Everyone was dancing, the place was going wild, and we got a few more drinks, and it wasn't very long before I felt something wet going down my neck." Ed chewed on a piece of backstrap before saying softly, "I had to do something about it."

"Someone poured a drink down your shirt," said Bill, running his fingers through his silvery hair.

"I had to do something," repeated Ed, "so I tipped over a table." He reached for the pitcher of syrup. "Well, the place just exploded. The next thing I knew, some one decked me." Ed reached up to touch his mouth, and then tilted his face up so his brother Bill could see the scar there. "A couple of Hoo-Hoos I knew, dragged me out to my rig and drove me home. One of my eyes was swollen shut, and I was leaking pretty badly around the mouth, and a couple of my teeth were loose, but I put on a clean shirt and got back in the rig with the boys."

"To finish your poker game."

"When the tournament got underway the next morning my eyes were swollen shut. The golf pro was going to start the tournament by shooting his shotgun in the air. And someone said, 'That guy's such a bad shot, I bet he couldn't even shoot Ed's hat.' Someone pulled that darn hat off my head and threw it up in the air, and the golf pro drilled it."

The next day, that Monday, Ed said, Hoo-Hoos were calling him on the telephone from all over Oregon saying: I hear you really tore that place apart the other night. Fighting everybody.

Ed spread open his palms out on the table. "Heck, I wasn't any hero. That guy decked me before I had time to get my fist clenched. But you know last year I was at a lumbermen's meeting down in San Francisco, and this friend of mine's son came up to me. Nice looking kid, and he said, 'Hello, Sir,' and I said, 'I know I should know who you are, but I don't remember you.' And he said, 'You know I want to apologize because I'm the guy who decked you at the Pioneer Club that night.' And I said, 'Are you the guy who poured the drink down my neck?' And he said 'No, but you tipped over that table on a bunch of girls.'"

Ed stood up from the table and walked over to the window to watch a China pheasant step out of the fields and onto his lawn. "Anyway, this young Hoo-Hoo fella says, 'It was a bunch of girls, Ed, and one of them was my girlfriend, and I felt like I had to do something.' Of course, I understood."

Bill leaned back in his chair, laughing. Ed shook his head just thinking about it: how he'd become famous for starting a fight when he hadn't had time to close his fist before he was knocked out, and how he'd ended up turning over a table on girls. It just went to show how quixotic fame was.

—Kit Duane

SOUTHERN OREGON

♦ HIGHLIGHTS

♦ AREA OVERVIEW

Between Eugene and Ashland, 162 miles to the south, even staid Interstate 5 turns a bit wild. It dips, rises and swings through hills, crosses the Umpqua and Rogue rivers and, just past 4,310-foot Siskiyou Pass, slips into California. The mountains here contain one of the state's most interesting natural features—Crater Lake—and one of its artistic highlights—the Oregon Shakespeare Festival.

Southern Oregon has retained its own inimitable flavor even as it has been settled by droves of retirees from California and other parts of Oregon. At a country store you might see three guys in a pickup truck, long hair sticking out from under their visored caps, thermal coffee mugs hanging from the gun rack; or a well-coiffed blond lady loading crates of groceries into a shiny truck with a Billy Graham bumpersticker. For while this is Oregon's Bible Belt, it's also the Marijuana Belt, where pockets of folk spread compost in organic gardens and keep a few plump goats in the back yard. Old timers keep cabins up their favorite rivers and fill them with fishing rods, trophy heads, and furniture hewn from gigantic logs.

Madrone, tan oak, cedars, hemlocks, unusual varieties of spruce trees, wild rhododendrons and, down near California, a few redwoods surprise visitors who expect solid walls of Douglas fir.

Climate: The Coast Range absorbs a surprising amount of moisture, leaving the inland valleys of southern Oregon dry. Fires often break out toward the end of hot interior summers. A summer day in Medford can easily reach 100 degrees; head east into the mountains for relief from the heat.

Food & Lodging: Though it's not the largest city, Ashland is southern Oregon's cosmopolitan hub, and that's where you'll find the best food and the priciest accommodations. (Budget-conscious travelers often stay in less-expensive Medford when they head down to the Shakespeare Festival.) Rustic riverside inns and cabin resorts are some of the region's best places to stay; see page 195.

Wizard Island, a volcanic cinder cone rising from the middle of Crater Lake.

SOUTHERN
OREGON

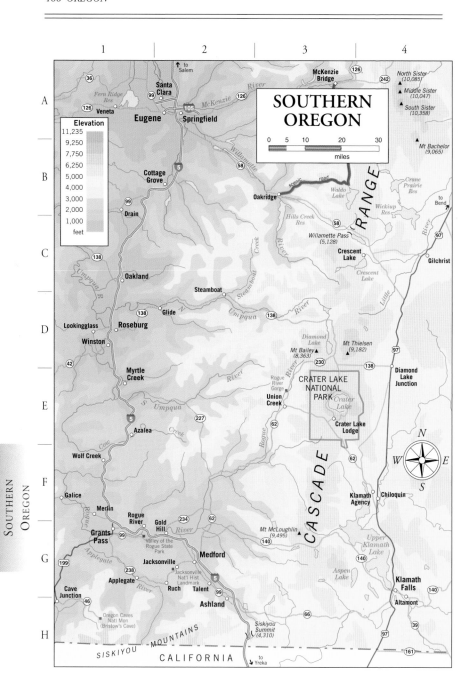

SOUTHERN OREGON

0   5   10   20   30
miles

Elevation
11,235
9,250
7,750
6,250
5,000
4,000
3,000
2,000
1,000
feet

to Salem

McKenzie Bridge
North Sister (10,085)
Middle Sister (10,047)
South Sister (10,358)

Santa Clara
Veneta
Fern Ridge Res
Eugene
Springfield
McKenzie River
Mt Bachelor (9,065)

Willamette River

Cottage Grove

Oakridge
scenic road
Waldo Lake
Crane Prairie Res
RANGE
Wickiup Res
to Bend

Drain

Hills Creek Res

Willamette Pass (5,128)
Crescent Lake
Crescent Lake
Little River
Gilchrist

Umpqua R.

Oakland

Steamboat

Steamboat Creek
Umpqua River
Diamond Lake
Mt Bailey (8,363)
Mt Thielsen (9,182)

Glide
Lookingglass
Roseburg
Winston

Myrtle Creek
S. Umpqua
River
Rogue River Gorge
Union Creek
CRATER LAKE NATIONAL PARK
Crater Lake
Diamond Lake Junction

Azalea
Cow Creek
Crater Lake Lodge

Wolf Creek
Rogue River
N
W   E
S

Galice
Merlin
Rogue River
Gold Hill
River
CASCADE
Klamath Agency
Chiloquin

Grants Pass
Valley of the Rogue State Park
Medford
Mt McLoughlin (9,495)
Upper Klamath Lake

Jacksonville
Jacksonville Nat'l Hist Landmark
Ruch
Talent
Aspen Lake
Klamath Falls

Applegate
Applegate River
Ashland
Altamont

Cave Junction
Oregon Caves Nat'l Mon (Bristow's Cave)
Siskiyou Summit (4,310)

MOUNTAINS
SISKIYOU
CALIFORNIA
to Yreka

■ UMPQUA RIVER *map opposite, D-1 to 3*

The two forks of the Umpqua River join up just west of Interstate 5, near Rose-burg; the combined waters flow west and empty into the Pacific at Reedsport.

The North Umpqua is famed for its summer steelhead runs and the Steamboat Inn, a top-flight but unpretentious fishing lodge with great food and a prime riverfront location. The river has its start high in the Cascades, near Diamond Lake and courses through a steep green canyon gushing with waterfalls. The South Umpqua flows through a broader, warmer, vineyard-draped valley that locals proudly refer to as "Oregon's Mediterranean."

◆ HISTORY

The Cow Creek Band of Umpqua Indians lived along the river and Cow Creek. Here they trapped deer and elk with iris-fiber snares, built weirs and funnel-shaped basket traps to catch salmon and steelhead, dug roots, dove into rivers and pulled lamprey off submerged rocks, gathered huckleberries, and made tea from yerba buena leaves. They lived in wood-roofed, semi-subterranean winter shelters, and less substantial brush-built summer houses. Men visited a dugout sweat lodge daily.

In 1846, as Oregon Trail emigration was reaching a fever pitch, Levi Scott and Jesse and Lindsay Applegate blazed a southern route to Oregon. Settlers in the southern Willamette Valley were anxious to beef up their numbers, partly because they were tired of being bossed around by the Methodist missionaries to the north. The Applegate party cut down to northern California, turned east and picked up Nevada's Humboldt River, then cut back up to Fort Hall. Jesse Apple-gate intercepted some migrants there, and persuaded them to try the new route. It wasn't exactly a cakewalk. Tabitha Brown, who was 63 years old when she joined the Applegate party, recounted:

> *W*e were carried hundreds of miles south of Oregon into Utah Territory and California; fell in with the Clamotte and Rogue River Indians, lost nearly all our cattle, passed the Umpqua Mountains, 12 miles through. I rode through in three days at the risk of my life, on horseback, having lost my wagon and all that I had but the horse I was on. Our families were the first that started through the canyon, so that we got through the mud and rocks much better than those that followed. Out of the hundreds of

wagons, only one came through without breaking. The canyon was strewn with dead cattle, broken wagons, beds, clothing, and everything but provisions, of which latter we were nearly all destitute. Some people were in the canyon two or three weeks before they could get through. Some died without any warning, from fatigue and starvation. Others ate the flesh of cattle that were lying dead by the wayside.

The opening of the Applegate Trail marked the beginning of hard times for the Cow Creek Indians, who soon found their game diminished and their fishing areas appropriated. Far worse than the early homesteaders were the miners who, after gold was discovered near Jacksonville, tore their way through every southern Oregon drainage, choking salmon streams with muddy debris.

The Cow Creek people signed a reservation treaty in 1853, which the government largely ignored. Settlers continued to move onto Indian land and harass the Cow Creeks, who retreated into the most remote areas. Many were rounded up by the government and sent to live on the Siletz Reservation on the central coast and

A large mule team hauls freight across southern Oregon. (Southern Oregon Historical Society)

PARADISE AND POPULATION

*O*nce Looking Glass had been a rich locality, with six big heavy-set ranches running cattle on the open grass, each making its proprietor ten times as big an
income as he needed to live on. The cinch was too good to last. The valley, along in
1890, had attracted some three hundred industrious colonists, who divided the open
grass-country between them and set out to make it pay as big for them as it had for
the original exploiters. Since it was only good for pasture, it went right on paying
the same as usual with the difference that, instead of giving six ranchers ten times
too much apiece, it gave three hundred ranches about one-fifth enough. The
colonists lived for a few years by borrowing, and when they could borrow no more
money they all got up and left...

—H. L. Davis, *Honey in the Horn,* 1936

Grande Ronde Reservation in the Willamette Valley.

Without consulting the Cow Creeks, the U.S. government terminated its relations with the band in 1956. In the government's eyes, they ceased to exist as a
tribe, and thus required none of the health care or educational benefits usually provided. In 1980, the supposedly non-existent Cow Creeks sued the United States for
treaty land stolen from them and won a $1.5 million settlement. The band put the
settlement money in an endowment using the earnings for tribal social service programs. In 1982, they were once again recognized as a tribe. Today they operate the
Cow Creek Bingo Center near the Canyonville exit on Interstate 5.

◆ TOURING THE UMPQUA

Most people approach the Umpqua River from Interstate 5 and Roseburg, where
the fresh smell of cut wood sharpens the air. Even with the river lending some
scenery, **Roseburg** is a little too rough-edged to draw many travelers. Across the
river is Mount Nebo—supposedly a resting place for the mythical giant logger
Paul Bunyan and his blue ox Babe. Perhaps they, like Scottish botanist David
Douglas, who visited the area in 1828, were fascinated by the long cones of local
sugar pines and the Oregon myrtle's bay-scented leaves. (Indians ate myrtle seeds
and made tea from the bark. Now the myrtlewood is the stuff of souvenir clocks
and monstrous coffee tables.)

SOUTHERN
OREGON

Just south and west of town, in the broad green valley of the South Umpqua and its tributaries, wine grapes flourish. Wineries range from the venerable Hill-Crest (Oregon's first real vineyard, est. 1961) to the upstart Palotai, which produces the traditional wines of the winemaker's native Hungary. Rieslings and gewurztraminers are regional bestsellers, and their vines predominate. Merlot and cabernet are also grown. Umpqua Valley non-varietal wines can be good quality for the price—Henry Estates makes a good red table wine from pinot grapes.

The fertile valley west of Roseburg was home to the pioneers in H. L. Davis's novel, *Honey in the Horn*. Davis's book won the Pulitzer Prize in 1936 and was cited by reviewers for its gutsy realism as it portrayed homesteaders moving from "built up" western Oregon to the wilds of eastern Oregon.

◆ NORTH UMPQUA   *map page 186, D-1 to 3*

Hikers and anglers should head east from Roseburg up North Umpqua Road (Hwy 138) and explore a river that's famous among fishermen, but little known to many others.

Boats are only allowed on the lower 35 miles of the North Umpqua (as far as Glide). From Rock Creek to Lemolo Lake (near the headwaters) only fly fishing is permitted. (Even on the unrestricted sections, pride keeps most anglers from using much else.) Steelhead are actually sea-run rainbow trout that migrate to the ocean when they're young and typically spend three years at sea. Summer steelhead return to their home upriver in May and stay there until the following March, when they spawn. Steelhead fishing is good from June through October, when the fish find the river's cool deep holes and fight like the dickens if any line tries to pull them away. Winter steelhead return to the river in November; fish for them from December through February. Both chinook and coho salmon come up the North Umpqua, and some wild brown trout live in the river's upper reaches.

Nobody's going to tell you exactly where to fish, but if you strike up a polite conversation in a campground or the lobby of the Steamboat Inn, someone's bound to get excited and drop a few solid hints. Fishing etiquette requires respect for others and a certain low-key conviviality. Boasting and whining are *out*.

One North Umpqua angler was Zane Grey, author of scores of Western novels and an avid sportsman. When steelhead were running, Grey would leave his Rogue River cabin and travel north to the Umpqua. He was, above all else,

SOUTHERN
OREGON

(opposite) The North Umpqua River at Deadline Falls and Rock Creek.

systematic in his fishing—he'd hire a fleet of "assistants," who'd get up before day-break to stand on specified river rocks. As the day wore on, Grey would relieve the assistants of their posts and fish the pools they'd saved for him. It was not a prac-tice that endeared him to the locals, who still sneer at the mention of his name.

A few miles upstream, near **Glide**, the jade-colored North Umpqua and the silty Little River lock horns at Colliding Rivers. The Narrows of the North Umpqua, just east of Glide, was a traditional fishing site for the Molalla Band of the Umpqua Indians. The steep gorge is still a popular place to fish for steelhead and spring chinook.

As it's traced east, the North Umpqua turns deep blue-green and magical. Trails, most leading to waterfalls, light out every few miles, and the riverside campsites are just as plentiful. A few miles past the Steamboat Inn on Hwy 138 east of Rose-burg, the road begins to climb, and the hills sprout huge basalt pillars. About 60 miles east of Roseburg, at the Tokatee Ranger Station, forest roads lead north to the one-pool, hike-in **Umpqua Hot Springs**. (Signs point the way to the parking area, but the trail is a little confusing. Hang a right at the trail's fork, head uphill, and be prepared to wait while others soak, naked of course. This spot is almost as popular as it is remote.)

Even non-anglers can become entranced watching fish struggle upstream past the underwater windows at the Winchester Dam fish ladder, three miles north of Roseburg (take exit 129 from Interstate 5).

Steamboat Inn. Cabins, cottages, suites, and houses are available at this terrific, popular establishment right on the river. Gourmet fishermen's dinners are served just after dark so fishermen can pull up that last catch; cafe-style breakfasts and lunches also available. Rustic, but reservations required for dinner. The Inn closes for January and February. Located 38 miles east of Roseburg on Hwy 138/N Umpqua Hwy; 541-498-2230 or 800-840-8825.

■ GRANTS PASS AND THE ROGUE RIVER   *map page 186, G-1*

Grants Pass is in the grip of the Rogue River, and the influx of travelers lured to the Rogue's whitewater has inspired residents to turn their historic homes into bed and breakfasts and open antique shops in venerable downtown buildings. On Sat-urday mornings, downtown streets take on extra color and fragrance and bustle with locals shopping at the farmers' market.

SOUTHERN OREGON

Despite a few surface frills, Grants Pass hasn't been tamed. There's still plenty of local color, some of it with a raucous edge. An organization called The Cavemen, who claim the Oregon Caves as their ancestral home, has been a slightly embarrassing civic organization for decades—there's even a postcard of a Caveman wedding inside the caves, with all the celebrants in Flintstone regalia.

In the fall, there's a substantial harvest that's not displayed at the Farmers' Market. Everyone in town knows that when the wild hill people start shopping, the marijuana crop is in. Grants Pass is, after all, a market town, and it gains a funny sort of prosperity when pot growers get some cash flow.

The Rogue River has its headwaters near Crater Lake. Along with its tributaries, the Illinois and the Applegate rivers, it drains the Klamath Mountains, a tectonic crazy quilt of ancient islands and chunks of ocean crust extending into Northern California.

Camelot and cavemen come face to face in Grants Pass. (Southern Oregon Historical Society)

◆ SEEING THE ROGUE

Zane Grey's cabin still stands at remote Winkle Bar. He spent hours staring at the river (probably feeling guilty that he wasn't inside writing Westerns) and described it:

> ...*D*eep and dark green, swift and clear, and as pure as the snows from which it springs . . . It is a river at its birth, gliding away through the Oregon forest with hurrying momentum, as if eager to begin the long leap down through the Siskiyous. The river tumbles off the mountain in mellow thundering music, racing between its timbered banks down the miles to the sheltered valley. Twisting through Grants Pass, it enters the canyoned wilderness of the Coast Range.

In 1926, Grey railed against Forest Service planners who wanted to build roads into Rogue River country. He was convinced that roads caused more fires than they helped to quash and that they led inevitably to destruction of wildlife habitats.

Grey's home stretch of the Rogue remains roadless; Congress declared the Rogue River "Wild and Scenic" in 1968, a classification that limits development.

A permit is necessary to raft the protected stretches of the Rogue. Permits are

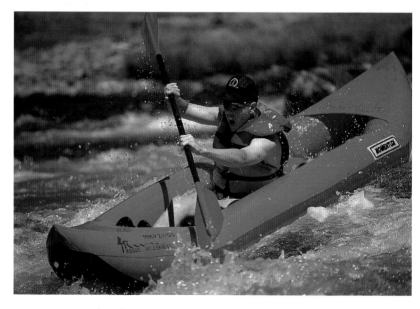

Kayaking the Rogue River near Rand in Hellgate Recreation Area.

parceled out by lottery each February and are sometimes available throughout the summer at the Rand Visitor Center just downstream from the town of Galice. (To enter the permit lottery, call 541-479-3735.) Rafting outfitters get a good share of the permits. Outfitters abound in Grants Pass and neighboring communities and offer everything from rides on guide-driven oared rafts to inflatable kayak rentals. Call the the same number for a list of river outfitters. (Also see page 292)

Jet boats are a common way to see the river's unprotected stretches. They leave from Grants Pass and the nearby town of Rogue River, or from Gold Beach, over on the coast. These boats buzz noisily along the surface of the water, slurping up water through the front, and shooting it out the rear of the boat. Evening jet boat trips usually include a dinner stop at a riverside lodge.

If you get the urge to travel a few river miles but can't stomach the idea of a jet boat tour, follow the Rogue out of Grants Pass through Merlin, headquarters of

---

LODGES ALONG THE WILD & SCENIC ROGUE RIVER
EAST TO WEST

The backcountry Rogue River National Recreation Trail runs from Grave Creek to Illahee. Several backcountry lodges offer accommodations and meals to hikers and boaters along this 40-mile stretch.

Black Bar Lodge.
    10 miles downstream from Grave Creek
    541-479-6507
May-Nov. Reservations required.

Marial Lodge.
    20 miles downstream from Grave Creek
    541-474-2057
Autos can reach this lodge via a primitive road. May–mid-Nov.

Paradise Lodge.
    24 miles downstream from Grave Creek, just below Blossom Bar

    800-525-2161 or 541-247-6022
Access by foot or boat. Open year-round.

Half Moon Bar Lodge.
    24.5 miles downstream from Grave Creek
    541-247-6968
Hike, boat or fly in. Open year-round.

Clay Hill Lodge.
    29 miles downstream from Grave Creek
    503-859-3772
Hike or boat in.

Illahee Lodge.
    32.5 miles downstream from Grave Creek, at the end of the Agness-Illahee Road, 7 miles upstream from Agness
    541-247-6111
Open year-round.

several river raft outfitters, to the tiny town of **Galice** where you can rent an inflatable kayak (a.k.a. "Tahiti"). Anybody with a modicum of paddling experience should be able to adapt to a Tahiti and be able to run a few unprotected miles of the Rogue, where a permit is not required, downstream from Galice.

Hikers will get a slower, more intimate look at the Rogue River over the 40 miles from Grave Creek to Illahe, 27 miles northwest of Grants Pass. The trail passes old gold mines and cabins. Summers are hot, so try to hike in the spring. Expect to see herons flying upstream, salmon jumping up rapids, and black bears fishing for salmon. Camp at a site along a trail or stay at backcountry riverside lodges. Some people ride a jet boat into a lodge, then hike out, often stopping to fish along the way. The Rogue is known for its spring chinook runs (May-July). Fish here, too, for summer steelhead (they're most plentiful in the fall).

North of the river, the Grave Creek to Marial byway follows an old mule road to the Rogue River Ranch, now a BLM museum. The quite rough Grave Creek–Marial road takes you into some of Oregon's wildest country, and provides access to the Rogue River Trail. Elk, deer, black bears, and wild turkeys are denizens of the Rogue country.

Wolf Creek Tavern between Roseburg and Grants Pass was built in 1857 as a stagecoach stop. The tavern has hosted Jack London, Sinclair Lewis, and Rutherford B. Hayes. 100 Front; 541-866-2474. **Galice Resort** at 11744 Galice Road is 12 miles past Merlin on right, 541-476-3818. Right on the Rogue, they offer raft rentals and guided trips, cabins, and a lodge.

For float trips, trips see listings on page 292.

■ ILLINOIS RIVER COUNTRY   *map page 186, F to H-1&2*

From Grants Pass, Interstate 5 heads off south and east through Medford and Ashland on its way to California. A smaller, forest-shaded road, US 199 leads west and south from Grants Pass to Crescent City, California. It traces the upper limit of redwood forests and passes a few wineries, many old mining sites and an uncommon number of long-haired, gauzy people with names like "Meadowlark" and "Doug Fir." What's now the scenic Redwood Highway has a rough history—military volunteers beat it into a hard path during their protracted 1850s Rogue Indian wars.

◆ ROGUE INDIANS

The Rogue and Illinois Rivers were home to two tribes of Takelma-speaking Indians, the Takelmas and the Latgawas, both called "Rogues" by early fur traders. Latgawas lived on the upper Rogue, in the Cascade foothills. They were fierce and had no compunction about eating crows, ant eggs, lice, and insect larvae. This diet made their Takelma neighbors shudder with disgust, but not more so than the fact that Latgawas sold Takelmas as slaves to the Klamaths.

The Takelmas lived along the Illinois and middle stretch of the Rogue. They ate fish and eels, deer and elk, acorns and seeds, and drank a manzanita berry-pine-nut shake. (The red-barked manzanitas have small, roundish evergreen leaves and fruit like small dry apples, which Indians ground into a fine meal and leached with water to produce a cider.) Winters they lived in pine-plank lodges. In the summer and fall, during fishing season, they lived in brush shelters near fishing sites. Takelmas kept a close eye out for rattlesnakes—they believed that it was fatal to have a rattler strike at one's shadow. To them, an eagle's cry predicted death by arrows.

Both Takelma tribes fought hard against intrusions onto their land. Applegate Trail migrants and miners on their way to California strikes feared them, and an 1850 treaty did little to calm down either side. When gold was discovered in southern Oregon, and miners rolled through the valleys, the Talkelmas and Latgawas joined forces with the Klamath and Shasta Indians, only to be defeated. In 1853 the Takelma tribes were moved onto a reservation at Table Rock.

Two years later, white volunteers, angered by clashes between the Shastas and miners, stormed the Table Rock Reservation and killed anybody within their range. The Talkelmas fought back hard, but their resistance cost them their reservation. Survivors were eventually sent north to the Grande Ronde Reservation, on the Yamhill River.

■ OREGON CAVES *map page 186, H-1*

A 45-minute, winding uphill drive climbs from the US 199 town of Cave Junction past steep downslope views of placer mining in Cave Creek and looks out onto the Siskiyou and Coast ranges. At the 4,000-foot high cave entrance to Oregon Caves National Monument, the cedar-shaked Cave Chateau, a huge rustic inn, snugs in against the waterfall-streaked hillside.

SOUTHERN OREGON

The entire Siskiyou Range is marble. Caves are formed when snowmelt and rainwater seep through plants, pick up carbon, and become a mild carbonic acid. When the acid hits the marble, it dissolves the rock, and forms tiny cracks, which grow larger as more acid splashes down, until room-sized chambers are eventually formed. Dissolved minerals recrystalize inside the cave, building stalactites, stalagmites, and other formations. Three miles of trails are mapped in the Oregon Caves, but the networks may be far more extensive.

The Siskiyou Range is locked in a tangled grip with northern California's Klamath Mountains. Along with northeastern Oregon's Blue Mountains, they contain the state's oldest rocks, dating from Triassic and Jurassic times. There are no lava rocks here and few traces of the inland sea that only briefly washed over the tectonic jumble. Instead, the Siskiyous are built from chunks of oceanic crust and old islands plastered onto the edge of the continental plate. When the Coast Range uplifted, Siskiyou rivers stood firm in their paths to the sea, cutting through the younger western Coast Range, and leaving steep slopes. The Klamath-Siskiyou complex was only lightly glaciated, which has allowed for the preservation of an amazing biodiversity. Buy your ticket for a cave tour next to the gift shop and join

The Oregon Caves Chateau is a National Historic Landmark.

a fascinating ranger-led tour through this labyrinth. Dress warmly; as this tour is strenuous, it is not recommended for anyone with heart or breathing difficulty or for very young children.

At **Oregon Caves National Monument** you'll find **Oregon Caves Chateau**, the rustic wood chalet open mid-June through Labor Day. It's built practically on top of a waterfall, and the entrance to the caves is just across the drive; 20000 Cave Hwy; 541-592-3400.

♦ KALMIOPSIS   *map page 186, G/H-4*

West of the caves at the heart of the Siskiyous, the rusty red peridotite and greenish serpentine of the Kalmiopsis Wilderness Area support only sparse vegetation. Plants that grow on these rocks are small, often uncharacteristic of the Northwest, and varied. Springtime lasts forever, marked by blossoms of rangy wild azaleas and rhododendrons, lovelier than any carefully tended pompom of pink or purple blossoms. Wild irises cover the hills, and late in the summer, tiger lilies tint roadsides orange. Rarer plants include the insectivorous cobra lily and the azalea-like *Kalmiopsis leachiana.* Shy black bears and about a million newts, salamanders, lizards, and skinks share the woods with rumors of Bigfoot (a.k.a. Sasquatch, the Northwest's shy version of the abominable snowman).

The Forest Service is trying to make the Kalmiopsis more "wilderness-like" by removing trail signs. The deeper into the Kalmiopsis you hike, the more essential a good map and compass skills become. There's a good chance of running into old mining claims, some still worked by miners who can drive their rigs in past the wilderness boundary.

■ MEDFORD AND VICINITY   *map page 186, G-2*

Medford, on Interstate 5 between Grants Pass and Ashland, is in a valley known for its temperature inversions and blanket of smog. While it may not be a place to linger, Medford has many reasonably priced accommodations, and many people who visit Ashland or Jacksonville save money by staying there.

The Oregon and California Railroad can claim Medford as its own. Tracks linking transcontinental railroad terminals in Portland and San Francisco were built in the 1880s. Jacksonville, then southern Oregon's largest town, was the obvious stop, but it was situated across some hills, which annoyed the flatland railroad builders. Thus, Medford grew up around a rail depot a few miles east of Jacksonville.

SOUTHERN OREGON

CHANGES IN THE FOREST

Logging was a first step to "progress" in most of western Oregon, where the trees and understory grew so thick as to make it nearly impossible to get around. In many places, it was even tough to find the room to fell a single tree without damaging its neighbors, which made clearcutting seem more practical.

Even as recently as the 1950s, the forest seemed boundless. Nearly 10 billion board feet of timber were cut in Oregon in 1952, keeping pace with postwar growth. Ever-vigilant silvaculturalists replanted the logged forests—originally a mix of Western hemlock, Douglas fir, and spruce—with solid stands of fast-growing, profitable Doug fir seedlings. Fine to harvest, perhaps, but not too long on biodiversity. And even fast-growing trees take more than half a century to reach harvestable size in the Northwest.

Once the private lands were cut to the quick, timber companies turned to the big trees on National Forest lands. These "lands of many uses" were, to some extent, intended for timber production, but starting in the 1970s, there were ever more restrictions. You couldn't sheer off the whole side of a hill, like you could on private land. You had to leave little fringes of trees around highways and riverbanks. And, starting in 1976, you couldn't diminish any species of wildlife within the logging area.

Logging, and replanting, proceeded apace anyway. It became obvious that there would be a span of years between the last harvest of the old-growth trees and logging the first flush of replanted trees. With what now seems a twisted logic, in the 1980s, the timber industry speeded up the cut of old growth trees. Oregon was then in a recession . . . mills were closing, and one way out was to feed more logs into the mills, putting people back to work. For a while, it worked. That the old growth was running out was a dirty little secret. The Reagan and the first Bush administrations continued to encourage heavy cutting on public lands.

All the while, mills were becoming increasingly automated, and unprecedented quantities of unmilled logs were being exported to Japan. Big timber companies were transferring many operations to southern states, where labor is cheaper and trees grow faster. The market dynamics changed. The construction industry had less use for high quality, knot-free old growth logs, and mills shifted to using lower grade southern lumber for wafer board, chip board, and plywood. With plywood operations shifted elsewhere, the Northwest mills produced mostly two by fours, which are much less labor intensive to mill.

In the 1980s environmentalists challenged the Forest Service's management of forest lands with lawsuits in federal court. Along with the suits came a petition to list the spotted owl, which nests in old growth, as an endangered species. It started an uproar—you could buy cans of "spotted owl pâté" from seething Roseburg vendors; pickup trucks had skewered stuffed owls dangling from gun racks. The owl, which to environmentalists was like the proverbial canary in the coal mine, signalling the forests' health, became a symbol of the increasing polarization between environmentalists and loggers.

By the end of the 1980s, some 25,000 logging jobs were lost in the Pacific Northwest. With approximately 10 percent of Oregon's old growth remaining, environmentalists feared the loss of these final stands and the diversity of life contained in them. For years, old growth had been considered "overmature," but more recent research showed that decaying trees supported a rich biodiversity. "New Forestry" techniques leave a few standing trees and fallen timber; foresters are talking more about ecosystem management and biological diversity; and clearcutting is increasingly frowned upon.

Clearcuts and logging roads were implicated in the slide activity that followed heavy rains in the late 1990s, and the concern reached far beyond traditional environmentalists when slides killed several Oregonians.

The controversy now centers on logging in burned areas, particularly the old-growth areas in southwest Oregon burned by the 2002 Biscuit Fire. Environmentalists have sued to stop the logging of areas designated primarily for fish and wildlife habitat under the 1994 Northwest Forest Plan, and it's likely that the logs will rot before the court battles are finished.

SOUTHERN OREGON

The northern spotted owl is at the center of the forest controversy because it (like many other species) can only survive in old-growth forest, not in tree farms.

Clear-cut hillside in Siuslaw National Forest.

Much of the timber debate in southern Oregon is wrapped up in the history of the Oregon and California Railroad. A mile-wide swath along the tracks was granted to the railroad in 1866 and some 2.5 million acres were later taken back by the government. The Bureau of Land Management now manages most of this land, which falls in a checkerboard pattern comprised of 640-acre squares alternating with private and Forest Service land, and it is that agency's biggest timber holding in the lower 48. The railroad land is designated for high-yield sustainable forestry. In lieu of taxes on these lands, counties have received 50 percent or more of the logging revenues, which makes up a substantial part of many local economies, leading to strong local support for the logging.

Critics maintain that the BLM'S management has focused so exclusively on commodity extraction as to make these checkerboard squares into "sacrifice land" and that ecosystem management of the adjoining private and Forest Service squares has been lax.

From Interstate 5 or Hwy 99 (roughly parallel to the Interstate), Medford presents a nearly impenetrable commercial strip, but it's worth a quick shot down past mobile home dealers and fast food joints to visit the **Southern Oregon Historical Society Museum**, 106 N Central, which features rotating displays, a fine photo archive, and a bookstore. Harry and David's pear emporium, south of town, is the retail "seconds" outlet of a big gift-basket fruit company and a good place to fill a picnic basket. Thus provisioned, venture off the main road, into fruit trees that grow to the horizon, to Jacksonville, five miles west of Medford.

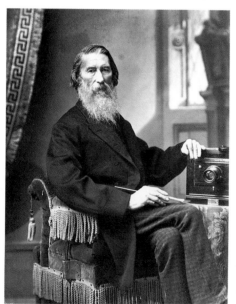

Peter Britt, photographer and painter of Jacksonville, was the first person to photograph Crater Lake. (Southern Oregon Historical Society)

SOUTHERN OREGON

Colorful fruit pack labels from Medford pear farms. (Southern Oregon Historical Society)

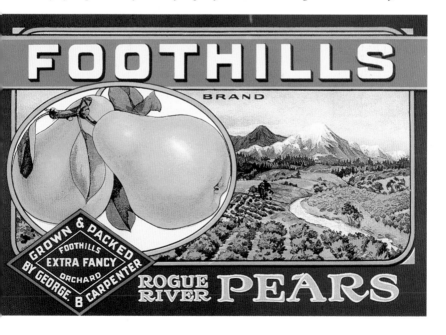

Pinto Colvig, creator of Bozo the Clown and the voice behind Disney's Goofy, sends a letter to a friend in his hometown of Jacksonville. (Southern Oregon Historical Society)

■ JACKSONVILLE   *map page 186, G-2*

Jacksonville's gold boom started in 1852, and within a couple of years it gained the veneer of a respectable town. According to legend, a night's take at the gaming tables once was donated to Godly causes. The money was used to build the Methodist church, where gold nuggets dropped weekly into collection plates.

Peter Britt, Jacksonville's most revered pioneer, was a Swiss-born photographer and painter. Back when photography meant heavy cameras and glass plate negatives, Britt lugged his equipment all over southern Oregon. (He was the first to photograph Crater Lake.) He was also an amateur horticulturist and vintner, remembered for introducing fruit trees that gave birth to the region's orchards.

After the first flush of gold brought prosperity, life quieted down. This serene image was punctured in 1923 when the D'Autremont brothers held up a train near Siskiyou Pass. They escaped, but left a jacket behind, with a receipt inside for Hugh D'Autremont. The brothers disappeared and weren't captured until 1927, when one of Hugh's Army colleagues recognized his "wanted" picture hanging in a post office. The other brothers were tracked down, and a trial date was set.

A festive spirit prevailed at the trial. The jury held an impromptu track meet, and witnesses played baseball. The D'Autremonts were sentenced to life in prison. The jail where they did time is now a **children's museum** where a surprisingly touching display chronicles the life of Pinto Colvig—a local boy who created the character of Bozo the Clown. Next door, at 206 N Fifth Street, the **Jacksonville**

Museum tells the story of the town's gold rush days. Call 541-733-6536 for more information.

Jacksonville once flirted with becoming a ghost town, but is now a paean to historic preservation with antique shops, pear trees, and the Britt Festival, a summer-long outdoor music festival. Like Ashland's Shakespeare Festival, the **Britt Festival** is hugely popular, and for good reason. The hillside setting lends itself to a relaxed, picnic-like atmosphere, and the good feeling rubs off on the performers, who run the gamut from bluegrass to pop to classical musicians. For tickets and information call 541-773-6077. To stay on, try the **Jacksonville Inn** at 175 E California Street; 541-899-1900 or 800-321-9344. This old eight-room hotel has a dressy restaurant downstairs.

■ APPLEGATE VALLEY   *map page 186, G/H-1/2*

The Applegate Valley, with Hwy 238 running down its midsection, connecting Medford and Grants Pass the long, southern way, has a pioneer feeling. The farmhouses pushed up against hillsides have streams meandering through their front yards. The **Valley View Winery** in **Ruch**, five miles west of Jacksonville is known

Valley View Vineyards in the Applegate Valley.

Chinese immigrant miner, Gin Lin, deposited over one million dollars of gold dust in Jacksonville banks in the 1880s before returning to China. (Southern Oregon Historical Society)

for its chardonnays, and its sunny, well-tended Applegate Valley setting is memorable. Call 541-899-8468.

Venture off the main road, and things get a touch less genteel. Hippie homesteaders are cheek by jowl with ex-loggers and transplanted urbanites—who show up astride their new horses, outfitted in stretch pants and bicycle helmets.

There's a dry, open look to the forests around the Applegate. The red-brown bark of the madrone trees and red-ochre soil glow against shiny green foliage. The land wears traces of southern Oregon's mining heritage. One of mining's more diligent practitioners was Gin Lin, whose mining site is still visible south of Ruch, just past the McKee Bridge, on the **Gin Lin Trail**. Gin Lin began mining here in 1881. It's staggering to imagine the amount of work involved in mining this site—miles of trenches dug, mountains reconfigured, and no small amount of gold washed into the sluices. By the time Gin Lin returned home to China, he had deposited over a million dollars worth of gold dust in the Jacksonville bank. According to one source, Gin Lin was robbed and fatally beaten as he got off the return ship to China.

Many Chinese men came to work in Oregon gold strikes. The Chinese didn't usually settle permanently—they faced discrimination, and they were expected by their own families to return to China.

■ ASHLAND   *map page 186, G/H-2*

Ashland is set on the banks of Bear Creek, which winds through town beneath steep Siskiyou peaks a few miles west of Interstate 5. North of town, a broad valley, checkered with pear and apple trees, stretches all the way to the Rogue River. A cultural hub, this theater town leads the Northwest in the number of Bed and Breakfasts per capita and is home to good bookstores, excellent restaurants, and espresso bars on wheels.

The half-timbered Elizabethan Theatre housed a Chautauqua series in the early 1900s—those traveling shows of popular education and concerts—but the building fell into disrepair and was condemned. It was being torn apart when Shakespeare aficionado Angus Bowmer noticed that, without the domed roof, it bore an

Shops and restaurants on Lithia Plaza near Main Street in downtown Ashland.

AUTHOR'S FAVORITE ASHLAND FOOD AND LODGING

Lodgings

Ashland Springs Hotel.
212 E Main Street
541-488-1700 or 888-795-4545
This historic downtown hotel has had its ups and downs. Built in 1925 as the Lithia Springs Hotel, its most recent incarnation was as the faux-Tudor Mark Antony. After a huge renovation, this is once again the place to stay in downtown Ashland.

Chanticleer Inn.
120 Gresham Street
541-482-1919 or 800-898-1950
Only a few blocks from the theatres, this B&B inn seems in its own peaceful world.

Country Willows.
1313 Clay Street
541-488-1590 or 800-945-5697
A short drive or bike ride from downtown, this comfortable B&B has a rural setting near hiking trails. Outdoor pool.

Mount Ashland Inn.
550 Mount Ashland Ski Road
541- 482-8707 or 800-830-8707
Head south of town to find this fabulous log inn on the road to Mount Ashland Ski Area. About 20 minutes from town; wonderfully scenic hiking.

Peerless Hotel.
243 Fourth Street
541-488-1082 or 800-460-8758.
Erstwhile roominghouse nicely renovated. Good restaurant next door.

Winchester Country Inn.
35 S Second Street; 541-488-1113.
Near the Shakespeare Festival theaters; rooms are attractive and uncluttered. Excellent restaurant.

Restaurants

Ashland Bakery & Cafe.
38 E Main Street
541-482-2117.
A good place to hear breakfast chatter about last night's shows.

Chateaulin.
50 E Main Street
541-482-2264.
French cafe near the Bowmer Theatre. Dinner only, but open for the after-theatre crowd, who appreciate the good bar menu.

New Sammy's Cowboy Bistro.
2210 S. Pacific Hwy., Talent
541-535-2779.
A few miles north of town, watch for the neon arrow and pink-doored cottage. Dinner Thurs.–Sun. Reserve well in advance.

Peerless Restaurant.
265 Fourth St.
541-488-6067.
Northwest cuisine at its freshest and finest.

(opposite) Lithia Park Pond and the Elizabethan Theatre in Ashland.

amazing resemblance to Shakespeare's Globe Theatre. Ashland residents swung into action: they built a 16th century–style stage, dug through attics for old-fashioned clothes to use as costumes, and put on a show. The first Shakespeare Festival was staged in 1935.

Since then, it's been unstoppable. Three theaters now run 12 plays in repertoire from mid-February through October, and a handful of smaller theaters fill in the winter gaps. Shakespeare is always represented in the **Oregon Shakespeare Festival**'s outdoor Elizabethan Theatre, but most of the plays staged in the large Angus Bowmer Theatre or the smaller Black Swan are by other playwrights. Call the box office for the annual schedule, 541-482-2111.

Actors know it's a good place to break into the business, and their obsession with their work gives Ashland an electricity amid its charming reservoir of Victorian houses, good restaurants, and bed and breakfasts.

Lithia Plaza, at the town's hub, has two fountains spewing alkaline lithia water. It's okay to drink the water, but it probably takes a truly refined palate to appreciate its stinky effervescence. Nonetheless, it stands as geological testimony to the fact that Ashland was destined to become an uncommon place.

Even actors and sophisticates need an occasional escape into the woods (and that's why they come to Ashland rather than New York). The closest escape from the crowded sidewalks is **Lithia Park,** a 100-acre corridor of trees, tennis courts, playgrounds, and Japanese gardens on the hillside overlooking the theaters. To walk in spectacular wildflower meadows and see views of distant Mount Shasta, head south of town and west of I-5 to Mount Ashland, where just past the ski area the vistas are glorious (and the roads bumpy).

During the Shakespeare Festival's November to mid-February off season, Ashlanders relax for a few months. Room rates plummet, and locals head south to Mount Ashland's ski slopes. As Interstate 5 drivers know, snow does pile up in southern Oregon's Siskiyou Mountains.

■ KLAMATH FALLS   *map page 186, G/H-4*

Once known for its bars and fist fights, Klamath Falls now attracts people perky enough to be up at dawn scouting the marshes for eagles, snow geese, and tundra swans.

It's worth taking a daytime stroll downtown, where the buildings are adorned with terra-cotta busts of Nefertiti and animal heads peering over doorframes. The **Ross Ragland Theater** is a multi-disciplinary performing arts center. The **Favell Museum** has a remarkably good collection of Western and Indian art. (It's hard to imagine a weapon more luminescent than the Favell's prized pink-and-blue fire-opal arrowhead, or a display quirkier than the miniature gun collection housed in a walk-in vault.) This museum showcases the best of Klamath Falls. Teddy Roosevelt once stayed at the nearby Baldwin Hotel. Now it's a cherished Main Street museum.

Klamath Falls leaders are working hard to change the city's rough and tumble image. Only one of the once-busy lakeside mills remains, and town is on its way to becoming a telecommunications and recreation center. The Running Y Ranch, a new resort with a golf course designed by Arnold Palmer, offers accommodations in a classy lodge and luxury homesites. Blue-green algae, claimed by its manufacturers to be "nature's most complete food," is harvested by a booming new age company based in a former Ford dealership at the Y intersection of Main Street and Esplanade.

Klamath Lake is Oregon's largest natural lake, but it covers only a small part of its former expanse. Shallow lakes and marshlands that attracted birds to the Klamath Basin have been tapped and diverted for irrigation since 1902. Today, in an effort to keep salmon and suckers alive, canals and reservoirs are tightly managed. They also draw enough water out to keep the Klamath Basin awash in potatoes, hay, and sugar beets. The tenuous balance is particularly difficult to maintain during drought years, when fishery biologists and farmers narrow their eyes at one another.

Every year, 20,000 acres in the Klamath Basin are flooded, then drained, to provide habitat for waterfowl. The basin's six refuges still attract incredible numbers of migrating waterbirds and, even in dry years, the basin seems awash with blue water lazing through perpetually spring-green flats. White pelicans nest in the Klamath Basin in March and stick around until late fall. During spring and fall, fields are carpeted with Canadian geese, snow geese, and swans.

Hundreds of eagles spend the winter in the Klamath Basin, roosting on sturdy old growth trees southwest of town. Every morning at sunrise they fly out for breakfast in a huge flock, with smaller hawks tagging along. Birdwatchers, wrapped tight in longjohns and puffy jackets, fumble between binoculars and

(following pages) Common egrets in the Lower Klamath National Wildlife Refuge.

Peace at Klamath

Chief Allen David of the Klamaths and Captain Jack of the Modocs make peace at Fort Klamath in December of 1869.

Allen David: I see you. I see your eyes. Your skin is red like my own. I will show you my heart. We have long been enemies. Many of our brave muck-a-lux (people) are dead. The ground is black with their blood. Their bones have been carried by the coyotes to the mountains, and scattered among the rocks. Our people are melting away like snow. We see the white chief is strong. The law is strong. We cannot be Indians longer. We must take the white man's law. The law our fathers had is dead. The white chief brought you here. We have made friends. We have washed each other's hands; they are not bloody now. We are friends. We have buried all the bad blood. We will not dig it up again. The white man sees us. Soch-e-la Tyee—God is looking at our hearts. The sun is a witness between us, the mountains are looking on us.

The pine tree is a witness, O my people! When you see this tree, remember it is a witness that here we made friends with the Mo-a-doc-as. Never cut down that tree. Let the arm be broke that would hurt it; let the hand die that would break a twig from it. So long as snow shall fall on Yainax mountain, let it stand. Long as the white rabbit shall live in the manzanita, let it stand. Let our children play round it; let the young people dance under its boughs, and let the old men smoke together in its shade. Let this tree stand there forever, as a witness. I have done.

Captain Jack: The white chief brought me here. I feel ashamed of my people, because they are poor. I feel like a man in a strange country without a father. My heart was afraid. I have heard your words; they warm my heart. I am not strange now. The blood is all washed from our hands. We are enemies no longer. We have buried the past. We have forgotten that we were enemies. We will not throw away the white chief's words. We will not hide them in the grass. I have planted a long stake in the ground. I have tied myself with a strong rope. I will not dig up the stake. I will not break the rope. My heart is the heart of my people. I am their words. I am not speaking for myself. I speak their hearts. My heart comes up to my mouth. I cannot keep it down with a sharp stick. I am done.

—Recorded by Jarold Ramsey in *Coyote Was Going There,* 1977

thermoses of hot coffee. When the first bird passes, unmistakable by its huge wingspan, there's a flurry of excited chatter. Soon the birds are coming in an almost steady stream, and the birders fall quiet, transfixed. In the late afternoon, the eagles straggle back to their roosts (under which there is usually a pile of feathers and bones), largely unheralded by humans. Also on the wing, coming in at sunset in great V formations looking for a place to rest are tundra swans who've flown thousands of miles to get here.

Oregon Department of Fish and Wildlife can give details about viewing the fly-out; 541-883-5734. The local Audubon chapter sponsors a big mid-February Bald Eagle Conference.

◆ KLAMATH INDIANS

Klamath Indians have lived here for 14,000 years harvesting wokas, or water lily seeds, from the marshes and shallow lakes. Traditional winter "pit" houses were based on shallow, saucer-like excavations, topped with broad cone-shaped wood roofs. Above-ground summer houses were framed with willow branches and draped with tule mats.

Klamaths were more compliant than their southern neighbors, the Modocs, about white incursions into their traditional lands. Little good it did them; whites generally lumped the two tribes together, treating them both as enemies. An 1864 treaty dealt the Klamaths a million-acre reservation where they were joined by some Modocs following the 1874 Northern California Modoc war with the United States.

The U.S. government terminated its relations with the Klamath tribes in 1954 (when there were over 2,000 tribal members) after a majority of the tribal members voted for this termination, partly because it meant that the tribe's assets were divided among individual members, to the tune of $50,000 apiece. Many recipients were taken advantage of by whites who saw a way of cashing in on the Indians' payments. Many Klamaths regretted both the loss of BIA services and the diminution of cultural identity that followed termination, and a group began working for reinstatement. The Klamath tribe was reinstated in 1991 and is now based in Chiloquin, north of Upper Klamath Lake. The tribe is reviving a culture that was neglected for many years, and hopes to prosper economically from their Chiloquin Casino (22 miles north of Klamath Falls). A First Fish ceremony (for a sucker), woka-gathering, and a Memorial Day weekend powwow in Klamath Falls

SOUTHERN OREGON

are regular events now. There are Klamath language study programs (the language almost died out), and the **Klamath County Museum**, at 1451 Main Street in Klamath Falls, has some fine displays of Klamath and Modoc culture and history.

■ CRATER LAKE   *map page 186, E-3*

Gold miners, looking for a strike to rival Jacksonville's, stumbled across Crater Lake in 1853. Of course, Klamath and Modoc Indians had known about the lake for thousands of years; their ancestors were living nearby when it was formed after the eruption of Mount Mazama 7,700 years ago.

Mount Mazama was 10,000 feet in elevation when small vents and cones on its flanks began to ooze lava. Deep inside the mountain, a huge pocket of magma

Emil Britt, son of noted photographer Peter Britt, ponders the beauty of Crater Lake on the day it was first photographed in 1874. (Southern Oregon Historical Society)

SOUTHERN
OREGON

This contemporary photograph of Crater Lake was taken not too far from where little Emil sits on the opposite page.

formed. A violent explosion blasted fiery ash all the way to Bend, followed by slews of red hot lava sliding down the mountain's sides. As the magma chamber emptied, the mountaintop lost its foundation, and collapsed into a 2,000-foot-deep pit. Even after the caldera formed, lava continued to pulse up from the bottom of the basin, building smallish cones, including Wizard Island, which now breaks the surface of the lake.

A thousand years later, the caldera was filled to within 1,000 feet of its rim with rainwater. No streams flow into or out of Crater Lake; it gains and loses water from precipitation and evaporation.

Now it's Oregon's only national park, and the country's deepest lake. The road from Klamath Falls climbs past big ponderosas until it reaches the crater's rim. There you can park, walk across the road past the beautifully renovated (but half-

SOUTHERN OREGON

heartedly tended) historic Crater Lake Lodge, and look down at the lake. It's a thousand-foot drop to the water, where blue sky is reflected in the lake water, which is 1,932 feet deep, a constant 39 degrees, and practically clear enough to read a book sunk six feet deep. Recently proposals to tap geothermal sources under lake waters have been countered by assertions that this may cloud the water.

It's not easy to get from the 33-mile rim road down to the water; a steep trail on the north rim is the only route. At the bottom of the trail, it is possible to catch the lake tour boat, the only craft permitted on the lake. (A boat leaves every hour, tickets are available at the dock.) Winter is incredible at Crater Lake. The southern entrance is plowed year round, but the rim road is closed to all but cross-country skiers (the lakeside concession rents skis). Within yards of the rim parking lot, crowds fall away, and the only sounds beyond the chatter of Clark's nutcrackers and gray jays are the woofs of snow falling from tree branches.

Accommodations in the national park are at **Crater Lake Lodge,** a historic lodge at the crater's rim; 541-830-8700. In nearby Prospect, try the tidy **Prospect Hotel** at 391 Mill Creek Road; 541-560-3664. **Union Creek Resort** is north of Prospect on Hwy 62 and offers rustic creekside cabins; 541-560-3565.

■ UPPER ROGUE AND DIAMOND LAKE   *map page 186, D-3*

It's not far from Crater Lake to the highest stretches of the Rogue River, less well-known but no less lovely than the section of the river between Grants Pass and Gold Beach. Stop off at the Rogue River Gorge, on Hwy 62 near Union Creek. Rock walls squeeze the Rogue into a narrow churn. Turn north to glacier-scoured Diamond Lake, popular year-round with southern Oregon families. In the winter it's possible to cross-country ski here and in the summer to boat and hike. Vigorous, non-agoraphobic hikers might wish to tackle the scree slopes of Mount Thielsen, the spikey-topped 9,182-foot peak that's always popping in and out of view from Diamond Lake's shoreline. Thielsen is the "lightning rod of the Cascades;" lightning-struck spots have metamorphosed into giant glassy carrots of re-crystalized rock.

(opposite) Mount Thielsen catches the first rays of dawn over Diamond Lake.

NORTHEAST OREGON

◆ **HIGHLIGHTS**

◆ **AREA OVERVIEW**

East of the Cascades, Oregon towns become more compact as the distance between them widens. Here space is definitely not at a premium. Big wheat farms and ranches share the open country, and the cowboys aren't just wannabes. Just when the landscape threatens to become a little too flat and dry, the Blue Mountains rise up, steep-sided and piney, followed by the Wallowas. On the state's eastern border is Hells Canyon, where the landscape suddenly becomes perpendicular.

Northeast Oregon is defined by big rivers: the Columbia separates Oregon from Washington and pours all the region's water toward the Pacific. The John Day courses west and north through fossil-laden rock formations and desert canyons. This river empties into the Columbia east of The Dalles. The Grande Ronde's headwaters are near Anthony Lakes, northwest of Baker City, and flow into the Snake River. The Snake cuts a steep gorgeous channel through layered basalt flows separating Oregon and Idaho.

Climate: Summers are clear with hot days and cool nights. Afternoon thunderstorms are common. Winters are cold and snowy.

Food & Lodging: Accommodations range from the surprisingly elegant Geiser Grand Hotel in Baker City to Halfway's colorful, big-hearted Pine Valley Lodge. If you want to stay at a guest ranch, you'll find several recommended in the text. Most small towns have very basic motels and cafes. Remote National Forest campgrounds are numerous.

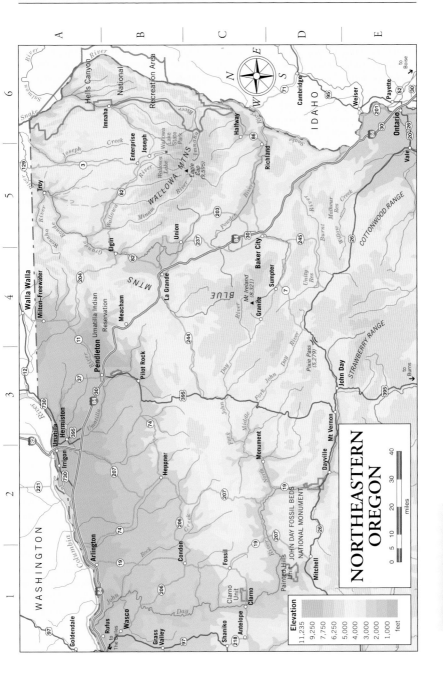

NORTHEASTERN OREGON

■ JOHN DAY COUNTRY

There are two approaches to touring the area around the John Day River—follow the fossil traces, or zigzag between towns with charming names—Fossil, Spray, Horse Heaven, Antelope, Fox. Not every dot on the map represents an extant town, but most places do have a little store, often with a lunch counter, where it's easy to catch up on the local gossip: who got caught poaching up in the Ochocos; who bought a promising new bull; who's over in Portland for the weekend, going to plays and shopping for art supplies; who hired the county road crew to put in a new gravel ranch road. People still tell strangers about the Rajneeshees, the red-clad guru-worshippers who took over Muddy Ranch and, for a few years in the 1980s, the town of Antelope. They'll reminisce about girlhoods in remote Blue Mountain mining towns, and tell you about fossils they've found in their backyards.

Fossil-hunting in Oregon dates back to the 1860s, when Thomas Condon, a Congregationalist minister and natural history buff, was posted in The Dalles. Encouraged by parishioners who became converts to geology, Condon explored the region's hillsides and river gorges, and began finding extraordinary fossils. His fossil collection was a must-see in The Dalles, and by the end of the 1800s, every East Coast paleontologist of note had made the obligatory pilgrimage to view John Day fossils. Condon became a bonafide geologist, and was a member of the University of Oregon's faculty from the college's founding in 1876 until his death in 1907.

◆ FOSSIL   *map page 223, C-1*

Fossil is a good place to begin a paleontological tour and is worth exploring for a couple of hours. Not near anything except the state road map centerfold, this well-preserved little town definitely shows signs of life. Stop by the store and walk the wood plank floor beneath mounted big game trophies and fish. Perhaps a kid will be learning to sew in the fabric section.

At the funky **Fossil Museum** an albino porcupine is displayed next to a primitive permanent wave machine, a jumble of bulldog clips dangling from frayed electrical wire. Traces of Rajneeshpuram are displayed with relief that the neighboring town is once again Antelope.

Across the street at **Asher's Car Museum** a phalanx of polished old-time cars rests in a double-wide(open on whim). In a small square, a sheepherder's wagon is displayed. This particular wagon, a leading compact of its day, was used until 1984—a dusty bottle of Tang rests with perfect historical accuracy on the kitchen counter.

Look for fossils behind the bleachers at the high school athletic field. (Pay heed to the sign, "Please don't break fossils on the bleachers.")

◆ JOHN DAY RIVER *map page 223, B/1-D/4*

For more fossil hunting, though not collecting, head west from Fossil to Clarno and the John Day River. A juniper-scented hike through the red bluffs, wind-carved arches and spires of the Clarno Unit of the John Day Fossil Beds reveals tropical plants embedded in mud flows 44 million years ago.

Put a canoe into the John Day River at **Clarno** for a 70-mile, three or four-day river trip through rugged basalt-pillared canyonland with sagebrush and cactus-strewn cliffs, some adorned with petroglyphs and studded with fossils. The silty John Day is one of the longest undammed rivers in the lower 48. Except when spring snowmelt is at its peak, it's an easygoing float with good fishing, camping, and wildlife—keep an eye out for golden eagles, chukars (partridges), wild horses, and coyotes. Late spring is the best time to float here; by July, the season's usually over. Put in at Clarno Bridge on Hwy 218 and take out at Cottonwood Bridge, Hwy 206. Call 503-261-9246 for flow conditions or 541-416-6700 for more details, including a list of shuttle drivers.

John Day himself was a Virginia woodsman who joined an overland journey to Astoria in 1811. He and a companion lost their way near the Snake River, crossed the Blue Mountains in the winter, and met helpful Indians as well as hostile ones who stole their clothing. The two putative mountain men were found naked and starving along the Columbia River. John Day went crazy, and died in Astoria. Along the river named for him, the colors are as soft as the eroded hills. Dusky green willows grow along the bank, where the river roars and birds call.

Wild erosion has occurred across the John Day country, including the magnificent Sheep Rock Unit west of Dayville. The hills are sculpted into fantastic forms, with castle-like cliffs of pale volcanic ash. Most of Oregon's volcanos spewed basalt lava from deep in the earth, but these pale rocks were originally sedimentary. The result is a unique volcanic scenery. Red, tan, and green striations cascade down the cliffs. Some are topped with little basalt berets that give them a proper Oregon heritage.

◆ BLUE BASIN   *map page 223, C-1/2*

Hike through the Blue Basin, on Hwy 19 about 10 miles north of Hwy 26, for a close look at the John Day formation's hallmark green ash. The sage-scented streambed is awash with green volcanic ash. A natural amphitheater, half a mile in, is quiet but for the echoing bird calls, crickets, and wind gusts rustling sparse grass. Many important fossils were unearthed from Blue Basin, and the verdigris cliffs continue to erode with each big storm, exposing new fossils, though they're widely scattered and difficult to spot. Oreodonts—sheep-size, leaf-eating mammals, akin to pygmy hippos—were numerous in the forests and streams of 25 million years ago. Sabertooth cats and hornless rhinoceroses lived here too, back before the Cascade Range rose high enough to block the flow of moist Pacific air. Replicas of basin fossils are placed strategically along the trail and covered with big plexiglas bubbles. The actual fossils are located in the expansive new Thomas Condon Paleontology Center Museum three miles east.

Continue up the John Day to **Dayville** (*map page 223, D-E/2*), where deciduous trees shade the highway through town, and the river runs along the north side of the road. You can walk across town in three minutes.

The Blue Basin area (above) in the John Day Fossil Beds National Monument,
and the Painted Hills (right).

◆ JOHN DAY *map page 223, D/E-3*

Upriver, near the southwestern edge of the Blue Mountains, is juniper-scented John Day, where the **Kam Wah Chung Museum** at 250 NW Canton Street provides an introduction to the region's gold mining history; 541-575-0028. As in Jacksonville (see page 206), Chinese miners were left with piles of rubble, which they found reasonably profitable to mine. In the 1880s there were twice as many Chinese as Caucasians in John Day, and the museum building was once an herbalist's office and Chinese social center. For more information call 541-575-0028.

From John Day, Oregon's gold belt runs east in a 50-mile swath to the Snake River. In 1845, an Oregon Trail wagon train ventured off the main trail route and found gold nuggets in the bottom of a water bucket (nobody could recall, at trail's end, exactly where the bucket had been filled). When California and Idaho proved thick with gold, Oregonians began retracing the eastern Oregon "Blue Bucket" route. By 1862 a thousand people were living in tents along Canyon Creek near John Day, placer mining the stream's abundant gold. In 1913, an 80-ounce gold nugget tumbled into a Blue Mountain placer mine. The U.S. Bank in Baker City now has this nugget, estimated to be worth between $30,000 and $40,000.

◆ SUMPTER

map page 223, D-4

"Ghost towns" in the rugged Blue Mountains run the gamut from the totally deserted to the trumped up. Sumpter, the most visited, has never been entirely deserted, and now does well by its past. At the turn of the century, 3,000 people lived in Sumpter, where hard-rock and placer mines were in full gear, and a narrow gauge

Miner David Briggs holds a nearly pure gold nugget extracted from the Briggs Pocket Mine. (Oregon Historical Society)

train carried gold and timber to Baker. As the mines played out, people moved on, though logging and gold dredges kept business alive until the mid-1950s.

The narrow gauge train is Sumpter's focus now. It shuttles visitors up from **Phillips Lake** all summer long and is a good family outing. For more remote and ghostly towns, head up County Road 24 to **Granite,** or north up Cracker Creek to **Bourne,** where gold is still mined. After a little poking around, it becomes clear that gold dredging has reconfigured the local topography. Combine these piles of rubble with hillsides covered with dead trees (victims of mountain pine beetles) and things look a little rough. For scenic respite, head to Anthony Lakes, high in the Elkhorn Ridge. The Elkhorns, on the fringe of the Blue Mountains, reach almost to the western edge of Baker City. There's great powder skiing, both down-hill and cross-country, at 7,000-foot **Anthony Lakes Resort.** In the summer, pitch a tent in the campground next to the ski area and spend a day taking a canoe tour of the lakes. Follow that up with a hike on the Elkhorn Trail.

■ BAKER CITY *map page 223, C/D-4/5*

Baker City was hatched from a gold nugget in 1863. A bar and hotel were built first, and a bank soon followed. Stage lines freighted merchandise from Baker to the mining towns until the Oregon Short Line Railroad arrived in 1884. According-ing to the WPA Guide:

> *T*ravelers passing through saw more exciting life in Baker City than in any town between Portland and Salt Lake. Miners, gamblers, *filles de joie,* ranchers, cowboys, and sheepherders frequented the dance halls and sa-loons or mingled on the board walks with the citizenry. Gambling halls, blacksmith shops, livery stables, and feed corrals were the principal in-dustrial establishments. Notwithstanding the two-fisted character of the town, the city commissioners in 1881 passed an ordinance prohibiting small boys from shooting marbles or riding velocipedes on the sidewalks, and required one citizen to remove his potato patch from a lot on a prin-cipal street.

The wide streets and sturdy stone buildings recall the town's grand ambitions. In a way, Baker City (which tacked the "City" back onto its name in 1989, after 77 years of being shortened to "Baker") is finding present-day prosperity in reliving

(following pages) Wheat fields stretch to the horizon in northeastern Oregon.

MEMORIES OF THE
WHITMAN MASSACRE, 1847

In the summer of 1847 a severe measles epidemic broke out in Oregon Territory. As Indians had no immunity to this disease, they almost invariably died. At first they tried to use a traditional method of healing that involved sitting in a sweat lodge, then jumping into a cold stream. When this and other methods failed, they came to a missionary and physician, Dr. Marcus Whitman at Waiilatpu, 26 miles from the Hudson's Bay fort on the Columbia. He tried to help them, but because many more of the Indians died than the whites, some Indians became convinced they were being poisoned. This provoked the Whitman massacre in which Dr. Whitman was killed along with several others. A Mr. Osborne, whose family was ill with measles and at the mission for treatment, was one of the survivors.

As the guns fired and the yells commenced I leaned my head upon the bed and committed myself and family to my Maker. My wife removed the loose floor. I dropped under the floor with my sick family in their night clothes, taking only two woollen sheets, a piece of bread, and some cold mush, and pulled the floor over us. In five minutes the room was full of Indians, but they did not discover us. The roar of guns, the yells of the savages, and the crash of clubs and knives and the groans of the dying continued till dark. We distinctly heard the dying groans of Mrs. Whitman, Mr. Rogers, and Francis, till they died away one after the other. We heard the last words of Mr. Rogers in a slow voice calling "Come, Lord Jesus, come quickly." Soon after this I removed the floor and we went out. We saw the white face of Francis by the door. It was warm as we laid our hand upon it, but he was dead. I carried my two youngest children, who were sick, and my wife held on to my clothes in her great weakness. We had all been sick with measles. Two infants had died. She had not left her bed in six weeks till that day, when she stood up a few minutes. The naked painted Indians were dancing the scalp dance around a large fire at a little distance. There seemed no hope for us and we knew not which way to go, but bent our steps toward Fort Walla Walla.

A dense cold fog shut out every star and the darkness was complete. We could see no trail and not even the hand before the face. We had to feel out the trail with our feet. My wife almost fainted but staggered along. Mill Creek, which we had to wade, was high with late rains and came up to the waist. My wife in her great weakness came nigh washing down, but held to my clothes. I braced myself with a stick, holding a child in one arm. I had to cross five times for the children. The water was icy cold and the air freezing some. Staggering along about two miles, Mrs. Osborne fainted and could go no farther, and we hid ourselves in the brush of the Walla Walla River, not far below Tamsukey's (a chief) lodges, who was very active at the commencement of the butchery. We were thoroughly wet, and the cold fog like snow was about us. The cold mud was partially frozen as we crawled, feeling our way, into the dark brush. We could see nothing, the darkness was so extreme. I spread one wet sheet down on the frozen ground; wife and children crouched upon it. I covered the other over them. I thought they must soon perish as they were shaking and their teeth rattling with cold. I kneeled down and commended us to my Maker.

—from the diary of a Mr. Osborne, 1847

Doctor Whitman appears oblivious to impending doom in this old print of the "Whitman Massacre" of 1847. (Southern Oregon Historical Society)

its past. The town, nearly moribund a few years back, has been largely revived by a route that passed a few miles away over 150 years ago, the Oregon Trail.

If you come to stay in Baker City and want old time flavor try the **Geiser Grand Hotel**, a beautifully refurbished downtown hotel at 1926 Main Street; 888-434-7374. Eat a surprisingly good dinner with the locals at **Barley Brown's Brewpub**, 2190 Main Street.

◆ OREGON TRAIL INTERPRETIVE CENTER   *map page 223, C/D-5*

The Oregon Trail Interpretive Center is several miles east of town on Hwy 86, at the top of Flagstaff Hill. The setting is spectacular, and though the outside looks like an expensive prefab house, the interior works. The Interpretive Center is a modern-day museum—one that imparts a sense of the experience rather than listing facts. Journal entries are everywhere—written out on the walls, voiced over in dioramas, included in film narrations. These pioneers, especially the women, were remarkable diarists, and they told astounding stories. They wrote of the birth and death of children, of disease, of river crossings and their party's arrival at trail landmarks. Wander through the museum, immersed in the private struggles of pioneers, then come up on a wall-sized window overlooking the mountains to the west. Gauge the wind and clouds and look down the path to the pioneer wagon ruts. For you, it'll be an afternoon's walk through sagebrush humming with cicadas—for them, it was the Blue Mountains, and the onset of fall. For more information, call 541-523-1843.

On curvy Hwy 86 east of the museum, tractors work the hay fields, trailing clouds of dust; irrigation sprinklers shoot off wildly in every direction, catching sunlight and reflecting it back. Magpies fly down and flash black and white across the road. Highway 86 picks up the loopy Powder River canyon and follows the dark blue water through green hills edged with mullein and foxglove. North of the highway, the southern border of the Wallowas soar, all ice-nipped and glaciated. Even the mountains rising around you don't hem this big country in.

■ HELLS CANYON   *map page 223, A-6*

Hells Canyon of the Snake River separates Oregon and Idaho. The canyon itself is 150 miles long, and includes 67 miles of undammed, free-flowing, and tumultuous river. Although it is the continent's deepest gorge, averaging 6,000 feet from

Hells Canyon is the deepest gorge in the United States. From Hat Point Lookout (right) the Snake River winds along some 6,000 feet below.

rim to river, it's not exactly easy to get to, and many Northwesterners know it mostly as a place to go for a scenic jet boat ride.

Hells Canyon's geologic origins date back to the collision of an ancient island group with the western edge of the North American continent. It's probable that a river gorge formed where the archipelago attached to the larger land mass, but the river didn't take its present route until it was rerouted by volcanic flows from the Columbia.

Hells Canyon remains wild and remote. The elevation changes with every step, springs come out of nowhere, and plants and animals fill every ecological niche. Dams have stilled some Snake River waters and destroyed salmon runs, but the most remote canyon areas with incredible whitewater are protected. It's a funny scheme, though. Floating permits are tightly regulated, though noisy jet boat travel remains unrestricted.

The Hells Canyon Preservation Council hopes to create a preserve managed by the National Park Service, claiming that the Forest Service has mismanaged the wilderness and recreation areas by allowing overgrazing and clearcutting. This is not a popular position with most locals, who fear increased restrictions as well as a loss of livelihood and personal freedom.

◆ HALFWAY *map page 223, C/5-6*

Halfway, 20 miles west of the Snake River on Hwy 86, is the closest real town to Hells Canyon. Located in the Pine Valley, near the Wallowa's southern edge, it shows up on maps because this hamlet is the only settlement for miles around.

Locals know they have a good thing going in this charming town but tend to downplay their good fortune. Ask a guy where to eat breakfast and he'll tell you, "Well ain't in this town much of a choice. There's a place on the right and a place on the left, Stockman's and Wild Bill's, and neither of them's much of anything." **Pine Valley Lodge** is a charming, quirky place to stay. Several rooms have kitchens, and a delicious continental breakfast is served in the lodge; 163 N Main; 541-742-2027.

Notices of funerals and garage sales are chalked on a blackboard on Main Street. You can make a U-turn on Main, and if you park, it's most likely fine to leave your keys in the car. If this seems like a slice of old-time America, it would be a mistake to think Halfway residents don't have their concerns. In the year 2000 the town raised some much-needed cash by striking a deal with an internet retailer and changing its name to Half.com. It was only a one-year gig and now all that remains of the venture is a scattered collection of Half.com coffee mugs.

◆ SNAKE RIVER DAM *map page 223, C-6*

At Oxbow, where Hwy 86 hits the Snake, the river is in the hands of Idaho Power. A dam, a motor home community, and a backed-up river full of jet boats is a recipe for disaster, but the Snake and Hells Canyon are powerful enough to overcome it all. The jet boats do offer the easiest passage to the heart of the canyon. The daylong buzz down the river passes pictographs, abandoned homesteads, and mines nestled at the bottom of steep canyon walls.

◆ SNAKE RIVER TRAIL *map page 223, C-6*

If jet boat trips seem noisy and rushed, drive north from Oxbow to the road's end (about eight miles on a bumpy dirt road) and pick up the Snake River trail. Scenic if not wild, the canyon slopes off into blue-green waters. It's a hot, dry trail, yet it's possible to climb down to the river in a few places and take a dip in one of the many pools of calm water. Take along drinking water and a swimsuit.

There's a good view of fish in the river, and of boats full of anglers fishing for bass, crappie, or trout. Gargantuan white sturgeon still live in the Snake. These primitive-looking fish, which can live for 100 years and grow to 1,000 pounds, used to migrate to sea. Now they are corralled in reservoirs between the dams. Dams have altered water flows and temperatures in ways sturgeon can't always deal with. Fortunately, only catch-and-release sturgeon fishing is permitted in the Snake.

A short riverbank day hike is an ideal way to see the canyon, or, if you prefer, consider a backpacking trip (jet boats will ferry hikers to and from riverbank trails). Drivers can catch Forest Road 39 eight miles west of Oxbow, and climb north toward the Imnaha River. This forested route rewards visitors with an openness not found west of the Cascades. The road climbs through bright, cool, wildflower meadows shaded by pines. (Call 541-742-7511 before planning a trip as Road 39 is not plowed during the winter and sometimes doesn't open until well into the summer.)

NORTHEAST

◆ HELLS CANYON RIM DRIVES *map page 223, A/6–C/6*

Hells Canyon Rim Drive spur leads to an overlook with spectacular views of the canyon and the Seven Devils Mountains, the Wallowa's stony Idaho lookalikes.

North of the Rim Drive viewpoint, Road 39 joins the upper reaches of the **Imnaha River** (known, along with the Lostine River, for its native trout). Continue along the Imnaha River to the town of Imnaha on 30 miles of dirt road, through a dazzling river valley where ranches are rimmed by steep hills. When you arrive in shady **Imnaha,** you'll be ready to hang out at the store, where wooden Indians repose on the front porch, and bar booths take up the center of the wood-floored store. Imnaha hosts an annual bear-rattlesnake dinner. It's usually in the spring, but the schedule depends on when the local hunters can buy a bear tag—sometimes they must wait until October.

◆ HAT POINT

If you are looking for a challenge, take the road to Hat Point. Twenty-four miles, seemingly straight up on a narrow dirt road with pixie-sized pullouts, make this Oregon's ultimate white-knuckle drive. For the first five miles, it's hard to enjoy the views. A driver needs concentration and plenty of nerve, and a passenger learns the real meaning of the word "cliffhanger." (Guard rails up here? Are you kidding?) Horse packers travel this route, and it's likely that any vehicle coming down is going to be bigger than a Toyota.

Is the drive worth it? You bet. Hat Point is up close to 7,000 feet, carpeted with wild strawberries and mint, Indian paintbrush, wild geraniums, and lupine, with a lookout and a no-frills campground. Early in the morning, cinnamon-colored black bears may forage in the bushes and coyotes trot through the meadows. There's a panoramic view of the Wallowas and Seven Devils from the Hat Point lookout tower. Don't let a climb up the tower substitute for a hike down toward the river, however brief. A steep trail traverses hills, wrinkled as a sharpei puppy, 5,500 feet and six hours down to the river. The bottom of the gorge is much warmer than the top; Indians found the canyon bottom made a good winter camp.

The top half of the hike has the best wildflowers and canyon views. Deeper into the gorge, the air warms, and the trail becomes quite steep and scrabbly. At the bottom, where the river is wild and tumbling, expect a jet boat to buzz by about once every hour.

◆ LOWER IMNAHA RIVER ROAD

Another trail to the Snake takes off 15 miles north of Imnaha on Lower Imnaha River Road, another steep drive into a canyon every bit as spectacular as Hells Canyon. The grueling five-mile NeeMePoo Trail traverses Lone Pine Saddle (great views here) before hitting the Snake River at Dug Bar. Here the Nez Perce crossed into Idaho when they were forced to leave the Wallowas in 1877. If you'd rather drive the final stretch of the Imnaha Canyon, the lower Imnaha Road continues to Dug Bar. Check the rocks for some of the region's best petroglyphs, and bring a fishing rod (winter steelhead run here, and there are trout the rest of the year). Four miles upstream from Dug Bar, at Deep Creek, are the remains of a Chinese miners' camp, where 32 gold panners were killed by white thieves in 1887.

■ WALLOWA MOUNTAINS *map page 223, B/C-5*

From Imnaha, it's one giant step south to Joseph and the remote Wallowa Mountains. Exposed granite sticks up from green meadows, and snow-topped peaks soar above the gentle hills to nearly 10,000 feet. It's hard to get into these mountains for a casual day hike. The spaces are so big, and the Wallowa's Eagle Cap Wilderness Area so remote, that horse packing fits in perfectly (see page 293). On or off a horse, it's easy to see why the Nez Perce loved the Wallowas.

Until the mid-1800s, this was Nez Perce country. Bands of Indians fished for late-summer salmon in Wallowa Lake, and, after acquiring horses in 1730, ran them nearby in the spacious valleys where there was plenty of prairie grass.

Explorers Lewis and Clark met the Nez Perce during their 1805 visit to Idaho. The friendly Indians kept the party's horses over the winter while the explorers traveled by canoe down the Columbia River. The Nez Perce took their pact of peace with these travelers from the east seriously, and Lewis and Clark considered them the finest people they met on their expedition. As more whites began using their land as a thoroughfare, the Nez Perce sought to make the best of it. Oregon Trail emigrants frequently traded their bony, tired cattle for Nez Perce horses. With a little rest and prairie grass, the cattle thrived, and the Indians became prosperous cattlemen. As the Willamette Valley filled up with homesteads, settlers began retracing their Oregon Trail journey. Eventually some settled in the Wallowa country, on land dedicated to the Nez Perce in an 1855 treaty. In 1863, the U.S. government cut the Nez Perce land allotment by about 90 percent, and the Christianized chief

Chief Joseph of the Nez Perce.

who signed the treaty didn't speak for all the people. The tribe divided into Christian "treaty" and traditional "non-treaty" factions.

Chief Old Joseph, an early convert to Christianity, was so opposed that he ripped both the treaty paperwork and his Gospel of Matthew to shreds. Old Joseph died in 1871, and his son, Joseph, became a leader of the non-treaty Wallowa Nez Perce. Joseph was not a warrior; he was a negotiator, and worked hard to maintain rapport with the white settlers and the army, even as Nez Perce were being killed in scuffles with whites.

In 1877, a government commission concluded that all the Nez Perce, even those who hadn't signed the 1863 treaty, must move onto the Idaho reservation. Joseph's band left the Wallowas, crossed the Snake River, and met with other non-treaty bands in Idaho, where they gathered camas before the inevitable trip to the reservation. It was a tense time, and tempers flared. Several Nez Perce men decided they needed to avenge the murder of a relative, and it led to the killing of more than a dozen white settlers.

The gathered non-treaty people, realizing they were all in trouble, broke camp. The army charged the Indians, who routed the soldiers and captured a good weapon supply. The army chased the Nez Perce through Idaho and Montana as the Indians tried to seek sanctuary first with the southeastern Montana Crow, then in Canada with Sitting Bull. They were 40 miles from Canada when Joseph and 431 of his people were forced to surrender their weapons.

The Nez Perce were sent to "Indian Territory" in Oklahoma, though some were later permitted to live on the reservation in Idaho with the treaty signers. Chief Joseph and some of his supporters were sent to Washington's Colville Reservation. The Nez Perce are still split—treaty people in Idaho, with the non-treaty mostly on the Colville Reservation. Old Joseph's grave was moved to the edge of Wallowa Lake in 1926, after a local dentist vandalized the original burial site.

◆ WALLOWA LAKE   *map page 223, B/C-5/6*

At azure, mountain-cradled Wallowa Lake, creeping development has begun. The nearby town of Joseph has just enough amenities and charm to make it attractive to urban refugees. Housing developments are taking over the west side of the lake. The state park campground on the lake's southern edge is nearly frenetic during summer weekends, when campers feed Doritos to deer wandering from tent to tent, and jet skis buzz out from lakeside docks. Up the road from Wallowa Lodge, a tram zips hikers and view-seekers on an ear-popping ascent of

Wallowa Lake with the Wallowa Mountains looming in the background.

Mount Howard. Purists and pennypinchers will roll their eyes and drive by, but on a clear day, alpine views from the tram's terminus extend to Montana's Bitterroot Mountains. Count in easy access to mountain hikes, and the cost of the ride is a real deal—a 10-minute ride to the top of the world.

◆ JOSEPH *map page 223, B-5*

The town of Joseph is lively, artsy, and beautiful. It's as trendy as northeastern Oregon gets, but hitching posts stand solid in a vacant lot between galleries, and locals still ride horses into town. Mongrel dogs lounge in the wildflower gardens planted on every street corner, and teenage boys, clad in bright western shirts and cowboy hats, come to town to gawk at girls.

The town takes its Nez Perce heritage seriously. And, like any full-blooded Western town, Joseph enjoys a party. Late in July, trail riders come down from Walla Walla and pickups come in from all over the Northwest for Chief Joseph Days. There's a three-day rodeo, a big ranch breakfast, a parade, an Indian encampment, and Indian dancing.

When team roping begins to lose its thrill, rodeo spectators drift downtown, where old brick storefronts feature a variety of bronze casting galleries. The literary arts also rear up at Wallowa Lake in July when the Fishtrap Writers Conference brings some of the Northwest's best writers to town.

To stay here try **Eagle Cap Chalets** which offer comfortable cabins near Wallowa Lake. Hwy 82; 541-432-4704. The historic **Wallowa Lake Lodge** has cabins and a main lodge; 660 Wallowa Lake Hwy (Route 1), 541-432-9821.

◆ ENTERPRISE *map page 223, B-5*

Located six miles north of Joseph, this town is, as its name suggests, a practical place. Only a couple of galleries are squeezed in among the stores selling utilitarian clothing, hardware, and computers. Enterprise proves its true Western mettle with the obligatory Stockman's Bar (nearly every Western town has one) and the old timers perched on benches, sizing up women and dogs. Stop by the Bookloft and gallery; it's the best bookstore this side of La Grande's Sunflower Books.

■ GRANDE RONDE VALLEY AND LA GRANDE *map page 223, B-C/4*

We came in sight of the Grande Ronde, a beautiful level valley, nearly round, I should think. But O! The getting down to it, over a long steep and stoney hill that equaled any getting downstairs I ever saw, and I have seen some on this road . . .

—Parethenia Blank, 1852

The Grande Ronde Valley is so perfectly contained and complete in its beauty it seems life could have begun here. Until the Grande Ronde River was diverted to make way for the first railroad, the broad, circular Grande Ronde Valley was marshy country. Nez Perce and Cayuse harvested camas from the blue-tinted marshes and soaked in the springs at **Hot Lake,** a spiritual place where quarrels were stilled.

When whites took over the valley, Hot Lake was developed as a vacation resort, then a sanatorium, drawing vacationers from as far away as the East Coast. A fire destroyed much of the resort in 1934, and now it's deserted, some say haunted. The huge brick building is shrouded in scaffolding; pigeons and snakes have the run of the place, adding to the spookiness. Glimpses inside reveal graceful banisters, tiled floors, the remains of a sunroom, and a bathhouse full of old clawfoot tubs. Boiling sulfurous springs gurgle in an octagonal stone outbuilding set on the edge of waterlily-studded Ladd Marsh. The marsh gives an inkling of what the entire valley was like before the river was diverted in the 1870s. On a cool spring morning, it's easy to imagine all the buildings gone and an Indian camp by the marsh's edge with sulfur mists rising above it.

Oregon Trail pioneers, intent on getting across the Blue Mountains, didn't linger in Ladd Marsh—they mostly stuck to the low ridges around the valley. Wagon trains hit the Grande Ronde Valley in the fall, and many pulled off the trail (present-day B Avenue near Birney Park) for a night's rest. Nez Perce or Cayuse were often around to trade.

An Oregon Trail commemorative sculpture in Birney Park describes the journey in pictograph-like images, photographic impressions, dreamlike images of carried objects, treasures, and the valley. Even if you don't really *get* it, you'll find the sculpture a break from the endless Oregon Trail kiosks with grainy historical photos and maps of the West.

MAGIC OF MUSHROOMS

Oregon's commercial mushroom business has been expanding rapidly. Mushroom buyers can be seen parking their trucks along some of the state's most remote roadways, ready to trade cash for mushrooms as pickers emerge from the forest. During the beginning of the season, a single pound of prime matsutake mushrooms can earn a picker more than $50. But while commercial mushrooming has boomed, few fortunes are being made in the woods. Most pickers earn the most modest sort of living, trading eight to ten hours of stoop labor for $20 to $100 dollars a day.

Professional mushroom pickers are necessarily migrant, moving with the seasons and following the rainy weather and the forest fires to places where the network of underground fungal mycelia promises to send up fruit. A good number of the pickers are virtually homeless, living out of their cars as they move up the coast.

Lars Norgren has been in the mushroom business since 1984. He began as an amateur, searching for psychoactive *Psilocybe* near his home town of Corvallis. Today Norgren is the proprietor of Peak Forest Fruit, a Portland-area company that buys and sells fresh boletes, morels, matsutakes, oysters, candy caps, and chanterelles. Norgren says the decline in other forest industries pushes more and more people into the woods to look for mushrooms.

"There is a geometric increase in the number of commercial pickers," Norgren explains. According to Norgren, some of the pickers are desperate for even the smallest amounts of cash. "A lot of these pickers do not have a home to go home to," he says. "I see these full-time drunks in Fort Bragg in late February, hanging around until every last mushroom is gone, and then I see them in the [Columbia River] Gorge in mid-April, living in these wrecks of cars. You can't figure out how they even keep them running and get up here." Another group of pickers come from stable but poor Cambodian and Laotian-American communities, where an extra couple of hundred dollars a week can provide a huge boost to a struggling family.

Due to the growing number of pickers, much of the Oregon mushroom crop finds its way into the hands of commercial buyers like Norgren, who estimates that up to 90 percent of the mushrooms in popular areas are now being found and taken. However, since pickers harvest only the fruit of the fungus, while leaving the mycelium undisturbed, there is little chance that the increase in commercial mushrooming will endanger long term health of the fungi. Still, there are other, more serious threats. Mushrooms are symbiotic with trees. No trees, no mushrooms. The future of Oregon mushrooming, like so much of the state's future, depends on the fate of its forests.

As a hobby, hunting mushrooms is an entertaining but not particularly easy pastime. Neophytes intending to test their skill might pick up David Arora's entertaining guide, *All that the Rain Promises and More* . . . . Arora is one of the leading experts on West Coast mushrooms. For those who prefer the final phase of the mushroom hunt, i.e., the feast, Lars Norgren sells his fresh mushrooms at the Portland Farmer's Market nearly every Saturday morning. During the height of the season fresh chanterelles can be had for as little as $6 a pound. Many of the other produce markets around Oregon have wonderful, seasonal mushrooms at a fraction of the price one pays at those gourmet food outlets that have the misfortune to be a much greater distance from the rainy woods.

—Gary Wolf

Do not eat the mushrooms pictured above!
Experience and knowledge are the essence of successful mushroom hunting.

Many emigrants were impressed by the valley's lushness and upon realizing that good land in the Willamette Valley was all but gone by the 1860s, returned east to the Grande Ronde. The Oregon Trail's first store west of the Rockies was near Birney Park. Unfortunately, the local fire department burned it down as part of a drill a few years back, and a big modern house was built in its place.

Today, logging and mill work figure heavily in **La Grande.** All over the east side, pine beetles have been killing trees, and salvage logging has become big business. Logging cutbacks in the western part of the state have accelerated cutting in the pine forests of the Blue Mountains.

This is not a well-to-do community, and many people do rely on seasonal pick-up work. In recent years, mushroom gathering has been a lucrative seasonal job for some. Stories vary—kids tell you they know someone who made hundreds of dollars a day when they lucked across a thick growth of morels, and that people have been shot for picking in somebody else's territory. Parents dismiss big money stories as nonsense. They insist that the only people getting rich off morels are the mushroom companies and brokers who buy rights to pick in recent clearcuts, where the mushrooms thrive. (Unfortunately, the shootings are for real.)

In **Ukiah,** southwest of La Grande, vans pull up in parking lots to buy morels from itinerant pickers. During late spring, peak mushroom season, Ukiah's population swells to near 600, up from the usual 250. In the nearby woods, blue plastic tarps are rigged up in roadside pickers' camps. (The only other time there's much happening here is during hunting season.)

No matter the price per pound, morels are tasty. They are out there for the picking, if you know where to go and have a permit from the Forest Service. Anyone who wants a good tramp in the woods through forests trimmed with delphinium, cat's-ear lilies, larkspur, calypso lilies, ladyslipper, lomatium, and shooting stars will enjoy searching for morels and cat's-brains mushrooms. (Needless to say, some mushrooms are deadly poisonous and their proper identification is not an area of expertise that should be treated with a laid-back attitude.)

Before leaving the area, stop in at **Lehman Hot Springs,** an old-time resort on Hwy 244 between La Grande and Ukiah. The giant swimming pool is divided into three chambers, with water temperatures ranging from relaxing to scorching hot.

West of the Grande Ronde Valley are the **Blue Mountains.** Driving through the Blues in the summer is a spree of curves and gear changes. Splashes of balsamroot light the hillsides, and pines and shrubs grow wherever a stream cuts a furrow between the hills. In the winter (and sometimes in fall and spring) even the freeway can be treacherous. Kiosks along Hwy 84 at rest stops and parks chronicle the Oregon Trail. At exit 248, west of La Grande, stop and visit the **Blue Mountain Interpretive Center,** where trails lead to wagon ruts still visible int he tall grass.

Near Pendleton, the Blue Mountains dissolve into folds and hummocks before flattening out into wheat fields.

■ PENDLETON   *map page 223, A/B-3*

Pendleton Round-Up has been held for four days in mid-September since 1910. The town cuts loose in a way that the November or April visitor would scarcely expect. It's a well-established tradition of festivity, as the 1940 WPA guide to Oregon reports:

> *As* Round-Up time approaches the city takes on all the appearance of a typical cow town of the Old West. . . . Here they are again, chapped and booted cowboys, saddles creaking, spur-chains jingling; cowgirls in fringed buckskin riding costumes; Indians from the nearby Umatilla Reservation, blanketed and moccasined, the bright-shawled squaws bearing papooses strapped to their backs. Mingled with them are hawkers of souvenirs and strangers from far and near.

What the WPA guide doesn't detail is the sense of hilarity, the frenzy of the Round-Up. As elimination rounds narrow the rodeo contests, spectators pour into town and the downtown cafes and bars fill and spill over onto the sidewalks. Main Street is cordoned off, and it becomes the domain of corn dogs, T-shirts, and Western music. On SW Court Avenue near the rodeo arena, you can buy a straw cowboy hat, and up behind the tipi village, Indians sell beadwork and jewelry.

As rodeo time approaches each afternoon, the pitch heightens and, under the grandstand, the Let 'Er Buck room begins to get crowded. As the events progress, and hot sun and dust roast and cake the audience in the bleachers, there's some solace to be found under the main grandstand. The **Hall of Fame Museum** is air-conditioned and quiet. Next door, the Let 'Er Buck room is darkened and pulsating with tight wranglers and beer. The phrase "gettin' Western" seems coined for this time and place. Evening brings the **Happy Canyon Wild West pageant,** a dance, and flat-out partying that engulfs the town. For Round-Up and Happy Canyon tickets and information, call 800-457-6336.

Even when the Round-Up's not happening, Pendleton's got a lively air. Like Baker City, Pendleton has found a good way to show off its history. At the **Pendleton Underground**, 37 SW Emigrant Street, are hand-dug tunnels that once led to barracks and businesses for Chinese railroad workers, and prostitution, gambling, and liquor for the masses. The Chinese sections are by far the most compelling— they recall the work the Chinese did in the West, and the bad treatment they received. Some speculate that they lived underground to escape harsh treatment they received on city streets. Call 800-226-6398 for information on tours.

A renowned guest ranch, **Bar M Ranch** lies 31 miles east of Pendleton in Adams at 58840 Bar M Lane; 888-824-3381. In Pendleton, at 209 S Main, you'll find the **Rainbow.** This restaurant and bar is open practically around the clock, and is brimming with Western spirit, especially during the Round-Up. **Raphael's,** a restaurant in a lovely old house, is where the locals go for a special dinner. 233 SE Fourth; 541-276-8500.

(above) Jillie Baldwin, champion lady buckeroo, shows off some fancy riding at the Pendleton Roundup in 1912. (Oregon Historical Society). Bull riding is one of rodeo's most dangerous and exciting events (opposite).

A grain elevator, a ubiquitous sight in the Pendleton area.

The agricultural business that gave Pendleton its start in the 1860s continues today. The city's grain elevators fill up, and flour and woolen mills hum. If you pull the car over at an eastern Oregon rest stop, you may find yourself chatting with a few members of the Pendleton Grain Growers Association—heading to Portland for business meetings and a visit with the grandchildren.

Pendleton Woolen Mills has operated for nearly a century out of a brick factory on the southeast edge of town. (Even before moving into this factory, the company had been making blankets for the Indian trade since the 1870s.) Take the colorful, clattering tour and watch brightly colored wool as it's carded, spun, then woven on looms that can weave a blanket in 15-20 minutes. The mill shop has a selection of seconds, which can make a blanket or fabric affordable.

Armchair Books, at SW First and Dorian Streets, isn't quite as well-entrenched as the Round-Up or Pendleton Woolens, but it's a good little shop with plenty of titles for those interested in the region.

NORTHEAST

■ COLUMBIA RIVER

Drop down to meet the blue water, hot breezes, and dug out gorge of the Columbia River. Center-pivot irrigation systems draw Columbia River water up and spray 125-acre circles of wheat and alfalfa. Irrigation has also made it possible to grow melons in sandy soils near Irrigon and Umatilla. This is also "Walla Walla sweet country." As these onions have half the sulfur content of regular onions they are less bitter; their farmers would like you to think of them as sweet.

Late in the day, the sun plays on the Columbia and the colors go purple-blue and ochre, with silver-tipped glints where sunlight hits choppy river waves. The wind can be ferocious, and it has generated sport way upriver. Even small riverside towns like Boardman and Arlington (where Portland's garbage ends up) fill up with windsurfers on gusty summer evenings.

Along the riverbank, it's easy to forget about the Oregon Trail, and reflect on Lewis and Clark's trip downriver. What roaring falls and rapids did they surf, what Indian villages lined these banks? What unimaginable numbers of salmon swam beneath their dugout canoes? Pull off the road, watch a sunlit skiff full of Indian fishermen tend their nets, and wonder what the future holds for them, for the salmon, and for this river.

Hat Rock was named by Capt. William Clark during the Lewis and Clark Expedition. It sits in a state park of its own namesake along the Columbia River just east of Umatilla.

SALMON RUNS

If the Pacific Northwest has a mythology, salmon is elemental to it. We fish for them, swap recipes for them, use them in designs for T-shirts and key chains, and, increasingly, worry about them. Once as plentiful as raindrops, salmon are now in decline.

An anadromous fish, born in fresh water, they travel to the sea, then back to their birthplaces to lay eggs and die. David Rains Wallace writes in *The Klamath Knot,* "the most they know of the forest is the taste of pine needles in the water and perhaps a glimpse of green boughs against the sky . . . That they die after spawning makes the quest seem all the more heroic, and all the more tragic the possibility that the quest will be thwarted by dams which will silt up and become useless in a century or two."

Fish that spawn near the ocean are less threatened than those who spawn far inland. Chinook, or king salmon, are the largest but least abundant of the family. They spawn far from the ocean, in inland streams. Their smaller relatives, the coho (silver salmon in supermarket-speak), spend a couple of years in freshwater streams, then run to the sea. During their youths, coho need shady pools. They're particularly sensitive to trampled banks (caused by cattle) and loss of streamside vegetation. Coastal coho habitats have suffered from heavy Coast Range logging, and their populations have declined sharply in recent years. Sockeye salmon spawn in lakes and rivers; kokanees are freshwater, landlocked sockeyes. Pinks head to the sea and stay there for most of their lives, as do chum, which also spawn near the ocean.

Steelhead (sea-run rainbow trout) commonly spend two years in fresh water, two at sea. They sometimes live through spawning, and doggedly repeat the cycle. Coastal cutthroat trout, also salmonids, run from the upper reaches of coastal rivers to the sea.

Before dams were built, 16 million salmonids a year used to return to the Columbia River Basin to spawn. Though favorable climatic and ocean conditions boosted salmon returns in the Columbia in 2001 and 2002, these strong runs have not persisted.

Hatchery fish are supposed to supplement or replace natural runs, but they cause a multitude of problems for their wild kin. They compete for limited food and habitat and can transmit diseases to wild fish. Salmon populations are rarely successfully restored by the addition of hatchery fish, but given the extent of the loss of natural runs on the Columbia, hatchery programs will continue. Some hatcheries are beginning to experiment with rearing, feeding, and release methods that approximate those found in the wild.

Most inland-spawning species must negotiate dams. The first encounter occurs when smolt, or young sea-going salmon, are ocean-bound. They're vulnerable to turbine blades, changes in the water's oxygen content, and northern pikeminnows which hang around the dams and prey on young salmon. The Army Corps of Engineers fills huge barge-top tanks with smolt, and tugboats push them downstream, through navigation locks at the dams. The smolt are released below the Bonneville Dam, with hopes that the ride hasn't altered the imprinting process necessary for their return upstream. All this work to restore salmon populations has made virtually no impact and, for the first time, people who suggest removing Snake River dams aren't necessarily being dismissed as lunatic environmentalists.

The ocean is like an open pelagic refrigerator to sea-run fish, who, as juveniles, make do with a buggy, riparian diet. The easy food and open space of the ocean allows fish to grow quickly and strengthens them for the long foodless trip back to spawning grounds. Predation by harbor seals, orcas, sea lions, and fishermen is the trade-off of ocean life. Salmon face the saltwater hazards in schools.

An entire school takes the cue to head upriver to spawning grounds at the same time. When they get near the stream where they were born, some fish nose around a little in neighboring streams before they choose the right one. They find their way by a sense of smell, but their olfactory drive can occasionally be overridden. When Mount St. Helens erupted in 1980, salmon that would have spawned in the ash-choked Toutle River swam up the nearby Kalama instead.

Spawning salmon often turn shades of red (sockeyes are the brightest). They eat little or nothing on the upstream pilgrimage, and their flesh begins to lose its tone. By the time they've swum and jumped to the gravel beds where they'll spawn, the fish are battered and emaciated, ready to breed and die.

Salmon attempting the falls on the North Santiam River.

SOUTHEAST OREGON

◆ AREA OVERVIEW

The clear air and sharp edge of southeastern Oregon's high sagebush country have always attracted reflective types. Distant dry views, the fluttery roar of wingbeats, and the smell of sage turn the mind inward and the eye to fine details of geology, plants, and animals. At first glance southeastern Oregon is frighteningly big and empty—an 1855 corps of engineers map fills in the spaces with "Barren Valley," "Great Sandy Desert," and "Broken Lava." The WPA guide calls this the "land of drought and distances." The sagebrush country is vast, and there isn't much to break the view. Reub Long, a Fort Rock rancher and writer, claims it's "10 good looks" across the high desert. To the uninitiated, these looks are uncompromisingly dull. But with a little attention, details come into focus. This place is for those who want to feel the space around them, to sit down on a rock and wait for waves of migrating birds, and hear the sound of wind rushing in through open windows.

Travelers looking for hip brewpubs or high culture had best see this country from an airplane window. Those with low-slung, well-polished cars should be aware that paved roads don't lead to the heart of southeastern Oregon.

Climate: Summer comes to southeastern Oregon sooner than it reaches the rest of the state, and it comes hard. Don't head out of town without full water bottles and a giant tube of sunscreen. Of course, at the top of 9,670-foot Steens Mountain, it's always a bit cool. In fact, the Steens Loop Road is commonly closed from November until late June or early July. Southeastern Oregon is the state's driest region, normally getting just less than 12 inches of rain a year.

Food & Lodging: If you think you need a "normal" motel, head for Burns, Ontario, or Lakeview. If you want to wake up to a morning dip in a hot springs pool, just bring a tent. In between, look for lodging (and good food) in old hotels in Frenchglen or Diamond, or stay in one of the area's low-key B&Bs. Most of these smaller places shut down for the winter.

Robinson Camp on the Hart Mountain National Antelope Refuge.

■ THE LAND

Volcanic basalt flows underlay the sagebrush. The basalt, once flat, is heavily fault-ed and has been lifted in large chunks. Both Steens Mountain, southeast of Burns and the Malheur Wildlife Refuge, and Hart Mountain, between the Steens and Lakeview, are fault blocks, heaved up on one edge and left propped in a tilted position. Hot springs gurgle all over southeastern Oregon—a clue that the earth's crust is thin here and that local faults are not finished creaking and scraping.

Most of southeastern Oregon is part of the Great Basin. Water drains into shal-low land-locked depressions with no outlet to the ocean. Giant lakes used to fill the flats, and rainy weather still brings broad, shallow lakes. But water evaporates faster than it falls here, and lakebeds quickly turn first into mud flats, then playas crusted with mineral deposits.

Not all of southeastern Oregon is desert. Trickles of water high on the Steens become the Donner und Blitzen River, channeling through the Malheur Wildlife Refuge into Malheur Lake. Seasonally, water is abundant. Wetlands turn brilliant green when winter snows melt into valley basins. More than anywhere else in the state, this land lets you know when it's been a wet year, as playas fill with a salty alkali brew and turn from hardpan desert to shallow lakes.

Many of southeastern Oregon's wetlands have been drained and turned into grain fields. Though this has disturbed animal habitats, wildlife still abounds. There are mice and rabbits enough to keep the hawks happy and a smattering of eagles from going hungry. Migrating water birds attract many of the region's tourists. And late in the summer, hunters begin poring over topo maps, imagining deer and elk waiting between the contour lines of the draws and ridges. Come Oc-tober, motels and campgrounds from Burns to Lakeview are filled with folks carry-ing rifles. (But, hey, if the number of guns is high, the murder rate is infinitesimal.)

■ HISTORY

Between 10,000 and 13,000 years ago, when lakes filled many now-dry basins, and wildlife was diverse and abundant, people were living in the Fort Rock Valley. Later, the Northern Paiute, members of the Uto-Aztecan language family, lived in small nomadic bands all across the Great Basin.

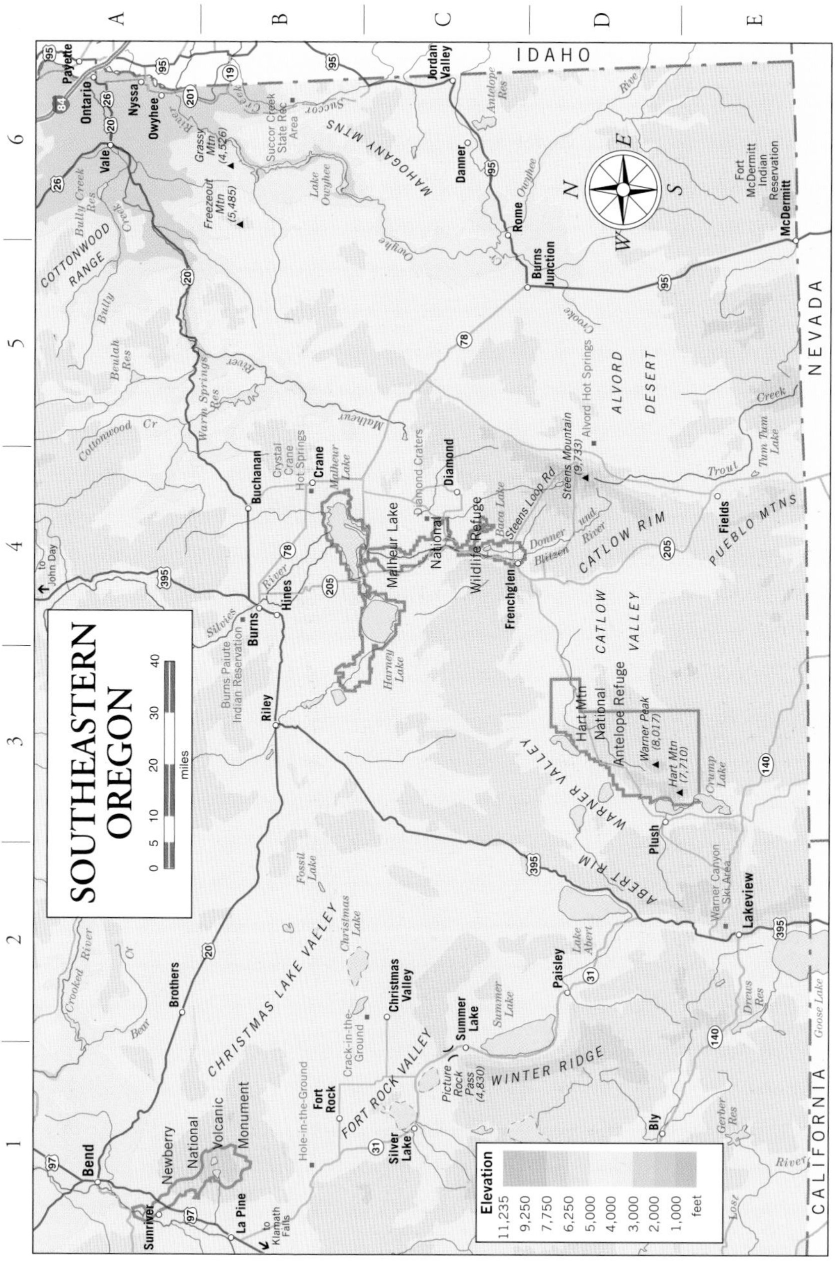

SOUTHEASTERN OREGON
0 5 10 20 30 40
miles
Elevation
11,235
9,250
7,750
6,250
5,000
4,000
3,000
2,000
1,000
feet
IDAHO
NEVADA
CALIFORNIA
Bend
Sunriver
La Pine
to Klamath Falls
Newberry National Volcanic Monument
Hole-in-the-Ground
Fort Rock
FORT ROCK VALLEY
Silver Lake
Crack-in-the-Ground
Christmas Valley
CHRISTMAS LAKE VALLEY
Christmas Lake
Fossil Lake
Brothers
Summer Lake
Picture Rock Pass (4,830)
WINTER RIDGE
Paisley
Lake Abert
ABERT RIM
Lakeview
Warner Canyon Ski Area
Bly
Gerber Res
Drews Res
Goose Lake
Plush
Crump Lake
WARNER VALLEY
Hart Mtn National Antelope Refuge
Warner Peak (8,017)
Hart Mtn (7,710)
Riley
Burns
Hines
Burns Paiute Indian Reservation
Harney Lake
Malheur Lake
Malheur National Wildlife Refuge
Buchanan
Crystal Crane Hot Springs
Crane
Diamond Craters
Diamond
Frenchglen
Steens Loop Rd
Steens Mountain (9,733)
Alvord Hot Springs
ALVORD DESERT
CATLOW VALLEY
CATLOW RIM
PUEBLO MTNS
Fields
Tum Tum Lake
Burns Junction
Rome
Danner
Jordan Valley
MAHOGANY MTNS
Succor Creek State Rec Area
Lake Owyhee
Grassy Mtn (4,526)
Freezeout Mtn (5,485)
Vale
Ontario
Nyssa
Owyhee
Payette
COTTONWOOD RANGE
Bully Creek Res
Beulah Res
Warm Springs Res
Fort McDermitt Indian Reservation
McDermitt
to John Day
A
B
C
D
E
1
2
3
4
5
6
N
E
S
W

SARAH WINNEMUCCA ON INDIAN AGENTS

*T*here are only two agents who have been kind to me, Captain Smith, agent at Warm Spring Reservation, and agent Parrish. It was because they did not steal. Captain Smith is the only agent who can truly say, "I have civilized my Indians." They are a self-supporting tribe, and very rich. When he first took them they were the poorest kind of Indians. We Piutes call them snake-headed Indians, for their heads are so flat that when they are turned sideways they look just like snakes' heads. Every year this agent gave from five to ten wagons, and the same number of farming implements, till every one of the Indians had farms. Dear Reader, if our agent had done his duty like that one, there would be peace everywhere, on every agency; but almost all the agents look out for their own pockets. Every agent that

we Piutes have had always rented the reservation out to cattle men, and got one dollar a head for the cattle, and if my people asked whose the cattle were, he would say they belong to the Big Father at Washington, and then my people would say no more.

—Sarah Winnemucca, daughter of a great chief, 1888

Sarah Winnemucca

What the buffalo was to the Northern Plains tribes, the sagebrush was to the Paiute. They used the herb for sandals, poultices, a lung-clearing tea, floor covering, bedding, blankets, and clothing. Each Northern Paiute band took advantage of the environmental peculiarities of its particular locale, and each was known to the other by a special dietary feature. The Warner Valley people were the Groundhog Eaters, the Paisley band were Pine Nut Eaters and east of Steens Mountain were the Berry Eaters.

John C. Frémont, Kit Carson, and Billy Chinook reconnoitered the area around what is now Lakeview in 1843, but white trappers and traders generally didn't make forays here. Wagon trains crossed the southeastern part of the state only occasionally, and they were often sorry they did.

Gold strikes in Idaho brought miners across the southeastern corner of Oregon in the 1860s, but few even bothered to slow down, much less settle. Yet it was spectacular ranching country, and as California's Central Valley became predominantly agricultural, California ranchers began looking to Oregon for grazing land.

The Homestead Act of 1862, which threw open 160-acre parcels of unappropriated land for a $10 filing fee, brought a new agenda to the high desert. Tensions mounted among ranchers and homesteaders and between Indians and whites in general. It seems there's never enough of anything to accommodate everybody —not even in southeastern Oregon.

Gen. George Crook arrived in 1866 to chase down the Paiutes, who'd been raiding white settlements. Many Paiute moved onto the large Malheur Reservation in 1872, but when whites found good grazing land and some gold on the Indian land, they began to steal back much of what they'd given away. In 1878, some Paiutes joined their Bannock neighbors and lashed out at the whites. Under the leadership of Egan, a Paiute, the tribes fought for two years, until Egan was beheaded by a Umatilla scout working for the U.S. Cavalry, ending the Bannock War. The Northern Paiute were sent to share a reservation in Washington state with the less-than-friendly Yakimas. Before long, Paiute began slipping away from the miserable reservation and returning to their homeland, drifting into the Burns area to look for a campsite or a menial job. Landless, they lived on small alkaline allotments or went to settle on the Warm Springs Reservation with Warm Springs and Wasco tribes from the Columbia River.

Thoc-me-tony (Shellflower) was a Northern Paiute who lived with a white family long enough to become fluent in English and Spanish and to pick up the name Sarah Winnemucca. When the Paiute were sent to reservations, she became their

interpreter. During the Bannock War, she tried to persuade the Paiute not to fight, and worked as an army guide.

After the war, Winnemucca traveled to the East Coast and lectured on the grim life of reservation Indians. She taught at the Indian school in Vancouver and wrote a book, *Life Among the Piutes.*

In 1935, a 771-acre reservation was established for the Paiute, but it was 1972 before the tribe finally gained title to the land.

■ CATTLE RANCHING

Once the Indians had been forced from the grasslands, the primacy of the cow was established. Cattle barons Henry Miller, Peter French, and John Devine claimed all the land they could and employed Latino cowhands, or vaqueros, to trail cattle north from California. In Oregon, the word vaquero (the Spanish "v" pronounced as a "b") evolved into buckaroo, still the regional name for cowboy.

Early ranchers paid little heed to high desert ecology—there was plenty of land and buckaroos to drive the cattle out where the grazing was good. When sheep entered the equation, the competition for grass stiffened, resulting in range wars and an even heavier burden on the grasslands. By the early 1900s, the thousands of cattle had destroyed native bunchgrasses and cleared the way for unbridled sagebrush growth.

Ranching is still about the only way to make a living in this country. The ranches are big, with supplemental grazing land leased from the Bureau of Land Management (BLM). Grazing rights are a chronic source of controversy.

More than in other western states, many ranchers in eastern and central Oregon have been willing to adapt their grazing practices to improve the quality of the rangeland and watersheds. Though some environmental groups see these efforts as token and politically motivated, other environmentalists are working with ranchers and BLM officials to map out future grazing strategies.

Nearly 175,000 acres on Steens Mountain were designated as a Wilderness Area by President Bill Clinton just before he left office. Thanks to a land exchange, grazing is prohibited on almost 100,000 acres of the wilderness.

(previous pages) Indians, settlers, and soldiers gather at a frontier trading post in the 1880s. (Southern Oregon Historical Society)

(opposite) Third generation cattle rancher Gary Miller at Frenchglen corral.

■ FORT ROCK AND CHRISTMAS VALLEY

Ice-age lakes once covered the Fort Rock and Christmas Valleys, in Oregon's big dry country southeast of Bend. Now it's all sagebrush flats, bleached alkali depressions, and quirky geologic features such as *maars*. One of these is **Hole-in-the-Ground,** which looks like a vast meteoritic crater. To see it, turn east off Hwy 31, 24 miles south of LaPine. A steep quarter-mile trail leads to the bottom of the maar, a pit excavated when groundwater flooded a pocket of molten lava, causing a violent volcanic blast.

◆ FORT ROCK *map page 255, B-1*

Though it's no Carcasonne, Fort Rock, southeast of Hole-in-the-Ground, is bulky and impressive. When the Fort Rock Valley was a pluvial lake, a volcanic island

Indians are thought to have inhabited this area near Fort Rock State Monument over 13,000 years ago.

erupted. Tuff blasted into the air, and settled back down in a donut-shaped ring. Years of erosion by waves chiseled the big orange ring into a steep-sided horseshoe.

Seventy-five sagebrush-bark sandals were found in a cave west of Fort Rock in 1938. Seeking to preserve the find, scientists lacquered the sandals, but unfortunately, the lacquer made testing by carbon dating—which came along later—impossible. Archaeologists tromped back to the cave and found another sandal, as yet unlacquered, which dated at 13,000 years old.

In the Fort Rock Valley, as in much of the arid West, homesteaders were lured by ads and bogus newspaper articles that waxed poetic about the potential and fertility of the land. All homesteaders had to do, according to promoters, was to follow the principles of dry-land farming and the rich growth of sagebrush would be succeeded by wheat fields and fruit orchards. A few good years in the early 1900s synergized the promotional campaign, and settlers came in droves. Fort Rock Valley's population topped out at 1,200 in 1916 (well, a drove here may not be a drove somewhere else), just before years of unrelenting drought began. People shooed out in a hurry, walking away from hundreds of homestead cabins. In 1949, over 100,000 acres in Fort Rock Valley were transferred to the BLM, putting the lid on dry-land farming. When electricity came to the valley in the 1950s, it meant more than electric percolators and late-night reading—it was possible, with electricity, to pump irrigation water. Soon alfalfa, one of the thirstiest and greenest of crops, was being grown in huge irrigated circles and perfect rectangles.

◆ CRACK-IN-THE-GROUND *map page 255, B/C-1/2*

With a name so mundane it's almost lyrical, Crack-in-the-Ground is a spookily impressive two-mile long, 40-foot deep cleave in the lava desert floor east of Fort Rock. Geologically, the crack is a tension fault, where the earth ripped apart like a broken zipper. A narrow path along the floor of the crack, where the halves could fit together as neatly as Africa and South America, leads to year-round pockets of ice, where pioneers came to make their Fourth of July ice cream. Take care driving to Crack-in-the-Ground: it's nine miles north of Christmas Valley (a town 27 miles southeast of Fort Rock) on a road that's rocky and rutted at best, and shouldn't be attempted when it's wet.

◆ CHRISTMAS VALLEY *map page 255, C-1/2*

The town of Christmas Valley is more substantial than its wide open desert setting far from any highway would suggest. This community is, in fact, a retirement Eden advertised in the 1960s. Real estate buyers snatched up the bargain-priced lots. Apocryphal stories tell of eager retirees driving out, cars packed full, and bursting into tears when they hit the platted streets of Christmas Valley, where a kitty litter mine keeps the economy afloat. After the initial shock, many residents decided that it wasn't such a bad place, and settled with their cats into high-desert modular home life, bringing a sturdy good spirit to the valley.

East of Christmas Valley, a sandy, rutted road leads to a trio of natural oddities. Flamingos, mammoths, and proto-salmon once lived at **Fossil Lake,** and the sharp-eyed will find traces of them still. Big inland **sand dunes,** many matted with sagebrush, are near the dry Fossil Lake. **Lost Forest** rises like Emerald City from the roller coaster dunes. This ancient ponderosa pine forest, also home to Oregon's largest juniper, survives despite little water thanks to a deeply buried, hard-bottomed ancient lakebed that holds water like a plate set under a potted plant.

The Fort Rock and Christmas Valley sights are all part of a BLM scenic byway. Pick up a brochure and map at their office in Lakeview.

Explorer John C. Frémont was sent west by the U.S. government to map the Oregon Trail in 1842. The following year, while searching for the mythical Buena Vista River (supposedly flowing from Klamath Lake to San Francisco Bay), he named Summer Lake and Winter Ridge. The weather atop the ridge was blustery when Frémont, Kit Carson, and Billy Chinook climbed it in December 1843; the lake below was lush and green.

> *We* traveled this morning through snow about three feet deep, which, being crusted, very much cut the feet of our animals . . . Toward noon the forest looked clear ahead, appearing suddenly to terminate; and beyond a certain point we could see no trees. Riding rapidly ahead to this spot, we found ourselves on the verge of a vertical and rocky wall of the mountain. At our feet—more than a thousand feet below—we looked into a green prairie country, in which a beautiful lake, some twenty miles in length, was spread along the foot of the mountains, its shores bordered with green grass . . . not a particle of ice was to be seen on the lake, and all was like summer or spring.

■ LAKEVIEW *map page 255, E-2*

Lakeview is closer to Reno, Nevada, than to Portland, Oregon, and far from any freeway, so it's no wonder that most Oregonians find it a little foreign. Unsuspecting visitors will also find it improbably pretty; Black Cap Butte shoots above the town, providing a jumping off place for hang gliders and a view all the way down to California. **Warner Canyon Ski Area** is a few miles out of town.

Lakeview is an agency town—the Forest Service, BLM, and Oregon Department of Fish and Wildlife have regional headquarters here, and it's also the county seat, home to a bustling courthouse. For entertainment, there's **Hunter's Hot Springs** on Hwy 395 N; 800-858-8266. It's an old resort with a hot springs pool and, just out back, a geyser. Oregon's only geyser is something of an artifact—it didn't exist until a drill bit into an underground spring and water started spurting every 90 seconds. During droughts, the geyser monitors the underground water supply; when the water table drops, the geyser sputters and dies.

No cartographer visiting the **Warner Valley** in the spring would dare label it "Great Sandy Desert" as early cartographers did. Sure, there are giant sand dunes here, and throughout the summer, salt-tolerant, deep-rooted greasewood provides

Hopeful homesteaders have come and gone in the vast southeast rangelands. A land drawing is pictured here in Lakeview in 1909. (Underwood Archives)

the only real glimpse of green foliage, but winter snows and spring rains bring the alkali lakes to a stinking life. As these wetlands have been drained and replaced with hayfields, their longtime visitors, the white pelicans, which once nested here in force, have diminished.

■ HART MOUNTAIN   *map page 255, D/E-2/3*

Hart Mountain, east of Lakeview on Hwy 140, then north to Plush, is a strikingly well-defined fault block mountain. A gravel road climbs the steep western face from the Warner Valley and the town of Plush to a high plateau, which shrugs off gently eastward to the Catlow Valley. From the top of 7,710-foot Hart Mountain, Steens Mountain crashes across the eastern horizon; to the west and 3,000 feet below, alkali-crusted Warner Valley lakebeds glisten like mirages.

The steep, gorged west side of the mountain is home to bighorn sheep (transplanted from British Columbia to replace the decimated native herd), golden eagles, and mule deer. Pronghorn antelopes prefer the lower east slopes.

Despite their common name and their appearance, pronghorns are not really antelopes; they're horned deer. The pronghorn's distinctive horn has a bony core covered by a sheath of fingernail-like keratin and fused hairs. Each fall, the horn sheath sheds off, and it doesn't grow back until late spring, leaving bare bone exposed all winter long.

The main road across Hart Mountain is a well-maintained gravel road, but a four-wheel-drive vehicle or a mountain bike is necessary on most of the side roads. Hike along the rimrocks at **Petroglyph Lake,** a couple of miles north of the main road to find Northern Paiute paintings (pictographs, actually) on sheltered cliffs.

The refuge's **Hot Springs campground** features 104-degree water in a roofless green cinderblock hut that's far less oppressive than it sounds. During the fall, the campground is favored by hunters.

Until 1992, Hart Mountain was, for a few days a year, the domain of the Order of the Antelope. This exclusive group, which included prominent male Oregonians, was formed to protect the pronghorn and was key in establishing the reserve in the 1930s. In more recent decades, the group strayed from conservation and used the annual retreat as an excuse for drinking and general hell-raising. Their annual rendezvous is now held on an adjacent parcel of land purchased by the group.

Plush, a small town under the mountain's western scarp, just hangs on. The

A TOPOGRAPHY OF SPIRIT

*T*hese are thoughts which come back when I visit eastern Oregon. I park and stand looking down into the lava-rock and juniper-tree canyon where Deep Creek cuts its way out of the Warner Mountains, and the great turkey buzzard soars high in the yellow-orange light above the evening. The fishing water is low, as it always is in late August, unfurling itself around dark and broken boulders. The trout, I know, are hanging where the currents swirl across themselves, waiting for the one entirely precise and lucky cast, the Renegade fly bobbing toward them.

Even now I can see it, each turn of water along miles of that creek. Walk some stretch enough times with a fly rod and its configurations will imprint themselves on your being with Newtonian exactitude. Which is beyond doubt one of the attractions of such fishing—the hours of learning, and then the intimacy with a living system that carries you beyond the sadness of mere gaming for sport.

The canyon would be shadowed under the moon when I walked out to show up home empty-handed, to sit with my wife over a drink of whiskey at the kitchen table. Those nights I would go to bed and sleep without dreams, a grown-up man secure in the house and the western valley where he had been a child, enclosed in a topography of spirit he assumed he knew more closely than his own features in the shaving mirror.

So, I ask myself, if it was such a pretty life, why didn't I stay?

—William Kittredge, *Owning It All*, 1987

town didn't get its name because it's a luxurious sort of place. Its name came about because of a card game, and a Paiute who got a royal flush and was subsequently nicknamed "Flush." He couldn't pronounce "Flush," so he called himself "Plush," and the town ended up with his name.

Oregon's state gemstone, the sunstone (a translucent pinkish feldspar), is for sale at the Plush store, but dedicated rockhounds should head 10 miles north of town. Turn off the road to Hart Mountain onto Road 6155 and follow the signs to the **sunstone rockhounding area.** (Pick up a brochure from the BLM office in Lakeview.)

■ BURNS AND VICINITY *map page 255, B-3/4*

Burns is far north of Plush, a long drive east of Bend on US 20. As the only city in Harney County, Burns has long been a market center, though it was never quite a social hub and Wild West cowtown as is, say, Miles City, Montana.

Burns' fortunes in the last hundred years have been linked to the prosperity of its twin city (or quasi-suburb), **Hines.** The railroad's arrival in 1924 made it practical for Edward Hines to build a sawmill to process Blue Mountain timber. Mrs. Hines, a de facto landscape architect, gave the mill town a touch of grace and green spaces missing from most company towns. The mill prospered for years, but when hard times hit the construction industry in the early 1980s, the mill closed and the Burns-Hines economy crashed. The mill was retooled and reopened a few years later, but there is still economic uneasiness here.

Burns is no tourist town, but it's a good supply stop for high desert travelers and residents. Don't even think of just driving right through—you might miss a

Harney County Sagebrush Symphony Orchestra performs al fresco near Burns.
(Oregon Historical Society)

(previous pages) Hart Mountain National Antelope Refuge
is a place of wild beauty and desert serenity.

mini-mart flirtation with a good-looking buckaroo in spurs. And, you'll certainly need to get gassed up and buy a six-pack of soda, a jar of peanut butter, and some crackers for the road.

The Paiute Reservation is just north of town. The **Burns Paiute Tribal Center** welcomes visitors, but it's best to call first at 541-573-2088. The tribe also runs a small casino.

East of Burns, the pancake-flat land is an old lakebed now filled with sediment. The eastern shore of the old lake is at **Buchanan,** now noted, peculiarly enough, for its shopping. Oard's, the crossroads store, carries an astounding selection of Indian jewelry, made by both the nearby Paiutes and other Indians of the southwest.

Backroads drivers will eschew US 20 and swing south to **Crane,** where the Mustangs represent Crane High School, one of the two public boarding high schools in the continental United States (the other is in Jordan, Montana). Just west of town, **Crane Hot Springs** on Hwy 78, open 9 to 9, offers a break from the road, with a natural outdoor warm pond and private tubs and rustic cabins; 541-493-2312.

■ MALHEUR WILDLIFE REFUGE *map page 255, B/C-4*

Thirty miles south of Burns on US 205, the Malheur Wildlife Refuge stretches another 30 miles south to Frenchglen.

Water streaming off Steens Mountain, just off to the southeast, into the Malheur Basin creates an oasis for the scores of birds that use the area for everything from a brief stop to a permanent home. Early settlers here ate their share of fowl dinners, but it took the milliners' plume hunters to threaten the swan, egret, heron, and grebe populations. In 1908, President Theodore Roosevelt went thumbs down on hats and established the Malheur National Wildlife Refuge.

Cycles of flood and drought mark the region's recent history—during the early 1980s, heavy snowpacks drained into the Malheur basin, raising lake levels until Malheur, Harney, and Mud lakes fused, flooding 36 ranches and a vital stretch of railroad. Ten years later, water levels were precariously low. Mud Lake was dry in the early '90s, and neither Malheur nor Harney lakes topped 1,000 acres, yet a few years later, a wet winter left the lakes brimful.

The spring migration of birds to Malheur is famous among birders looking for a quick infusion to their "life lists." Spotting scopes in hand, they'll follow a schedule that goes something like this: Stay overnight at the comfortable cheap compound at **Malheur Field Station** (541-493-2629); zip over to the **refuge headquarters** and scan **Malheur Lake** with an ear cocked for migrant songbirds; cruise down **Center Patrol Road** to inspect ducks in the ponds; drive further south to **Frenchglen,** keeping an eye out for red-tailed hawks and golden eagles. At the Frenchglen Hotel note little gray birds in the trees. After a quick stop in the funky general store, it's on to **Page Springs Campground,** for a look to the junipers for Brewer's blackbirds and on to the rimrocks for cliff swallows. Next it's Peter French's **P Ranch** for bobolinks and an occasional woodpecker; back up north to **Benson's Pond** where the trees may shelter warblers and waxwings, and osprey soar over the pond. Swing past the **Krumbo Reservoir** for another eyeful of waterbirds (loons, grebes, and all manner of ducks); and return home to the field station on Hwy 205.

On the right spring day a good birder can see more than 100 species.

More casual birders, and easygoing nature-lovers, will find the refuge equally well suited to a slow drifting tour past the rolling sunlit fields, swampy lakes, and brushy thickets. Stop in at the refuge headquarters for birding tips and a visit to the museum, where drawers full of birds are mounted on wooden sticks, popsicle-style. Spend a few hours tooling down Center Patrol Road. Even the most casual birdwatcher will do well to pack along a field guide and binoculars—it's a thrill to recognize a kingfisher, backlit into silhouette on a telephone wire, or see a covey of California quail bustle into roadside weeds.

In late February, male sage grouse begin strutting across their *leks,* or ritual mating grounds. As part of their sexual come-on, air sacs in the birds' necks puff up so full that their throats sag almost to the ground. During the strut, wing and tail feathers are rigidly spread, and a frantic head-jerking swings the distended air sac every which way. This frenzy goes on until May, when less favored males are nearly ready to collapse into a heap of bird bones, and the females get on with the business of nesting.

Wildlife biologist Gary Ivey checking Canada goose eggs on the Malheur Wildlife Range.

■ PETER FRENCH LAND

It's not all feathers and field guides around Malheur. Much of the land was once part of Peter French's cattle kingdom. French trailed cattle up to Oregon in 1872 for Hugh Glenn, a big time California doctor and rancher. He quickly purchased a few head of cattle, great grazing land, and the P brand from a man named Porter. French had a knack for acquiring land, and soon had cattle running all over the Catlow and Blitzen valleys on the western flanks of the Steens.

French married his boss's daughter, but Hugh Glenn was killed a few days after the wedding, and his daughter, either bereaved or relieved, never left the Bay Area for the big P Ranch house built for her in Oregon. Gossips claimed her child bore little or no resemblance to Pete French.

French may have given up on his marriage, but he never lost his love for running cows and managing his land. French, Henry Miller, and John Devine controlled most of southeast Oregon's rangeland, leaving little room for homesteaders who tried to squeeze in around ranch holdings.

French made life difficult for homesteaders. He was determined to extract a toll from Ed Oliver, who had to cross some of French's land to reach his own homestead. Oliver was ornery enough, and poor enough, to refuse to pay. On December 26, 1897, rather than ante up, Oliver put a bullet through French's head. A

Young cowboy rope chasing cattle during a round-up near Crane.

Peter French's ranch crew chows down. (Oregon Historical Society)

jury acquitted Oliver of murder, but people still take sides and debate whether French was a pig or Oliver a weasel.

The **P Ranch headquarters**, two miles east of Frenchglen, still has the original barn, beef wheel, and willow fence. An even more compelling remnant, the Round Barn, is north of a hamlet called Diamond. French and his cowboys spent winters breaking horses inside this cavernous barn. The juniper construction has held up well; birds use the Round Barn now—look for mud-spackled swallows' nests on the ceiling, and a great horned owl perched at the barn's peak. Today you can stay at the small and tidy **Hotel Diamond** with its rip-snorting history and good food; 10 Main Street; 541-493-1898. Be sure to spend some time at **Frazier's,** a small pub adjacent to the hotel. **McCoy Creek Inn** is an old ranch with outbuildings converted to comfortable lodgings, near splendid trails; McCoy Creek Road; 541-493-2131.

Recent volcanism has left the **Diamond Craters** area sculpted with domes, lava flows, "bomb" craters, rimrock, and Malheur Maar, a spring-fed lake. It's a good place to leave the car and hike around the ropey, fresh-looking pahoehoe lava. The BLM office in Burns publishes a detailed guide to Diamond Craters; 541-573-4400. Copies are also stocked at the Malheur Refuge Headquarters.

■ STEENS MOUNTAIN *map page 255, D-4*

It's easy for a person to feel small and insignificant anyplace in southeastern Oregon, but there's no place more humbling than Steens Mountain. Though people often refer to "The Steens," Steens Mountain is really just one immense thing—a 30-mile long, 9,700-foot-high fault block. Major Enoch Steen chased Indians to the top of the mountain (and, the story goes, over the east rim) in 1860, and left his name behind. During the 1920s, cowboys and Basque and Irish sheepherders brought livestock to graze the mountain slopes. Perhaps it was romantic—sheepherders' wagons, Irish music, chorizo for dinner—but it was rough on the land. By the time they were through, bunchgrass was gone, replaced by sage.

From the eastern scarp of the Steens, where the rocks were heaved up, it's a mile-long drop to the Alvord Desert. Geologists probing the base of Steens Mountain reckon that the fault block, which started its push at least ten million years ago, is still rising. Pleistocene-era valley glaciers scoured four big U-shaped gorges

(above) A Basque sheepherder's family poses for a photographer. Many Basques came to "The Steens" in the 1920s. (Oregon Historical Society)
(left) Interior of Round Barn built by Peter French near Diamond.

(above) View from the east rim of Steens Mountain towards Alvord Lake and Desert.

on the Steens' western face: Kiger, Little Blitzen, Big Indian, and Wildhorse.

Oregon's highest road climbs the gentle western face of the Steens fault block and stops a half mile shy of the summit. The 66-mile **Steens Loop Road** starts at Frenchglen and, in good weather, is passable in any passenger car that can take a few bumps and ruts. The southern half of the loop is not as well maintained as the northern part. Spur roads off the loop have deeper ruts than the Oregon Trail, but are worth a careful drive, mountain bike ride, or hike.

Ecological life zones are easily seen on a trip up Steens Mountain. Gray-green sagebrush expanses at the base of the mountain are topped by dense stands of darker, purple-shadowed juniper. Above the juniper, quaking aspen and mountain mahogany grow to timberline, where alpine bunchgrass takes over. By the time the loop road is passable (July 1), wildflowers are blooming at the lower elevations. August brings stubby, intricate alpine wildflowers and hummingbirds high on the mountain; the aspens turn gold in September. Bighorn sheep live high on the mountain in the summer; look for them from the East Rim viewpoint.

DESERT SERENITY

These are the signs of the Desert:
A buzzard serenely circling high in air;
Alone, between two infinities . . .
The sage-brush ocean breaks against
A far coast. Where purple mountains dream.
White alkali-flats shimmer a mirage of blue lakes,
Which constantly retreat from the pursuer.

—Charles Erskine Scott Wood, *The Poet in the Desert*, 1929

Peer into the **Kiger Gorge** and imagine it filled with glacial ice (the notch on the gorge's rim is from a smaller glacier). From the **East Rim** viewpoint, there's a drop straight down to the vast **Alvord Desert**. Steens Summit is topped by a wind-buffeted weather station. A steep trail from the summit leads to Wildhorse Lake, worth an icy plunge on a summer afternoon.

Lower on the mountain, a popular trail runs up **Big Indian Gorge**. Another good hike starts at the Page Springs campground and follows the wet path of Page Springs.

The Steens Loop makes a great mountain-bike trip; make this a two- or three-day trip and camp on the mountain. More casual mountain bikers will want to pull their cycles off car racks and ride the jeep trails and spur roads off the main loop.

A good base for a tour of Steens Mountain is the **Frenchglen Hotel**, a simple hotel with hearty meals (including family-style dinners) served in the lobby; Hwy 205; 541-493-2825.

A schoolhouse is moved by a ten-horse team near Alvord in the early 20th century.
(Oregon Historical Society)

Chinese laborers mining borax in the Alvord Desert in the 1890s. (Oregon Historical Society)

■ ALVORD DESERT   *map page 255, D/E-5*

Steens Mountain casts a rain shadow east over the Alvord Desert. Only six inches of rain falls annually here, compared with 25 inches on the western slope of the Steens. Although it is now one of the driest spots in the state, it's not hard to imagine the Alvord Basin during wetter times 12,000 years ago. Surrounded by scarps and lacking a drainage outlet, the basin became a lake. Today spring run-off occasionally floods the chalky white, dry, rock-hard playa.

At the end of the 19th century, Chinese laborers mined borax from the dry lake bed surface. Borax crystals were refined from the crude alkali sludge in vats and crystallizing tanks; the by-products were cast into bricks and used to build houses for the workers. Mule teams carried loads of purified borax crystals 130 miles to the railroad in Winnemucca, Nevada.

Dirt tracks lead down to the Alvord Desert floor. Drive down, but, rather than taking a car onto the hardpan, park and walk onto the dry cracked alkaline mud. (Pick a set of tire tracks to follow out and back, or bring a compass along—it's easy to become disoriented. Needless to say, savvy desert rats always carry water.) To turn your trip into a pilgrimage, take along a copy of C. E. S. Wood's *The Poet in the Desert,* and remain until Truth appears.

On weekends this spiritual proving ground becomes a sports arena. Bright sails scud across the playa. They're no mirage—they belong to "landsailors." These windsurfer cousins strap themselves into a seated position on an overgrown skateboard base, reducing the chance of a hard fall onto the unforgiving playa.

◆ FIELDS *map page 255, E-4*

It's still no Hood River (home of windsurfing), but Fields, a crossroads hamlet due south of Steens Mountain, is now Landsailing Central. No trip to the dry side of the Steens is complete without pausing in Fields for a tank of gas or a burger. (The road between Frenchglen and Fields is paved, but the road between the east face of the Steens and the Alvord Desert is well-graded gravel.) Even if you choose not to spend the night here (the Frenchglen Hotel some 50 miles north is a better bet), check out the local great horned owl and linger long enough to feel the rhythm of the desert.

Even folks who aren't enchanted by the desert may find **Alvord Hot Springs** worth a visit—and it's free. A short path from a roadside pullout 22 miles north of Fields leads to a sheet-metal shack. It's none too glorious from the road, but once you're immersed in the outdoor concrete pool, the desert and the east face of the Steens take on a new luminosity.

■ DESERT TRAIL

Walking the game trails and sheepherders' paths of the Desert Trail introduces you to a unique wilderness experience. The trail's six sections run from northern Nevada, to Hwy 78 east of Malheur Lake. (The trail is planned to extend to Farewell Bend State Park on the Snake River near Huntington, but progress is slow.)

Eventually, the Desert Trail Association, in conjunction with the BLM, plans to establish a desert hiking trail from Canada to Mexico. The southern portion of the trail will cut across Nevada to southern California, where a trail already exists. To the north, the trail will go through the Blue Mountains, across Hells Canyon and Idaho, and connect up with the Continental Divide Trail to Canada.

Hikes or backpacking trips along the Desert Trail are in remote open country where few other hikers venture. There's no specific footpath along much of the trail. In order to preserve the fragile soil and vegetation, the trail is a borderless corridor marked by rock cairns. Conceptually, it's not a track, but a trail of information. Order maps and trail information from www.thedeserttrail.org.

■ OWYHEE UPLANDS *map page 255, A/B-6*

The southeastern-most corner of the state is not part of the Great Basin; the Malheur and Owyhee rivers drain water from this area into the Snake River, and eventually the Pacific Ocean. Its wild rivers and streamside scenery rival the coast or Cascades, but it's known more to truckers than tourists.

Basque sheepherders and Japanese farmers found traditional occupations here. Hawaiians learned to be trappers, and Irishmen became cowboys. The **Owyhee River** takes its name from a couple of Hawaiians who learned the art of trapping on the "mainland" (there were no mammals to trap in Hawai'i). They were sent to explore this uncharted tributary of the Snake River in 1819 and never returned; presumably they were killed by Shoshone.

The Vale Reclamation Project, a '30s-era Bureau of Reclamation project created a series of dams and diversion canals that flushed fields with water from the Malheur River.

Vale on US 20, just 12 miles from the Idaho border, is an agricultural hub. Potatoes, alfalfa, mint, wheat, sugar beets, onions, and corn all thrive here, thanks to the irrigation canals *(see map page 255, A-6)*.

Ontario's surprises are cultural as well as agricultural. There's a Japanese-American community on the Snake River about 15 miles from Vale. It was created primarily because many Japanese were interned here during World War II. After the war, some internees stayed to farm potatoes, sugar beets, and onions. Ontario's Japanese-American community hosts an **Obon Festival** each July, with traditional dance and crafts and an open house at the Buddhist temple.

The **Four Rivers Cultural Center,** at 676 SW Fifth Avenue in Ontario, celebrates the region's multiethnic heritage; in addition to Japanese-Americans, Ontario is home to Native Americans, Mexican-Americans, and people from the Basque country.

◆ LESLIE GULCH AND SUCCOR CREEK *map page 255, B-6*

Head south from Ontario to reach the Owyhee River. Water has sculpted volcanic ash and lava into rugged, fantastic forms in the Owyhee country. Most Oregonians would think they'd landed in southern Utah if they dropped into the steep bedrock canyons of Leslie Gulch or Succor Creek, which are accessible from Hwy 95 near the state line. To get there follow the 52-mile gravel and dirt road BLM scenic byway near the state's far eastern border. Find thundereggs, Oregon's state rock, along Succor Creek. The rough, dirty-concrete-colored spheres are typically sawed in half, exposing agate and quartz crystals in inner cavities.

Long stretches of the Owyhee River, which has its headwaters in northern Nevada and flows into the Snake near Owyhee on the Idaho border, are accessible to floaters. Several outfitters run trips down river. The BLM office in Vale has the details at 541-473-3144. During the summer, 30-mile-long **Lake Owyhee** is abuzz with motorboats and waterskiers.

◆ JORDAN VALLEY *map page 255, C-6*

Remote Jordan Valley, on a turn in US 95 near the Idaho border, is the oldest settlement in southeastern Oregon. It was founded in 1864, when a hotel and store began catering to gold miners travelling to Idaho strikes. By 1880, the region had gained a reputation as sheep country, and Basque sheepherders arrived hard on the heels of Scotch and Irish herders. Jordan Valley's Basque heritage is not readily apparent—the landmark pelota court is in disrepair. **The Old Basque Inn** serves a few Basque-inspired entrees along with standard American dishes. 308 Wroten Street (Hwy 95); 541-586-2800.

Jean Baptiste Charbonneau, born on the 1805 Lewis and Clark expedition, is buried in Danner, west of Jordan Valley. His mother, Sacagawea, a Shoshone kidnapped by a tribe from the Missouri River country, was won by her husband, the half-French Toussaint Charbonneau, in a gambling game. At 16, she was acting as an interpreter for Lewis and Clark, who took her past her native village. An indefatigable traveler, she gave birth to Jean Baptiste at the Fort Mandan winter camp in February 1805; two months later, she was carrying him to the Pacific.

William Clark took control of Charbonneau's education and sent him off to study in Europe. Later Charbonneau returned to guide and gold-pan in the West. He was traveling from California to a gold strike in Montana when he died at Inskip's roadhouse (now a tumbled relic) across from the Danner cemetery.

Just north of **Rome,** the clay **Pillars of Rome** catch the sunsets. Hard to get to, the upper reaches of the Owyhee River, southeast of Rome, are worth the trip.

(opposite) Lake Owyhee at Leslie Gulch.
(following pages) Dramatic rock formations in the Owyhee Uplands.

O F   I N T E R E S T
S T A T E W I D E

■ WEATHER

Location and season must both be considered when packing for a trip to Oregon. Generally speaking, the Cascades, which run north to south through the western part of the state, block moist Pacific air, leaving wet weather on the western side of the mountains, while the east side remains drier. **The coast** is the rainiest part of the state. It's typically stormy in the winter and foggy in the summer, though warm, sunny summer days are certainly not unheard of. It rarely gets below freezing here, but winter drivers over the Coast Range should check on snow and ice conditions. For road conditions throughout the state call 800-977-6368.

Western Oregon valleys are slightly less rainy than the coast, and typically enjoy dry summers. Snow falls occasionally.

CITY	FAHRENHEIT TEMPERATURE						PRECIPITATION	
	Jan. Avg.		July Avg.		Annual		Avg. Total	Avg. Snow
	High	Low	High	Low	High	Low	Per An.	Per An.
Portland	44	33	79	55	107	-3	37.6"	7"
Astoria	47	35	68	52	101	6	77.4"	6"
Eugene	45	32	81	50	108	-12	47.3"	7"
Crater Lake	33	17	69	41	100	-21	66.9"	540"
Burns	35	15	86	51	103	-32	11.8"	47"
Pendleton	39	25	88	59	119	-28	12.3"	18"
Medford	45	28	90	57	110	-10	16.5"	15"

The **Cascades** get cold weather and snow in the winter, with generally cool summer weather. Year round, there are distinct west slope–east slope climates; if it's cloudy west of a pass, the sun may be shining to the east.

Central and eastern Oregon get less rain and more extreme temperatures than the west. The mountainous areas do catch a lot of moisture, especially as snow, and summer thunderstorms are no rarity here (as they are west of the Cascades).

Every year brings some unusual weather—sometimes it's a wet and cold summer, other years a sun-drenched Portland winter. It's never a mistake to pack a wool sweater and an umbrella, and it's also smart to include sunglasses.

■ ABOUT LODGING

There is a wide range of accommodations in Oregon, and sometimes the unlikeliest locations have great places to stay. Included in this book are we've included a selection of lodgings and restaurants that we know from personal experience that either have historic or cultural interest, or are simply fine places to abide in a beautiful area. In Oregon country towns, we might include a cafe where we like to hang out, as much for the conversation and local feel as for nourishment. These days a complete listing of motels and hotels can be had by town or region on the web at www.traveloregon.com.

Camping is one of the best ways to get the feel for some of the state's wilder areas. Oregon State Park campgrounds are fairly developed (read, showers) and on well-beaten paths. Check www.oregonstateparks.org for information or call 800-452-5687 for reservations. National Forest and BLM sites are generally more primitive (pit toilets), more remote, and less expensive.

■ ABOUT NORTHWEST FOOD

While much Oregon food might best be described as "old-fashioned American," a new generation of cooks has created a distinctive Northwest cuisine, a style that emphasizes local products and produce. And the Northwest is a place of gustatory abundance: fresh, delectable oysters, crabs, and clams; Oregon spot prawns, tuna, and chinook salmon; local lamb and beef; chanterelle and morel mushrooms collected in the forests; apples and pears so crisp and juicy they are famous the world over; flavorful blackberries, cherries, raspberries, cranberries; and fine cheeses such as Oregon blue. The wine industry in Oregon is growing and producing varietals such as pinot gris, chardonnay, and zinfandel, but pinot noir is the local favorite. Microbreweries are all over the map, specializing in well-crafted beers, ales and stouts. The orchards of the Columbia Gorge produce apples, pears, and peaches. Clear Creek distillery in Portland uses these beautiful fruits to create world-renowned brandies. As for coffee, a real Northwest coffee house will make some of the best to be found anywhere.

FACTS ABOUT OREGON *The Beaver State*

The Land

CAPITAL: Salem

STATE FLOWER: Oregon grape

STATE BIRD: Western meadowlark

STATE TREE: Douglas fir

ENTERED UNION: Feb. 14,1859

FIRST SETTLED: 1811

SIZE: 10th Largest State
97,073 sq. mi./251,420 sq. km

HIGHEST POINT: Mount Hood
11,235 feet (3,405 meters)

NATURAL RESOURCES/INDUSTRY:
Leading U.S. timber producer
Leading in nickel production
Greatest profusion of agates

The People

POPULATION: *(2000):*

Census 2000: 3,421,400

White	92.8%
Black	1.6%
Hispanic	4.0%
Asian/Pacific	2.4%
American Indian	1.4%

LARGEST CITIES:

Portland (city)	513,325
Portland (metro)	1,800,000
Eugene	136,800
Salem	131,385
Medford	62,030
Springfield	53,700
Bend	53,040
Corvallis	52,215

FAMOUS OREGONIANS:

Chief Joseph ◆ Joaquin Miller ◆ Matt Groening ◆ John Reed
Linus Pauling ◆ Alberto Salazar ◆ Ken Kesey ◆ James Beard

■ OUTFITTERS, RAFTERS, AND WINDSURFING

DESCHUTES RIVER
map page 152, A to E-3

All Star Rafting. Maupin; 800-909-7238. Raft the Deschutes from Maupin.

Ouzel Outfitters. Bend; 800-788-7238. Also runs trips on the McKenzie, Rogue, Owyhee, and North Umpqua.

HALFWAY, HELLS CANYON, WALLOWAS
map page 219, A to C-5&6

Eagle Cap Wilderness Pack Station. 541-432-4145. Horse packing trips, both short and long,into the Wallowas.

Hells Canyon Adventures. Oxbow, Oregon; 800-422-3568 or 541-785-3352. Jet boat tours and whitewater rafting.

Wallowa Alpine Huts. Joseph; 800-545-5537 or 541-432-4887. Hut-to-hut backcountry skiing in the Eagle Cap Wilderness Area.

Wallowa Llamas. Halfway; 541-742-2961. Llama packing in Hells Canyon and the Wallowas; spectacular country, nice people, noble beasts.

Wallowa Outdoors. Enterprise; 541-426-3493. Historical, wildlife, wildflower tours of Hell's Canyon and Eagle Cap Wilderness; also fishing and custom tours.

Wing Ridge Ski Tours. 800-646-9050 or 541-426-4322. Telemark tours in the Eagle Cap Wilderness.

HOOD RIVER   *map page 138*

Rhonda Smith's Windsurfing Center. Port Marina Park; 541-386-9463. Sailboard, kiteboard, and kayak rentals and lessons.

MOUNT HOOD   *map page 138*

Mazama Club. Portland; 503-227-2345. Mountaineering club that offers climbing and skiing lessons.

Timberline Mountain Guides. Bend; 541-312-9242. Mountaineering classes and guided trips.

COAST, NORTH
map page 100

Columbia River Kayaking. Skamokawa, WA; 360-795-0895. Paddle Nehalem Bay or the lower Columbia River.

Cleanline Surf. Cannon Beach: 171 Sunset Blvd.; 503-436-9726. Seaside: 719 First Ave.; 503-738-7888. Surfboards, wetsuits.

NORTH UMPQUA
map page 182, D-1 to 3

North Umpqua Outfitters. Roseburg; 800-789-7152. Rafting.

OREGON DUNES
map page 100

Sandland Adventures. 85366 US 101, south of Florence; 541-997-8087. Dune buggy rentals and tours.

Sand Dunes Frontier. 83960 US 101, south of Florence; 541-997-3544. Dune buggies and a theme park.

PORTLAND AREA   *map page 51*

Alder Creek Kayak and Canoe. 250 NE Tomahawk Island Drive (Jantzen Beach exit off I-5) 503-285-0464. Canoe and sea kayak lessons and rentals.

Friends of the Columbia Gorge. 503-241-3762. It's not their main thing, but this conservation group offers guided hikes in the gorge during the spring.

Audubon Society of Portland. 5151 NW Cornell Rd.; 503-292-6855. A variety of short classes and outings.

Fat Tire Farm. 2714 NW Thurman; 503-222-3276. Bike rentals.

Portland Parks. 1120 SW Fifth, offices in the Portland Building; 503-823-7529. Guided hikes in city parks twice a week.

Portland River Co. Riverplace Marina; 503-229-0551. Guided sea kayak tours on the Willamette River.

ROGUE RIVER
map page 182, F-1 to 3

Galice Resort. Galice; 541-476-3818. Guided trips or rentals.

Jerry's Rogue River Jetboats. Gold Beach; 541-247-4571 or 800-451-3645. The quick way to get upstream.

Orange Torpedo Trips. Grants Pass; 541-479-5061 or 800-635-2925. Inflatable kayak trips from one to three days.

River Trips Unlimited. Medford; 541-779-3798 or 800-460-3865. A variety of trips, some with stays at backcountry lodges.

Rogue River Outfitters. Gold Beach; 541-451-4498 or 888-235-8963. Guided fishing and whitewater trips.

SMITH ROCK, CENTRAL OREGON CASCADES   *map page 152, F-3*

First Ascent Climbing Services. 1136 SW Deschutes Ave., Redmond; 541-548-5137 or 800-325-5462. Smith Rock women's and teens' programs.

Timberline Mountain Guides. At the Smith Rock parking lot; 541-312-9242. Climbing gear and guided trips.

■ FLY FISHING

BEND   *map page 152, G-2/3*

Fly Box. 1293 NE Third; 541-388-3330.

ENTERPRISE   *map page 129, B-5/6*

Wallowa Outdoors. 110 S River St.; 541-426-3493

EUGENE   *map page 88*

The Caddis Fly. 168 West Sixth Ave.; 541-342-7005.

PORTLAND   *maps pages 51 and 54*

Countrysport. 126 SW First; 503-221-4545

Kaufmann's Streamborne Flies. 8861 SW Commercial, Tigard; 503-639-7004 .

WELCHES   *map page 138*

Fly Fishing Shop. Hwy. 26; Welches; 503-622-4607 or 800-266-3971.

■ FESTIVALS AND RODEOS

FEBRUARY

Ashland: Shakespeare Festival. P.O. Box 158; Ashland 97520; 541-482-4331. Runs mid-February through October; three theaters with 11 plays in repertory.

Klamath Falls: Bald Eagle Conference. Contact Klamath County Department of Tourism; 800-445-6728 or www.eaglecon.org.

Newport: Seafood and Wine Festival. Contact Newport Chamber of Commerce, 800-262-7844.

APRIL

Fishing season begins.

Celilo: Celilo-Wyam Powwow and Salmon Feast.

Hood River: Blossom Festival.

MAY

Bend: Pole Pedal Paddle Race. 541-382-3282.

Brookings: Boatnik-Azalea Festival, Memorial Day weekend.

Keizer: Iris Festival, third week.

Klamath Falls: Klamath Indian Rodeo.

Prineville: Timber Carnival.

Tygh Valley: All Indian Rodeo.

JUNE

Cannon Beach: Sandcastle Contest, early June.

Jacksonville: Pioneer Days, mid-June. Peter Britt Festival. 800-882-7488. Runs late June through early September. Classical, jazz, country, and pop concerts in an outdoor pavilion.

Portland: Rose Festival. 503-227-2681. Two big parades, a waterfront carnival, and roses blooming in Washington Park are the main attractions at this festival, which runs through the first half of June.

Portland: STP (Seattle to Portland Bike Ride).

Warm Springs: Pi-Ume-Sha. 541-553-1161. Powwow and celebration of the heritage of the three tribes sharing the Warm Springs Reservation.

JULY

Elgin: Elgin Stampede, mid-July.

Hood River: Hood River County Fair.

Irrigon: Watermelon Festival, late July.

Joseph: Chief Joseph Days. 503-432-1015. Rodeo and parades, last weekend.

Madras: Jefferson County Fair.

Ontario: Obon Festival, mid-July.

Paisley: Mosquito Festival, end of July.

Portland: Blues Festival, early July. Oregon Brewers Festival, late July.

St. Paul: St. Paul Rodeo, early July.

Veneta: Oregon Country Fair. Hwy. 126, west of Eugene; 541-343-4298. Weekend-long fair with hippie crafts, music, and a vaudeville blowout.

JULY *(cont'd)*

Wallowa: Friendship Feast and Powwow, mid-July.

Wallowa Lake: Fishtrap Writers' Conference. 541-426-3623. Early July. Jazz at the Lake, mid-July.

Yachats: Smelt Fry, early July.

AUGUST

Crater Lake: Crater Lake Rim Run.

Redmond: Deschutes County Fair and Rodeo.

Steens: Steens Rim Run, six miles (10 km), from Fish Lake campground to East Rim (elevation 9,730 feet), early August.

Sunriver: Sunriver Music Festival. Call 541-593-1084 for tickets. Series of classical music concerts.

Tygh Valley: Wasco County Fair.

SEPTEMBER

Cycle Oregon. 503-224-7335. A popular week-long group bike ride (with vans to carry gear). The route changes every year, providing regular participants a chance to see every corner of the state.

Eugene: Eugene Celebration.

Hood River: Columbia River Cross Channel Swim, Labor Day.

Lakeview: Lake County Fair and Roundup, Lakeview, Labor Day weekend.

Mount Angel: Oktoberfest.

Pendleton: Pendleton Round-Up. 800-524-2984. A big traditional rodeo. Pendleton becomes a giant cowboy party for four days in mid-September. Indian encampment and an evening pageant.

Portland: TBA Festival. "Time-Based Art" is lively and cutting-edge.

Salem: Oregon State Fair, Labor Day Week.

OCTOBER

Oxbow Park: Salmon Festival. East of Portland.

Portland: Trail Blazers' season starts.

Weston: Umatilla County Potato Show, late October.

Portland Center Stage. 1111 SW Broadway; 503-248-6309.
Contemporary and classical productions between November and April in the Intermediate Theater.

Portland Opera. 1516 SW Alder St.; 503-241-1802.
Five productions annually at the Portland Civic Auditorium.

Artists Repertory Theater. 1516 SW Alder St.; 503-241-1278.
A variety of commissioned plays, regional premieres, and classics.

RECOMMENDED READING

■ HISTORY

DeVoto, Bernard, ed. *The Journals of Lewis and Clark*. Boston: Houghton Mifflin Co., 1953. A good abridged version.

Schlissel, Lillian. *Women's Diaries of the Westward Journey*. New York: Schocken Books, 1982. Gripping stories and insightful analysis.

■ LITERATURE

Berry, Don. *Trask*. Sausalito: Comstock Editions, Inc., 1960. Oregon classic about a mountain man seeking vision and land.

Cody, Robin. *Ricochet River*. New York: Albert A. Knopf, 1992. Nice boy comes of age in timber town.

Davis, H. L. *Honey in the Horn*. New York: Harper & Brothers, 1935. (Recent reprint by Oregon State University Press). Epic Pulitzer Prize-winning novel of turn-of-the-century homesteaders and other Oregonians.

Duncan, David James. *The River Why*. New York: Bantam Books, 1983. Young man obsessed with fly fishing finds his own way to live.

Gloss, Molly. *Jump-Off Creek*. Boston: Houghton Mifflin Co., 1989. Novel about a woman homesteader toughing it out in northeastern Oregon. Taken from diaries.

Irving, Washington. *Astoria Adventure in the Pacific Northwest*. New York: KPI, 1987, first published 1839. Written by America's first man of letters, this American classic was commissioned by John Jacob Astor to chronicle the establishment of his fur-trading company.

Kesey, Ken. *Sometimes a Great Notion*. New York: Penguin Books, 1963. Oregon's grandest novel, about a family logging business near the coast.

Kittredge, William. *Hole In The Sky, A Memoir*. New York: Alfred A. Knopf, 1992. Memoir of a youth spent changing the landscape of southeastern Oregon.

Lesley, Craig. *River Song*. New York: Dell Publishing Co., 1989. A good story revolving around Indian fishing on the Columbia River.

Lopez, Barry. *River Notes: The Dance of Herons*. New York, Avon Books, 1979. Intense communion with wet green landscapes.

Ramsey, Jarold, ed. *Coyote Was Going There: Indian Literature of the Oregon Country.* Seattle: University of Washington Press, 1977. Indian stories from all across the state.

■ NATURAL HISTORY

Evanich, Jr., Joseph E. Jr. *The Birder's Guide To Oregon.* Portland: Portland Audubon Society, 1990. The state's best birding spots.

Houle, Marcy Cottrell. *One City's Wilderness: Portland's Forest Park.* Portland: Oregon Historical Society Press, 1987. Natural history and hiking trails.

Mathews, Daniel. *Cascade-Olympic Natural History.* Portland: Raven Press, 1984. The number one field guide for the western part of the state. Great reading.

Nehls, Harry B. *Familiar Birds of the Northwest.* Portland: Portland Audubon Society, 1981. Easy-to-use handbook of common birds.

Norse, Elliot A. *Ancient Forests of the Pacific Northwest.* Washington, D.C., Island Press, 1990. Readable discussion of old-growth forest ecosystems.

Wallace, David Rains. *The Klamath Knot: Explorations of Myth and Evolution.* San Francisco: Sierra Club Books, 1983. Natural history of Klamath/Siskiyou area.

■ RECREATION

Casali, Dan and Madelynne Diness. *Fishing in Oregon.* Portland: Flying Pencil Publication, 1984. How to fish Oregon's rivers and lakes.

Garren, John. *Oregon River Tours.* Portland: Garren Publishing, 1991. The best whitewater tours.

Jewell, Judy. *Camping! Oregon.* Seattle: Sasquatch Books, 2001. The state's campgrounds rated and described.

Schreeber, Corey. *Wildwood Cookbook.* Oakland: 10 Speed Press, 2000. Creative Northwest cooking. Lovingly written and lavishly photographed.

Sullivan, William L. *100 Hikes in the Central Oregon Cascades.* Eugene, Oregon: Navillus Press, 1993. Sullivan writes thorough, detailed hiking guides.

Sullivan, William L. *Exploring Oregon's Wild Areas.* Seattle: Mountaineers, 1988. Excellent, information-packed book on the best natural areas.

Vieberg, Klindt. *Cross-Country Ski Routes of Oregon's Cascades.* Seattle: The Mountaineers, 1984. A little out of date, but still useful.

I N D E X

■ ABOUT THE AUTHOR

Judy Jewell has lived most of her life in Oregon, and has traveled widely around the Pacific Northwest. She's a regular participant in the Columbia River cross-channel swim, has cycled almost the entire Oregon coast, and has summited Mt. Rainier. Judy is also author of *Camping! Oregon*, and co-author of the *Moon Handbooks* to Montana and Utah, and *Lonely Planet Pacific Northwest*. She lives in Portland with her husband and dog, and tries to hike in Forest Park daily.

■ ABOUT THE PHOTOGRAPHER

Greg Vaughn is a freelance photographer specializing in travel and nature. His award-winning imagery has appeared in magazines such as *Travel & Leisure, National Geographic, Sunset, VIA, Travel-Holiday, Natural History,* and *Outside.* Greg provided the photography for Compass American Guides' Pacific Northwest and was a major contributor to several books on Hawaii. Greg and his family live in Eugene, Oregon. For more information, or to contact Greg, see his website at *www.GregVaughnPhoto.com.*